THE HARṢA-CARITA OF BĀṆA

THE HARṢA-CARITA OF BĀṆA

Translated by

E.B. Cowell

F.W. Thomas

MOTILAL BANARSIDASS PUBLISHERS
PRIVATE LIMITED • DELHI

First Indian Reprint : Delhi, 1968
Reprint : Delhi, 1993

ISBN : 81-208-0791-X

Also available at :

MOTILAL BANARSIDASS

41 U.A. Bungalow Road, Jawahar Nagar, Delhi 110 007
120 Royapettah High Road, Mylapore, Madras 600 004
16 St. Mark's Road, Bangalore 560 001
Ashok Rajpath, Patna 800 004
Chowk, Varanasi 221 001

PRINTED IN INDIA

BY JAINENDRA PRAKASH JAIN AT SHRI JAINENDRA PRESS
A-45 NARAINA, PHASE-I, NEW DELHI 110 028
AND PUBLISHED BY NARENDRA PRAKASH JAIN FOR
MOTILAL BANARSIDASS PUBLISHERS PVT. LTD.
BUNGALOW ROAD, DELHI 110 007

TO

THE RIGHT HONOURABLE

THE EARL OF NORTHBROOK, G.C.S.I.

this work is dedicated in sincere gratitude for the kindly sympathy and generous help which he has given to the New Series of the Oriental Translation Fund. To that generosity is due the publication of this translation of Bāṇa's old historical romance.

PREFACE.

THE book of which an English translation is now for the first time presented to those who are interested in Hindu literature and antiquities, appears to have been almost forgotten in India. One writer on rhetoric mentions it by name in his Sāhityadarpaṇa as an example of the kind of prose composition called Ākhyāyikā, and a verse passage is quoted from it in the older treatise on rhetoric, the Kāvyaprakāça; yet few native scholars had seen it for many years, although rare copies did linger unknown in some native libraries. Professor FitzEdward Hall first introduced it to the knowledge of European Orientalists in the Introduction to his edition of Subandhu's Vāsavadattā, published at Calcutta in the Bibliotheca Indica in 1859; he discovered three MSS. more or less complete. An edition with an excellent Commentary was published at Jammu in Kashmir in 1879 (Saṃvat 1936), and this was reprinted with some variations in Bombay A. D. 1892 (Çāka 1814), and an independent edition of the text appeared in Calcutta in 1883, prepared by Pandit Vidyāsāgar. Professor Führer has promised a new edition of the text from a careful collation of all the MSS. available in India, but his numerous engagements in connection with the Lucknow Museum have hitherto hindered him in carrying his undertaking to completion. We have had to do our best with the imperfect materials at our command, and we shall mention at the close of this preface the additional help which we have received in our task from other quarters.

The great merit of the Harṣa-carita consists in the fact that it is a very early attempt at an historical romance. Bāṇa's other work, the Kādambarī[1], and Subandhu's Vāsavadattā deal with mythological fiction, and everything is viewed through a highly poetical atmosphere; and the Daça-kumāra-carita is equally based on pure imagination, although its characters, as in the *picaresco* literature of modern Europe, are the exaggerated pictures of the vulgar rogues and ruffians of every great city. But the author of the Harṣa-carita has taken his own sovereign as his hero and has woven the story out of the actual events of his reign. The narrative can be often illustrated by contemporary inscriptions,—in fact it is as much based on real events as Scott's Quentin Durward or Waverley. This gives to it a peculiar character which distinguishes it from all other works of Sanskrit literature. In studying any other classical Sanskrit writing we are generally obliged to infer the date of its composition by a careful examination of the accidental allusions or the peculiar words and phrases which it may contain, or by tracing the earliest quotations from it in subsequent authors; it is the special interest of the Harṣa-carita that it treats of a period, which happens to be almost as familiar to the student of Indian history as the reign of any of the early Muhammadan monarchs of Northern India.

Çrī-harṣa, who gives his name to the story, was the ruler at whose court the Chinese Buddhist traveller Hïuen Thsang for a time resided, who has left us such a precious description of India as he actually saw it in the early part of the seventh century (A.D. 630—644); and, fortunately for us, Çrī-harṣa was a king who well deserved to have this strong light thrown upon his reign. He was the Akbar of the 'Hindu period' of Indian history; and under his wise toleration the adherents of

[1] Translated by Miss Ridding in the present series.

the contending religions, Brahmanism and Buddhism, seemed to forget their rivalries in a common feeling of loyalty, just as Rajputs and Muhammadans served Akbar with equal devotion. The one great difference is that Akbar's reign is presented to us in broad daylight by such full contemporary narratives as those of Abū'l Faẓl and 'Abd-ul-Ḳādir Badāūnī, which give us a detailed account of every great event and biographical notices of all the leading personages of the time; while we learn the events of Çrī-harṣa's reign only by the passing allusions of the Chinese visitor or the brief records of some inscription. Now here our romance comes in to supply a living and contemporary picture, wherein we can see something of the India of that time, just as we see in Arrian and Plutarch something of the India of Alexander's time; but we long in vain for some chronicler who would have filled in the imperfect sketch with a thousand details now for ever lost.

Bāṇa's style resembles the *estilo culto* of Spanish literature; it abounds with double meanings in the words and veiled allusions in the sentences, so that the reader is apt to be bewildered by the dazzling coruscations which keep flashing across his path[1]. Most of these puns and under-meanings refer to mythological stories, or well-known poetical superstitions like the parted ruddy-geese on the opposite banks of a river, or the cakora's red eyes at the sight of poison; but some of them undoubtedly refer also to the events of his time and can only be unriddled now by patient research and critical insight. Thus Hofrath Prof. Bühler has shewn that in p. 76 the words at first sight might seem to mean only "that the supreme Lord (Çiva) took

[1] We have tried to preserve this characteristic feature of our author's style by continually explaining the puns in our notes; but we have often omitted them out of consideration to the English reader. Many of these will be found in the 'Additional Notes and Corrections' in Appendix B. Appendix A. also contains two long descriptions omitted from the text.

the hand of Durgā the daughter of the snowy mountain"; but under this mythological allusion is concealed a reference to a contemporary conquest, since the words may be also translated, "in our monarch a supreme lord has taken tribute from an inaccessible land of snowy mountains"; and there are several similar allusions to the king's exploits in the same passage. Prof. Bühler remarks that the inscriptions of Aṃçuvarman (three of which are dated Saṃvat 34 and 39) prove that the Çrī-harṣa era was introduced into Nepal during the lifetime of the great King of Thānesar and Kanoj, who held the whole of Northern India from 606 to 648 A. D. "If an Indian prince adopts a new foreign era, especially one founded by a contemporary, that may be considered as almost a certain proof that the borrower had to submit to the Çaka-kartṛi or establisher of the era[1]." Similarly in p. 57 where we have a description of Harṣa's reluctance to become king, till the Goddess of the Royal prosperity herself forced him to mount the throne, in spite of his previous vow of austerity,—we are at once reminded of Hiuen Thsang's story that Harṣa at the advice of a Bodhisattva, refrained from mounting the siṃhāsana. So too in p. 168 where "the rising clear-flecked moon (*çaçāñka*) shone like the pointed hump of Çiva's tame bull, when blotted by mud scattered by his broad horns," the commentator himself supplies us with the allusion, as he tells us in his note on the opening verses of chap. vi., that Çaçāñka was the name of the dishonoured Gauḍa king against whom Harṣa was marching. Hiuen Thsang states that Rājyavardhana was treacherously killed by Çaçāṃka (*Che-chang-kia*), the ruler of Karṇasuvarṇa in Eastern India.

But beside these veiled historical allusions, the work has another interest from the vivid picture which it offers of the condition of Indian society and the manners and customs of the period. Bāṇa is not a mere rhetorician; his descriptions

[1] *Ind. Ant.* XIX. 40.

of court and village life abound with masterly touches which hold up the mirror to the time. Not even the Pali Jātakas introduce us more directly into the very heart of the period or give us a more life-like picture. The court, the camp, the quiet villages, which then, as now, contained the great mass of the population, and the still more quiet monasteries and retreats, whether of Brahmans or Buddhists, are all painted with singular power; and his narrative illustrates and supplements the Chinese traveller's journal at every turn.

The first chapter gives the mythological history of Bāṇa's family, the Brahmanical Vātsyāyanas, until we come to his own birth and education, and his spending some years in travel partly for pleasure and partly to acquire learning. At length he returns to his home Prītikūṭa on the Sone, where after a while he receives (ch. 2) a summons from King Harṣa's half-brother, that he should repair to the court and renew an intimacy which had been interrupted by some former acts of indiscretion. He obeys the request and repairs to the royal camp near the Ajiravatī river (on which Çrāvastī stood, though it is not alluded to). The King at first receives him coldly, but Bāṇa soon makes his way and becomes a favourite. After a while (ch. 3) he revisits his home at the beginning of autumn, and at the request of his cousins proceeds to relate the history of the King's reign. This narrative fills the remainder of the book (pp. 79—260), and is left unfinished at the end of the eighth chapter.

Prabhākara-vardhana[1], the king of Thānesar, had, by his queen Yaçovatī, two sons Rājyavardhana[2] and Harṣa, and a daughter Rājyaçrī, who was married to Grahavarman[3], the

[1] Prabhākaravardhana is described as "a most devout worshipper of the Sun" in the Sonpat Inscription.

[2] Rājyavardhana is described in the Madhuban inscription as "a most devout worshipper of Sugata."

[3] The genealogy would seem to be Grahavarman, Avantivarman (*infr.* p. 122), Susthitavarman, Çarvavarman, Içānavarman, Īçvaravarman, Ādityavarman, Harivarman; cf. the inscriptions Nos. 42, 46,

son of the Mukhara king of Kanyākubja. The king dies while his elder son is absent on an expedition against the Hūṇas, but the prince returns at his brother's earnest summons; and in his overwhelming grief, he determines to become an ascetic and to leave the throne to Harṣa. At this moment, however, tidings arrive that Grahavarman has been killed by the king of Mālwa[1], who has also thrown Rājyaçrī into prison. Rājyavardhana at once determines to avenge his brother-in-law's death and marches with his cousin Bhaṇḍi[2] and the army, leaving Harṣa as his vicegerent. After a time news is brought that he had easily conquered the Mālwa army but had been treacherously assassinated by the King of Gauḍa[3]. Harṣa himself now marches against this new enemy; on his way he accepts offers of friendship from Bhāskaravarman[4], the King of Prāgjyotiṣa (Assam). Soon afterwards he meets Bhaṇḍi, who is returning loaded with spoil and bringing the Mālwa troops prisoners; he announces that Rājyaçrī has escaped from prison and fled into the Vindhya forest. Harṣa sends Bhaṇḍi against the Gauḍa king and hastens himself to find his lost sister. By the help of a Buddhist mendicant he comes upon her, just as she is preparing to mount the funeral pile, surrounded by her female attendants. Harṣa rescues her from the pile and takes her with him to the camp, after making a vow that he and his sister will assume the dress of Buddhist mendicants as soon as he has conquered the Gauḍa traitor and consoled his subjects in their sorrow for his deceased father.

Harṣa's partiality for Buddhists and Buddhist doctrines

47, Corpus Inscr. Ind. III. Adityavarman had as his queen Harṣaguptā, sister to Harṣagupta, of the same Guptas of Magadha, who were similarly connected with Harṣa's family.

[1] Professor Bühler suggests that this is the Northern Mālwa about Fatehpur. He would identify the king with the Devagupta of the Madhuban Inscription.

[2] Poni in Hiuen Thsang.

[3] Cf. Hiuen Thsang, (Julien), II. 248.

[4] Bhāskaravarma Kumāra, in Hiuen Thsang.

is frequently brought out in our story, as the foregoing sketch will shew,—he seems indeed to be more than half a Buddhist at heart; and it is remarkable that we find a similar view of his character in Hiuen Thsang's account, although he may naturally exaggerate the amount of favour shewn. His language might indeed imply that the king almost professed himself a Buddhist; but his narrative clearly shews that he was equally tolerant to both the great religions of his subjects.

Thus, when he held a great assembly at Kanyākubja, twenty kings attended it, with the most distinguished Çramaṇas and Brahmans in their districts. An immense *saṅghārama* was erected with a tower and a golden image of Buddha, and every day viands were presented to the Çramaṇas and Brahmans; and, in the disciples' account of the second assembly held at Prayāga, we find that on the first day they installed the statue of Buddha, on the second that of the Sun, and on the third that of Maheçvara. Hiuen Thsang says of the inhabitants of Kanyākubja, "une moitié suit la vraie doctrine, et l'autre s'attache à l'erreur"; and our narrative similarly shews us the two religions existing side by side; and in the elaborate description in the eighth chapter of the Vindhya forest, we find Buddhists and Brahmans of every sect, "all diligently following their own tenets, pondering, urging objections, raising doubts and resolving them." When we read these accounts of India in the seventh century they lend some support to the theory that later Brahmanism was itself a *renaissance*, and was separated by a chasm from the ancient cult, just as the Sassanian religion was a later revival (after the long Parthian domination) which turned a longing eye to the past glories of the Zoroastrian creed under the Achæmenidæ.

For our translation we have chiefly used the Bombay text (though with a corrected punctuation), but we have collated it with the Calcutta and Kashmir editions. Pandit

Kailāsacandra Datta Çāstrī[1] had published the text and translation of the fifth book (Benares, 1883), with an original Sanskrit commentary of his own; this has often helped us in obscure passages and we have frequently quoted it. Pandit Ravaji Rāmacandra Kale has also published (Bombay 1882) a very useful volume of English notes to the whole work; this only came into our hands when our translation was more than half printed, but we gladly acknowledge our obligations to the author as he often supplements or improves upon the printed commentary. When our translation was partly printed we obtained the help of the valuable MS. (A) which Hofrath Prof. Bühler has presented to the India Office Library, and he also lent to us a collection of the various readings of another MS. and a native scholar's notes on the first book. The MS. A has been of great assistance to us and we have frequently quoted it in the later part of our translation and in the Notes in the Appendix, but as we were not re-editing the text, we have chiefly consulted it where the native editions seemed corrupt.

We are painfully conscious of the imperfections of our translation; but we offer it to Oriental scholars as an honest attempt to help the student in reading a difficult Sanskrit work which will well repay the trouble of mastering it. The book is full of Sanskrit lore of every kind; but its author was not (as Gibbon says of Libanius) "a recluse student whose mind, regardless of his contemporaries, was incessantly fixed on the Trojan war and the Athenian commonwealth." He was by no means the mere lover of what was abstruse and difficult; he had also an eye for the picturesque and the pathetic, and he could sympathise with the men and women of his own time;—like Apollonius Rhodius, he was a poet as well as a grammarian.

[1] [He was an old pupil in the Calcutta Sanskrit College. E. B. C.]

THE HARṢA-CARITA.

INTRODUCTORY VERSES[1].

[1] 1. Adoration to Çambhu, who is the main pillar in the building of the city of the three worlds,—beautiful with the moon hung on him like a white royal chowrie[2], as it kisses his lofty brow.

[2] 2. I worship Umā, whose eyes are closed with the delight of grasping Hara's neck as if she were fainting at the touch of the Kālakūṭa poison which stains it.

3. Adoration to the omniscient Vyāsa, the creator among poets, who made the Mahābhārata holy by his speech as the Bhārata continent is hallowed by the river Sarasvatī.

4. Most commonly the poetasters of the world have their perceptions ruled by desire, loquacious and wilful like red-eyed kokilas;

[3] 5. Countless such there are like dogs, following their own vile nature from house to house[3],—not many are there like Çarabhas, possessing creative power[4].

6. A poet is not reckoned among the good[5] and is detected as a

[1] The Kashmir text inserts another verse at the beginning; "Hail to the holy Sarasvatī, hail! that goddess, who, having her power manifested as the enlightener of the all, through the gradually evolving faculties commencing with 'desire,' illuminates the nature of her mansion, the lotus-hearts of the sages,—her, even Sarasvatī, I praise."

[2] Chowries and flags are hung on triumphal pillars; cf. *trailokyamahāgṛihastambha* (of Viṣṇu), C. I. I. iii. 159 and 160. Note that this verse occurs entire in an inscript. *Ind. Ant.* xiii. p. 92.

[3] Or "those are of no account who only give bald descriptions (*jāti*) from house to house."

[4] There is a pun in *utpādaka*, which is also a synonym for the fabulous animal called the *çarabha* as having eight legs, four of which are said to grow on its back (*Vācaspatya* lex.).

[5] Or "is counted as no man," *a-nā*.

'thief'[1] by his only changing the words of former writers[2] and by his concealing the signs of different styles[3].

7. In the North plays on words are mainly admired, in the West it is only the sense; in the South it is poetical fancy[4]; in Gauḍa pomp of syllables.

8. A new subject, a diction not too homely, unlaboured double meanings, the sentiment easily understood, the language rich in sonorous words—all this it is difficult to combine in one composition.

[4] 9. What has that poet to do with poetry, whose language, going to the furthest limits of metrical skill[5], does not fill the three worlds like the Bhārata story?

10. They upon whose lips abides Sarasvatī, unwearied even at the end of their 'fits,'[6]—how can such writers of romances[7] escape being praised as the princes of poets?

11. The pride of poets verily melted away through Vāsavadattā[8] (when it came to their ears), as the pride of the Brāhman seers[9] through the (Indra-given) spear of the Pāṇḍavas when it came near Karṇa[10].

[5] 12. The prose-composition of the revered Haricandra stands pre-eminent as a sovereign, luminous with its employment of words, delightful[11], and preserving rigidly the traditional rules of letters[12].

13. Sātavāhana[13] made an immortal refined treasure of song, adorned with fine expressions of purest character[14] like jewels.

[1] Does this allude to the *Caura-pañcāçikā*; or only to plagiarists generally? For the poet Caura see *Vāsavad.* Comm. p. 33.

[2] Or "by his changing colour through fear," or "by trying to change his low caste."

[3] Or "by his concealing the marks of his chains." For *bandha* cf. *Kāvyād.* i. 47.

[4] *Utprekṣā*, where the comparison is introduced by 'as it were' or 'methought.'

[5] Or "embracing all narratives." For the literary history contained in the following lines compare Prof. Peterson's Introd. to *Kādambarī*, pp. 68—96.

[6] *Ucchvāsa* means 'a breathing out' and also 'a division of a narrative.' The sk. contains puns in *vaktre* (also the name of a metre), and *kaviçvara* = Brahmā, on whose lips the goddess rests; cf. *Kād.* Introd. *v.* 11.

[7] For the *ākhyāyikā* see *Sāh. Darp.* § 568.

[8] See Dr Castellieri's paper in the Vienna Oriental Journal, vol. I., where he shews that Bāṇa wrote his work especially to surpass Subandhu's Vāsavadattā; see also our Appendix, notes to pp. 67, 74, 233.

[9] Droṇa, &c.

[10] Does this refer to Arjuna's attack on Karṇa with the Aindra weapon, *Mahābh.*, VIII. 4720?

[11] Or "not stealing from others" (*ahārī*).

[12] Or as applying to a king, "glorious by the rule of his territory, and preserving all the caste-regulations."

[13] Another reading is Çālivāhana; both Sātavāhana and Çālivāhana have been identified with Hāla the author of the Saptaçataka, but see Weber, *über das Saptaçatakam*, p. 3.

[14] Or "of pure description."

14. The fame of Pravarasena[1], bright like a lotus[2], has gone to the other shore of the ocean by his 'bridge,' like the army of monkeys.

15. Bhāsa[3] gained as much splendour by his plays with introductions spoken by the manager, full of various characters, and furnished with startling episodes, as he would have done by the erection of temples, created by architects, adorned with several stories, and decorated with banners.

16. By whom is not delight felt at the beautiful expressions uttered by Kālidāsa as at sprays of flowers wet with honey-sweetness?

[6] 17. To whom is not the Vṛihat-kathā[4] a marvel like Hara's sportive exertions of power,—by both of which Love is kindled[5], and glory done to Gaurī?

18. My tongue seems checked and drawn within my mouth by Āḍhyarāja's[6] *utsāhas*, even when they are only remembered as abiding in my heart[7], and so it does not attain to a poet's success.

19. Yet still through my loyalty to my lord, undismayed and eager in the hope of gaining my end, I venture audaciously to plunge with my tongue into the ocean of narrative.

[7] 20. A narrative, like a bed, which is to wake up its occupant happily refreshed, is set off by its well-chosen words like feet, luminous with the clever joinings of harmonious letters[8].

21. Victorious is Harṣa who guards the world by a wall of fire of glorious majesty,—a mountain of good fortune[9] for fulfilling the desires of all his friends.

[1] He seems to have written the Prākrit poem the Setubandha.

[2] Kumuda is also the name of one of Rāma's monkeys.

[3] See Weber's *Indian Literature*, p. 205.

[4] The Vṛihat-kathā is alluded to in Kādambarī (Bombay ed. p. 40).

[5] In the one by Kāma's being consumed,—in the other by the amatory legends of the poem; or it may mean that Kāma is personified in the latter, as Naravāhana, one of its heroes.

[6] An unknown poet, unless it refers to Guṇāḍhya, the author of the Vṛihat-kathā. *Utsāha* seems to refer to a pantomimic recitation as well as to general energy.

[7] I.e. even though they are not immediately present to me; or perhaps "which though mentioned abide in my heart." This is a hard çloka.

[8] Or "with the fastenings of gold." For *çayyā* cf. *Kād.* introd. 8.

[9] Çrīparvata is also the name of a range of mountains in Telingana. Cf. Hall, Introd. to *Vāsavadattā*, p. 11.

CHAPTER I.

THUS runs the tale:—In former days the Holy One, the Most High, enthroned in his own sphere, [8] was reclining on his full-blown lotus couch surrounded by Indra and the other gods; and on a certain occasion he was holding a session, framing questions on the lore of Brahma[1] and enjoying other blameless discussions. As he so sate, adored of the three worlds, the Prajāpatis headed by Manu, Dakṣa, and Cākṣuṣa, and all the great sages with the seven Ṛiṣis worshipped him. Some in chorus chanted the Ṛik hymns apt for psalmody; some recited the Yajus sentences of worship; some sang aloud the Sāman strains of praise. Others rehearsed the Mantras that reveal the ritual of the sacrifice. And there, arising from the differences of their studies, quarrels one with another we heard among them.

Now there was a certain sage, a great ascetic, by nature excessively choleric, a son of Atri and brother of the moon, by name Durvāsas, and he, while brawling with a second sage named Mandapāla, [9] being blinded by passion made a discord in singing a Sāman. At this silence fell on all the other sages through fear of a curse, while Brahmā in the sport of another conversation heeded not. But the divine Sarasvatī, a maiden of tender years, now doffing her girlhood and arrayed in youthful beauty, was fanning the great Father with a fly-flap held by her arm's waving tendril. Those sprays, her feet, glowed with a natural red as though flushed by furious stripes, and her steps were musical with a

[1] Cf. Manu, III. 231.

pair of anklets keeping time with them like two disciples intoning the Veda word by word. Her legs produced the illusion of being the pillars of the portal to the city of Love[1]. Her left hand, like a bud, was laid in sport on the chain of her girdle, which tinkled like the murmur of love-sick *kala-haṃsas.* Her body was made pure by a Brāhmanical thread, which, hanging from the shoulder, seemed like a coil of virtues that had clung to her through dwelling in the Mānasa[2] of the wise: while her necklace, studded with many a pearl and having a brilliant central gem, suggested the path of renunciation, leading midway the sun and lined by many liberated souls[3]. Her quivering lips glowed red as with lac from the feet of all the sciences, which had entered her mouth. In her cheek was reflected an image of Brahmā's black deer-skin, as if the moon's deer were come down to hearken to her honeyed song. [10] One eyebrow like a creeper was raised in a disdainful curve, and a stream of tears flowing from the outer corner of her eye seemed to be washing one ear soiled by the discord[4]; while the other ear, revelling in a white full-blown *Sindhuvāra* flower, betokened as with a gleaming smile the intoxication of knowledge[5]. In the flowers of her ear-ornament tribes of devoted bees attended upon her like repeated Oms accompanying the Çruti. Her form was clad in a silken robe fine and spotless

1 Cf. Spenser, *Faery Queen*, Bk. II. c. iii. 27, 28,

'And her straight legs most bravely were embayled
In gilden buskins of costly cordwayne...
Like two fair marble pillours they were seen
Which doe the temples of the gods support.'

Also *Vāsavadattā*, p. 54 (Hall).

2 There is a pun on *mānasa* = (1) mind, (2) lake Mānasa.

3 The Sanskrit here has puns on *mukta* 'released' and 'pearl' and on *madhyanāyaka* 'central gem' and 'spiritual guide through the centre.' The Comm. quotes a passage to the effect that 'the ascetic who attains *yoga* and the warrior slain face to face with his foe pass through the centre of the sun': cf. the last note to this chapter.

4 The eyebrow is compared to a spray used in sprinkling the ear.

5 A laugh is often called by the Hindus 'white,' cf. Wilson, 'Hindu Theatre,' II. p. 197: and Sarasvatī as the goddess of learning is naturally spoken of as intoxicated therewith.

as the fabric of thought. In this guise, shedding on all sides the moonlight of her teeth, pure as if of the substance of speech, the goddess Sarasvatī, hearing the discord, smiled.

Seeing her so smiling, 'Wretch!' cried the sage, 'vain in the conceit of a grain of ill-got knowledge, dost jeer at me?' With these words, shaking his head so that his matted locks, streaming[1] from the broken fillet, seemed by their outpouring yellowness to flood the heavens with an issuing fire of passion; gathering a frown that darkened the chess-board[2] of his forehead, like the presence of the god of death, and recalled the crocodile embellishments upon the faces of Yama's wives; with a red eye offering, as it were, an oblation of his blood to the goddess of pitilessness; imprisoning [11] the gleam of his teeth, as if it were his voice flying in terror at the merciless biting of his lip; altering the tie of the black antelope skin—a scroll of cursing as it were—which was slipping from his shoulder; clasped in every limb by gods, asuras, and sages, who, reflected in his drops of sweat, seemed to have come for refuge in their alarm at the curse; with a hand whose fingers shook with an angry tremor spurning his rosary as though it were a string of syllables clinging with supplications to him; thus, having first rinsed his mouth from his earthen pitcher, he took the water of cursing.

Meanwhile the great goddess Sāvitrī was seated in corporeal shape near to the Self-existent, wearing a robe of the silken bark of the tree of paradise and white as a mass of ambrosia foam. A shawl of lotus filament was tied in a *svastika* knot between her swelling bosoms. Three sectarial lines of ashes, banners of triumph, as it were, over the three worlds vanquished by ascetic force, brightened the courtyard of her forehead. Her *Vaikakṣyaka* scarf consisted of a hermit's wrap which hung from her shoulder, white as ambrosia foam, like a Ganges stream bent to a circle by

[1] *Viçarāru* apparently = 'bursting.'

[2] *Aṣṭāpadam: caturaṅgaphalakam*, Comm.: perhaps so called from its furrowed lines. Regarding this and the next allusion *vide* further note in the appendix.

ascetic power. Her left hand held a crystal water-vessel like the lotus calyx whence Brahmā arose; and her right, encircled with a rosary and studded with rings of shells, was raised aloft, the finger of scorn being scornfully waved as she cried:—'Fie on thee, sinner, prey to anger, evil of heart, reft of reason, ignorant of self, [12] false Brāhman and pretended sage, outcast, excommunicate, how comes it that, bewildered by thine own offence, thou wouldst curse the divine Sarasvatī, mother of the three worlds, fit adoration for throngs of gods, asuras, sages, and mortal men?'

So she spoke, and abandoning her ascetic's pillow arose, and with her the four incarnate Vedas left their cane seats in wrath, clad in bark garments and holding delicate chowries of *Kuça* fibres, bearing their hermit's staves, and grasping their round water-vessels like weapons. Under the guise of sweat *soma* juice, as it were, oozed from them: their foreheads gleamed with the pure ashes of the *Agnihotra* oblation: their voices echoed the sacred syllable: the quarters of the heavens were oppressed by the weight of their angrily agitated matted-locks: the daylight was darkened by the bulging of their black antelope skins flung round as they girt up their loins: and the world of Brahmā vibrated with the coming and going of their passionate panting.

Whereat in vain besought to mercy by the gods, 'O reverend sir, be merciful, she is no victim for a curse'; in vain implored by suppliant disciples, 'Master, forgive one fault'; in vain restrained by Atri, 'Balk not, my son, the fruit of thine asceticism'; the sage, beside himself with passion, let fall the water of that curse, crying:—'Ill-mannered girl, I take away from thee this state of pride by knowledge won. Begone downward to the world of mortal men.' But when Sāvitrī would have answered curse with curse, 'twas Sarasvatī that hindered her, saying:—'Dear friend, restrain thy wrath: even to Brāhmans by birth merely, uninitiated in heart, respect is due.' [13]

Thereupon, seeing Sarasvatī thus cursed, the Lord Brahmā uplifted his form, which wore the white sacrificial thread, as though his birth from the lotus had left a fibre clinging about him. With his right hand, which, as its signet ring sent up a spray of emerald rays, seemed to grasp a cluster of *Kuça* grass for staying a world-dissolution[1], he allayed the tumult of the curse; while his teeth shot out pure penetrating rays like plummet lines[2] for the building of a coming aeon of bliss, and his voice echoed through the spheres like a drum heralding with honour the departure of Sarasvatī, as in deep tones he spake:—'Brāhman, the path thou hast followed is one not frequented by the good. Its final goal is death. The dust upraised by the steeds of passion in their unbridled onrush is wont to cloud the vision of such as be not masters of the senses[3]. How limited indeed the scope of the eye! for 'tis by the purified intellect that the perfected behold all things good and evil. Nature rejects this union of piety and wrath as of water and fire. How dost thou, leaving the light, sink in darkness! for the root of all asceticism is patience. Skilled in discerning the faults of others, thy angry mind, like an eye inflamed, perceives not the frailty of its own passion[4]. How can censoriousness consort with commerce of great penances? [14] Blind verily is that seeing man who is over-wrathful. Clouded with passion, the mind distinguishes not what should and what should not be done. First of all the wisdom of the angry man is darkened; then his frowning brow. The flush of passion assaults first the senses, last the eyes. In the beginning the store of merit dissolves away; then the oozing sweat. The flash of dishonour flickers; then comes the trembling of the lip. How ruinous to the world was the growth of thy matted locks and bark dress, shoots and bark as it were of the poison tree! Like a pearl necklace, this graceless[5] impulse of thy mind is out of

[1] The origin of *darbha*=*kuça* grass from a world-convulsion is stated *Ath. V.* 19. 30. 5, and its power to allay passion, id. 6. 43. 1–

[2] *Sūtrapātam*, cf. *Kathās.* 14. 30, 24. 93: this passage has a bearing on the derivation of *sūtradhāra*.

[3] There is a pun on two meanings of *akṣa* (1) axle, (2) sense. Cf. *Kād.* p. 37, l. 14.

[4] *Doṣa* means either 'sin' or 'inflammation of the eye': *kupita*='inflamed' in both senses.

[5] *Vṛittamukta* has also *per paronomasiam* the sense of 'having round pearls': *parivartulamauktikā* Comm.

harmony, surely, with thy sage's dress. With a heart void of resignation idly like an actor dost thou wear the counterfeited semblance of an ascetic. Nought free from taint can I detect in thee. Even to this hour thy levity floats but on the surface of the sea of knowledge. None of these great sages are deaf and dumb, impotent and dull of wit. Why hast thou checked the sinless Sarasvatī, when thine own heart, the haunt of angry sin, should rather have been checked? These are the follies born of their own heedless slips whereby the undiscerning fall into reproach.'

Then to Sarasvatī he spake again:—'Dear child, be not dejected. Sāvitrī here shall accompany thee and solace the pain of severance from us. And the curse shall end when thou shalt behold the lotus face of thy child.'

So much decreed, Brahmā, having dismissed his court of gods, asuras, sages and mortal men, laid his hand upon the shoulder of Nārada, who hastily approached, and arose for the performance of his daily rites. [15] Sarasvatī, too, a little discomfited at the curse, letting fall upon her bosom a mingled glance of light and dark like a streak in a black antelope skin, led on by thronging bees caught, like the incarnate letters of the curse, in the incense of her fragrant sighs, her hands nerveless with sorrow at the curse, went with Sāvitrī to her mansion, her path to the world of men being pointed out as it were by the down-bent rays of her nails. And swarms of *kalahaṃsas* of the palace, convoked by the prattle of her anklets, followed after her like the hearts of the dwellers in Brahmā's world.

Meanwhile, as though to bear the tidings of Sarasvatī's descent, the light-coroneted sun went down to the middle world. Gradually waned the day, his pools all saddened by the calamity of the closing of all their lotus beds. Quickly, as though stung by the angrily bent side-glances of wine-flushed beauties, the world's sole eye, ruddy as a young monkey's mouth, lighted upon the peaks of the earth-propping hills. White were the environs of the heavenly hermitages with milky streams flowing from herds of cows with dripping udders; as though washed by the surge of the milky sea in uproar at the near rising of the moon. Let out for his evening ramble, the *chowrie*-crowned Airāvata was dashing his tusks at will against the banks of the heavenly stream, while the sound went up of their crashing against its sides of gold. The sky displayed a rosy tint, as though smeared with lac from the feet of thousands of mistresses of the Vidyādharas gone forth to their trysts. Like the sweat of Sandhyā in her delight at Çiva's worship[1], the evening glow streamed forth of saffron hue, flushing the heavenly spaces and filled with the sunset offerings of the saints on their journey along the sky. [16] Resplendent was the world of Brahmā, where crowds of noble worshipping sages clasped a forest of hands in evening adoration; as though all the lotus beds were come to show honour to that lotus whence Brahmā sprang. And loudly from the Brāhmans[2] uprose the chorus of the third libation hymn. In the temples of the seven sages the courts were all tressed with the flames of the lighted *Vaitāna* fires; as though a camp lustration had commenced in an army devoted to Dharma. Light were the hermits from the removal of the poison taint of sin which the Aghamarṣaṇa hymn[3] had stolen away. The sand isles of Mandakinī's stream were purified by rows of ascetics seated at evening prayer, and the line of its waves was broken by the gleam[4] of Brahmā's floating *haṃsas*. Fragrant with the scent of their own honey, the night-lotus beds, to the joy of the bees, commenced to open, like umbrellas of the water nymphs, seraglio mansions for the wives of the feathered tribes. Satisfied with their symposiums on the sweet honey of day-lotuses now languid at day's close, the flamingo swarms sank to sleep, arching their necks to be scratched by the soft fibres, and fanning the blue lotus beds with rows of flapping wings. The evening breeze, soft as the sigh of night, came making grey the river with the pollen of flowers

1 Çiva's evening worship is described in the Meghadūta çl. 38.
2 Or 'loud in Brahmā's praise' or 'loudly from Brahmā.'
3 The Aghamarṣaṇa hymn is the last in the Ṛig-Veda.
4 Literally 'betoothed by the smile.'

on the bank and bearing perfume from the jasmine[1] in the curls of the matrons of the City of Saints. [17] Throngs of bees reclined in huts formed by the cavities of lotuses barred by the tips of filaments erect and stiff as they closed.

Like clustering *Kuṭaja* buds in the forest of Çiva's hair when it tosses in the dance, the star-swarms filled the sky with their clusters. About the earth the new-born darkness closed, coppery-hued from the after-effects of the twilight, coloured like the skin of a ripe date, and thick as the cloud of doomsday[2]. Sharply piercing the mass of soft dusk, the scattered lamps peeped forth like clusters of *Campak* buds about the ear of the goddess of night. Paling with the lovely effulgence of the crescent moon's rays, the eastern quarter began to narrow the dusk, like a young sandbank by Yamunā's banks when the dark water retreats as it dries. Perturbed, like the spirit of a proud beauty, by the moon's fingers[3] clutching its tresses, the darkness, in hue like a jay's wing, a very cluster of curls belonging to the Gipsy[4] of night, dissolved and abandoned the sky, and cast its gloom upon the pools of blossoming blue lotuses. The form of the Lord of White Splendour, now uprisen, assumed the glow of the Udaya mountain, resembling the lip of the nymph of night; and his redness was as though he were covered with blood oozing from his own deer, now slain by a stroke from the rending paws of the lion that dwells in the caves of the valleys of Udaya's peaks. The gloom had waned, as if washed by the flow of the moonstone's ooze from[5] the Eastern hill. Like a great ivory crocodile-mouthed conduit bearing a stream of milk trickling from the world of cows, the moon's circle had commenced to fill the ocean. [18]

At that clear evening time Sāvitrī thus addressed Sarasvatī, who, vacant in heart as it were, was lost in tearful thought:—'Friend, my tongue is ashamed to prate to thee,

1 *Mallikā = bhūpadī*, opens at night.

2 Or 'a black cloud.'

3 I.e. 'rays.'

4 Her beauty hangs upon the cheek of Night
Like a rich jewel in an Ethiop's ear. *Romeo and Juliet.*

5 Read *acalacyuta* with the Calc. and Kashmir texts.

whose wisdom may instruct the three worlds. Thou knowest already what are the ill-mannered ways of fate, unstable, heedless, like a lowborn person, even of the worthy, inconstant, not to be evaded, in no wise pleasurable[1]. A mere grain of undeserved humiliation, coming from an inferior, makes turbid the spirit[2] even of the wise. Even an atom of misfortune, when watered with ceaseless tears, like a leafless tree, puts forth a thousand shoots. An over-delicate soul, like a *Mālatī* blossom, is withered by the particles of fiery pain. Like the elephant's goad, even a slight prick of trouble, assailing the great, suffices to torment. Moreover our native home, linked to us like a kinsman by the knotted ties of natural affection, is hard to abandon. Separation from approved friends, dreadful as the stroke of the wood-cleaving saw, leaves a fissure in the heart. But thee it befits not to be thus afflicted. Thou surely art not the soil in which should spring up the shoots of the poison plant of pain. Also, seeing that before and behind us like a ruler stand our past deeds, potent whether good or evil in producing their fruit, [19] what occasion have the wise for sorrowing? Why, pray, do these inauspicious tears defile a face which is the single lotus of auspiciousness for the three worlds? Enough now of this: say what part of the world thou wouldst adorn. On what blest spot is thy heart fain to alight? What holy bathing-places dost thou desire to grace? In what fortunate forest seclusions wouldst thou live the ascetic's life? Here am I ready to descend to earth, a loving friend, well-skilled to serve thee, tried in friendly offices when we played together in the dust. Cast thyself henceforth in heart, voice and deed, seeking no other refuge, upon the author of all knowledge, the bestower of paradise, the dust of whose feet makes pure both gods and asuras, whose earring is formed of the moon's digits, even on Çiva, god of gods, preceptor of the three worlds. In but a little time he will give thee release from the woe of the curse.'

[1] The ways of fate are here punningly compared to the caprices of women, cf. *vāmāḥ: striyaçca* Comm.

[2] There is a pun on lake Mānasa made turbid by a falling particle.

To these words Sarasvatī, letting fall a pearly white tear-drop, replied:—'Dear friend, if I go with thee, neither severance from Brahmā's world nor grief at the curse will cause me any distress: 'tis only that the happiness of serving the lotus-throned fills my heart with soft regret. Furthermore 'tis thou who knowest the abodes where Dharma can be followed[1] upon earth, the means of mystic meditation, and how to practise the postures of ascetic rapture.' So much said she ceased to speak: and that night she spent with unclosed eyes, sleepless through agitation.

Next day as, heralded by the dawn [20] rosy as an old cock's comb, the adorable sun, the world's diadem, Mount Udaya's crest jewel, arose with a form red as with blood scattered from the mouths of his own steeds cut by the tossing clanking bit, the keeper of the goose tribes that draw Brahmā's chariot[2] sang aloud in Aparavaktrā metre as he strolled along not far away:—

'Wherefore trembles thine anxious glance,
'O nursling of pellucid Mānasa as thy home?
'Descend, O *kalahaṃsa*, to the pond;
'Again shalt thou return to the abode of lotuses.'

Hearing this Sarasvatī thought: ''Tis I, methinks, to whom he appeals. So be it! I must respect the sage's sentence.' So she arose resolved to descend to the earth, and having left her attendants prostrate at the separation, parted from her kindred, and then, like one cut off from the herd, passed thrice round the four-faced god. At last, courteously turning back crowds of pursuing devotees, she set forth accompanied by Sāvitrī from Brahmā's world.

Straight she came to the steady-flowing[3] loud-roaring river Mandākinī with milky udders downward streaming[4] like the cow of Dharma, a very *Mālatī* wreath for the head

[1] As e.g. Madhyadeça, Manu ii. 21.

[2] The Kashmir and Bombay texts insert here *vivicya*: *vicārya* 'having reflected.'

[3] Or 'descended from Dhruva,' i.e. from the star of Dhruva or the firmament or Viṣṇu; cf. Comm.

[4] The Sanskrit may also mean 'with down-raining white clouds.'

of Çiva[1]. Thick covered were its banks with close-clinging Bālakhilyas[2]. The bark of its trees had been washed by Arundhatī. [21] The clear stars were tremulous as they crossed its high-leaping waves. Its sand-isles were bristling beds of floating sesamum seeds and water[3] offered by ascetics. All white were its banks with offerings to the manes let fall by Brahmā when purified by bathing. *Kuça*-grass beds of the seven Ṛiṣis, who had slept hard by, gave token of the birth-fast for the sun's delivery from eclipse[4]. Dappled was it with abundant flowers from the service, let fall by Çacī's lord when purified by rinsing his mouth. It had garlands of *Mandāra* blossoms, dropped as the remains of the sacrifice from Çiva's city. Scornfully had it cleft the rocks of Mandara's caves. Rippled was its surface with the cup-like bosoms of unnumbered beauties of Indra's court[5]. Its waters were resonant with its tumbling over myriad stones and crocodiles. Masses of the moon's ambrosial dew bestarred its banks, flowing down from the sun's Suṣumṇa ray. Grey were its sands with smoke from the fire of Dhiṣaṇa[6]. Vidyādharas were flying in terror at its leaping over the sand *liṅgas* erected by the saints. Such was the river, the cast slough, as it were, of the sky serpent, the sportive forehead-ornament of the jester of Indra's world[7], the bazaar street of the wares of Dharma, the shot bolt of the gate of Hell's city, the silken turban wrap of Sumeru's king[8], the cloth banner of Kailāsa's elephant, the track of liberation, the wheel-rim of the aeon[9] of goodness, the bride of the lord of the seven oceans[10].

Passing along its banks Sarasvatī descended to the world of mortals; and just as she stood on the edge of the sky she

1 The heavenly Ganges falls on Çiva's head.
2 Liliputian munis concerning whom many stories are told.
3 For the *tilodakam* cf. Manu III. 210.
4 An eclipse involves impurity to all people, and so necessitates a fast.
5 I.e. Apsarases.
6 Bṛihaspati, the purohita of the Gods, and the planet Jupiter.
7 Gaṇeça ?
8 =Çiva.
9 Yuga=(1) age of goodness, (2) chariot.
10 =The Milk Ocean or a Mount Candra (Comm.).

spied a great river brimming with water, pure, cool and sweet, a daughter of Brahmā, by name the Stream of Gold, but by men called Çoṇa, the pearl necklace, as it were, of Varuṇa, the ambrosia cataract of the moon mountain, the ooze of the Vindhya's moon-gem, a flood of camphor sap from the Daṇḍaka forest, the streaming loveliness of the world, the crystal couch of the sky's beauty[1]. [22] At the sight her heart was taken captive by its beauty, and there upon its bank she resolved to dwell; so she said to Sāvitrī:—'Pleasant to me, friend, is the neighbourhood of this great river, which makes dull the lustre of Mandākinī. Here are honeyed voices of peacocks, trees having stocks besanded with heaps of pollen, the entrancing hum of lute-like clusters of scent-intoxicated bees. My heart prompts me to abide even here.' So as Sāvitrī welcomed her words, saying, 'Thus let it be,' she alighted with her friend upon the western bank: and for a dwelling she fixed her mind upon a certain fair creeper arbour by the shore containing a slab of stone. Then after resting she soon arose, and having with Sāvitrī gathered flowers for worship, bathed: next, having in Çiva's honour erected sand *liṅgas* on the sand-isles, she with deep devotion performed in full the ritual of clasping of fingers together with the Dhruvā hymn and preceded by the Pañcabrahma prayer[2]; lastly after long meditation on the eight incarnate forms, earth, wind, water, sky, fire, sun, moon, sacrificer, she presented the eightfold[3] offering of flowers, and refreshed her body with easily gathered roots and fruits and Çoṇa water, cool and of a sweetness surpassing even ambrosia. That day passed, she made a couch of flowers and slept on the stone floor of the creeper arbour. On the morrow she spent night and day in the same routine.

[23] Now as the days in this wise sped on and time passed, one morning, when the sun was risen only one watch, she heard in the northern quarter the deep clear sound of horses' neighs

[1] I.e. as mirroring the sky. Çrī often reclines on a slab.

[2] A prayer addressed to Sadyojāta, Vāmadeva, Aghora, Tatpuruṣa and Īçāna. Comm. (We have divided this sentence in our translation.)

[3] As symbolising the eight forms.

filling the thickets of the woods with echoes. Her curiosity aroused, she came forth, and looking abroad from the bower beheld at no great distance and speeding towards her a cloud of dust grey as the leaf which contains the blossoming *Ketakī* flower. In due course, as proximity gave birth to distinctness, she saw a troop of horse floating in that huge mass of dust grey as a *Çapharа's* belly, like a school of crocodiles in water. Before it ran an army of foot about a thousand strong, mostly young men, with clusters of crisp hanging hair upon their foreheads, and cheeks laughing with the bright gleam of their ear-ornaments: girt with scented jerkins spotted with a powder of black aloe wood paste; their upper garments formed into turbans; sparkling golden bracelets on their left forearms, daggers fastened in strong knots in their sashes of doubled cloth; tirelessly with bodies thin and hard from incessant exercise leaping like the deer of the winds and spurning smooth and rough ground, holes, and clumps of bushes; clubs at their sides, swords in their hands; laden with various wild flowers, fruits, roots, and leaves for worship; and making a ceaseless hubbub with cries of 'On, on, make speed, make speed, away, away, make way in front.' In the midst [24] she discerned a youth in age about eighteen years, shaded by a sky-reaching umbrella, which with its half-moon, its girdling heaps of pearls, its inlay of pieces of various precious stones, and its whiteness as of shells, milk and foam, resembled the milky ocean voluntarily come to present Lakṣmī. All about him was the sparkling light of his ornaments, as if the horizon of the heavens were keeping close out of passion for the sight of him. Down to his loins from his topknot hung a wreath of *Mālatī* flowers, like a pennon of beauty won by a world conquest. The red rays uprising from the ruby in his crest[1] seemed delicate sprays carried by an invisible goddess to cleanse his travel-soiled form. His hair, wreathed in clusters of crisp curls and charmingly adorned with a coiled coronet[2]

[1] *Çikhaṇḍakhaṇḍikā: cūḍābharaṇam.* Comm.

[2] *Muṇḍamālā*, which occurs several times in the book, seems to mean originally Durgā's wreath of sculls, and then a wreath of white flowers. The black hair in contact with the white flowers is compared to the darkness swallowing the day.

of white *Vakula* buds, appeared to be swallowing up the day's contracted blaze. His forehead, all yellow as with arsenic paste, cast the glow of its beauty upon the heavens, and being clasped by its natural loveliness, seemed composed of a second[1] portion of the moon which forms the coronet of Çiva's matted locks. His wide eyes, whose glances bold in the confidence of fresh youth's commencement made nought of the whole world, appeared to create an autumn, clothing the heavens in myriad pools of opening white, blue and red lotuses. His long nose was like a river of beauty's water, flowing from beneath the moonstone of his forehead, and bridged across the stream of his long eyes. His mouth, breathing a fragrance of mangos, camphor, *Kakkola*-fruits, cloves, and coral trees, and resounding with a hubbub of intoxicated bee-swarms, seemed to emit a very spring together with a Nandana forest. His innocent smiles, bathing the heavens with the light of his teeth as he uplifted his face to catch the jests of his friends around him, [25] created incessantly a kind of moonlight roaming about the sky. A dangling three-pointed ear-ornament—an emerald set between a pair of pearls big as *Kadamba* buds—emitted a sheen which suggested a pendant of green jasmine leaves with their flowers. His arms, decorated with painted lines of scented civet powder, resembled a pair of Kāma's pennon poles with rampant crocodiles girdling their tops. His body was divided by a white Brahmanical thread, like Mandara encircled by the stream of Ganges indignant at the churning of the ocean[2]. His breast, a broad sandbank with two shapely swelling bosoms for ruddy-geese, and with a coating of camphor powder in handfuls for dust, seemed a horizon spread out before him and kept within bounds by the length of his stout arms. His slim waist was marked off by a tight-

[1] The *first* portion having been used for Çiva, the *second* remains for this hero. The Sanskrit words for 'natural loveliness' may also be translated 'connate Lakṣmī,' referring to the birth of Lakṣmī along with the moon from the ocean.

[2] The Ganges is imagined as seeking to stay the churning by clinging fast to the mountain.

drawn lower garment of *Hārīta*[1] green, of which one corner was gracefully set in front a little below the navel and the hem hung over the girdle behind, and which on both sides was so girt up as to display a third of his thigh. His stout thighs, glistening with a thick smearing of bright sandal, seemed to scoff at the length of Airāvata's trunk, being very stone pillars for supporting the granite platform of his great chest; while his knees issued from huge 'crocodile mouths[2]' with hard flesh accumulated by incessant exercise. His shanks were somewhat slim, as if from the fatigue of supporting the weight of his vast thighs. His feet, which hung on either side, were red as two young shoots of the tree of paradise, and the waving light of their nails formed as it were a row of chowrie ornaments for his horse.

[26] He was mounted on a great steed, swift as thought, in colour like a dark *Sindhuvāra* flower, and with a coat as black as a *golāngūla* ape's cheeks. As it advanced its high prancing hoofs seemed to rest awhile in the air when it coiled its legs, and falling to tear up the earth. Every moment the hard bit clanked when released by the teeth. Upon its forehead dangled rings of fine gold and the end of the bit rested against its long nose. It was adorned with tinkling trappings of gold. Close on either side with their hands grasping the saddle cloth, two attendants shook white chowries. In front chanted a bard, whose eloquence caused the hairs on the young man's cheeks to bristle with delight, as though tiny stamen filaments from his ear-wreath had become attached to them. He seemed to reveal a descent of a Kāma's aeon, to produce a cosmos of moonlight, to beget an animate creation of the substance of smiles, to pave his path with devotion, to frame a day all of love, to inaugurate a kingdom of affection. He was to the eye, as it were, a collyrium of allurement, to the heart an attracting spell, to the senses a powder able to affect the healthiest; for desire a never-cloying delight, for

[1] The *Hārīta* is a kind of pigeon.

[2] *Makaramukha* is a name given to the upper part of the knee; *makaramukhaṃ : jānunor uparibhāgaḥ.* Comm.

bliss a never-failing charm; the resurrection day of Love[1], the elixir of youth, the unshared rule of loveliness, [27] the triumphal pillar of shapeliness, the capital sum of grace, the fructuation of the world's good deeds, the first bud of beauty's creeper, the fruit of Prajāpati's studies in creation, the glory of graciousness, the high-tide of sparkling wit.

By the young man's side, on a horse not close to any other, was a person wearing a white[2] jerkin and a white silken turban round his head. Tall, in aspect like a pillar of molten gold, with a frame hardened in spite of advanced years by exercise, with short nails beard and hair, bald as a shell, somewhat stout, hairy-bosomed, dressed handsomely but with little display, he seemed one to teach even old age to be decorous, to add weight even to great qualities, to convert magnanimity itself to a disciple, to provide deportment itself with a monitor.

When the young man heard of that pair of divinely shaped maidens—for the footmen in the van took it all in at a glance and in astonishment made their report—his curiosity was aroused, and putting his horse to a gallop, he rode up to the bower, eager to see them. While still at a distance, he alighted from his horse, and staying his suite, approached respectfully on foot attended only by the second noble personage. [28] Greetings made, Sāvitrī and Sarasvatī duly received them with the usual hospitality of forest life, beginning with the offer of a seat of twigs and ending with presents of fruit with flowers. They being seated, Sāvitrī sate down, and after a not over-prolonged silence addressed herself to the second of the two, the man of advanced years :— 'Sir, to make the first address ill becomes women, whose innate modesty is their all, more especially noble girls, innocent as woodland fawns. Yet hearing, greedy to learn the news and emulous of the eye which has been gratified with seeing, moves me thereto. And indeed even at first sight the good proffer confidence like a gift. Like wine, the

[1] Kāma was killed in anger by Çiva.

[2] Read *valakṣa* (for *dhavala*) with Comm. and the Kashmir text.

feeling inspired by the courtesy[1] shown by a superior makes even the timid talkative. In the very meek confidence easily reaches its highest point, like a string passing to the very end of a plaint bow[2]. Moreover, even in the profoundly wise the previously unknown masterpieces of creation visible in the world occasion astonishment; for the beauty of this high-souled youth is beyond anything in the universe. It is not the levity natural to young women that compels me to speak, but the exceeding grace, handmaid of high birth, that appears in this darling of heaven[3]. Therefore relate what hapless region has through your coming been desolated by the spreading plague of separation. What is your destination? Whose son is this young man, a second Kāma humbling the pride of Çiva's roar? How named the sire, rich in austerities, whose heart this youth gladdens, as the Kauṣṭubha jewel gladdens the heart of Viṣṇu, with an ambrosial shower? [29] Who was his mother, worthy of the worship of the three worlds, the parent, like the morning twilight, of a great splendour? What fortunate syllables make up his name? To inquire concerning your honour also is the next proceeding of a heart compliant to curiosity.'

She having so spoken, the other courteously replied:—'Lady, kindly speech is a hereditary art among the noble. Not merely your face, your heart also is moonlike, bestowing delight by words cooling like ambrosia dew. Women like you come into the world as the native soil of nobility, nay, a greater glory, as the fine arts for forming noble characters[4]. Not to mention conversation, even interchange of glances with the noble is a great exaltation. Listen then: This young man, Dadhīca by name, the pride of the Bhṛigu race, is the externalized life of the sainted Cyavana[5],—that forehead-

[1] Or—of the wine—'courteously offered by a superior.'

[2] The pun here turns on the double sense of *atinamre*=(1) 'flexible,' (2) 'very submissive.'

[3] The term used here (*devānām priyasya*) is that which Açoka uses of himself in his inscriptions.

[4] 'To know her was a liberal education,' Steele.

[5] For the story of this mythical sage cf. Wilson, 'Hindu Theatre' I. p. 263 n. and reff.

mark of the triad Bhū Bhuvas and Svar, whose invincible might paralyzed the pillar-like arm of Indra, whose lotus feet tread rudely on the couch formed by the jewelled crowns of gods and demons, and who blasted Puloman by the outpouring of his splendour. His mother was a princess, Sukanyā named, a gem among the maidens of the universe, daughter of the world-conquering Çaryāta, whose train is of unnumbered monarchs. Observing her to be with child, her father took her in the birth-month from her husband's side to his own dwelling, there to bear her child[1]. The son borne by the princess was this young man—long life be his. [30] And in the king's house he in good time grew up, lotus-eyed, the delight of his kindred, like the young lord of stars[2]. Even when his daughter returned to her husband's house, the grandfather parted not from this cheery-faced[3] grandson of his, a solace to the heart. There accordingly he was trained in all the sciences and the circle of the arts.

'In time, observing him to have attained to youth, his grandfather, reflecting that his father too should have the delight of gazing on his lotus face, has now prevailed upon himself to send him away to his father's presence. But me let your highness understand to be one named Vikukṣi, the least of servants, minister of the will of my auspiciously-named lord Çaryāta. My master appointed me his attendant on the way to his father's feet. Our royal house follows the rule of heredity, and length of service produces in the great a certain kindly feeling even towards a dependant[4]. Unfailing indeed is the store of good feeling in the great.

'Some two leagues hence across the Çoṇa is the abode of the sainted Cyavana, a forest rivalling Caitraratha[5] and by him entitled Cyāvana, an appellation derived from his own

[1] The custom should be noticed.

[2] I.e. the moon.

[3] '*Na jāyate yatra tṛiptis tad āsecanakaṃ viduḥ.*' Comm. 'that of which we are never satiated': cf. A. K. *Viçeṣyanighnavarga*, 53.

[4] The office of minister was frequently hereditary in Hindu times, cf. Wilson, 'Hindu Theatre' II. p. 208 n.

[5] The grove of the god Kuvera.

name. That is our journey's goal. If now this is a time for an act of grace, and your heart is void of contempt towards us, if such as we are fit recipients of favours and worthy to hear, let not this our first solicitation of curiosity meet with a repulse. We also are fain to hear your highnesses' story. Your aspect in no way falls short of divinity: but our hearts are eager to hear your lineage and names. Say therefore what stock was made enviable by your birth. Who is this lady near your highness, a coinherence as it were of mutually exclusive qualities? Thus:—with the darkness of her locks close by, she has a radiance as of the sun; [31] with the face of a lotus[1] the eye of a fawn; wearing the brilliance of the young day, she has yet the smile of a night-lotus; the voice of a lovesick *kalahaṃsa*, yet swelling bosoms[2]: hands soft as day-lotuses, yet hips broad as the rocks of the mountain of snow[3]; thighs like a young elephant's trunk, yet a languid gait; she has not passed the season of girlhood, yet she has the swimming eyes of love[4].'

Sāvitrī answered:—'You shall hear, my lord, in good time. Our hearts are fain to stay here many days: and the distance is slight. Intimacy will make all clear. Let my lord not forget people seen only by chance.' After which reply she became silent. But Dadhīca, with a voice which, resembling the deep mutter of clouds laden with new rain, set the peacocks dancing in the creeper arbours, gravely said:—'My lord, her highness being conciliated will be gracious to us; now let us visit my father. Rise, let us proceed.' Then, the other assenting, he slowly arose, and with a bow moved away. As he mounted his horse and departed, Sarasvatī gazed for a long time after him with an eye with straight rigid lashes and pupil motionless as in a

[1] The contradiction turns on the double sense of *puṇḍarīka* = (1) lotus, (2) lion.

[2] *Payodharāḥ* may also mean 'clouds'; the *kalahaṃsa* migrates during the rainy season.

[3] Snow kills the lotus: hence the contradiction.

[4] The words may also mean 'not faithless to Kumāra and yet loving his enemy Tāraka.'

picture[1]. Crossing the Çoṇa, Dadhīca quickly reached the site of his father's seclusion. But when he disappeared Sarasvatī stood for a long time gazing in that direction, and could hardly cease looking [32].

Then, when she had remained quiet one short moment recalling that perfection of form, her heart was filled more and more with astonishment. Her eye longed to see him again; and something involuntarily drew her glance in the same direction as before. All uncommissioned her heart went away with *him*. Like a new spray upon a young wood-creeper, love somehow[2] sprang up in her heart. She passed the day as it were languid, empty, and heavy with sleep. But when with westward inclining circle the sun's radiant form, lover of the lotus beds, sprung from the three Vedas, was nearing the west, with colour golden as a cluster of *Lāṅgalikās*, and brilliance red as an old crane's head, while the gathering dusk sky-enveloping was befouling the firmament with a blackness like the bark of a young *Tamāla*, and slowly slowly the moon was creeping up the heavens, like a swan of Mandākinī, in pursuit of the tinkling anklets of the roaming mistresses of the saints,—at that hour, the very outset of night, Sarasvatī, her twilight worship done, fell with languid limbs on her couch of young shoots and there remained. Sāvitrī also, having performed the evening ritual, in due course took to her couch of leaves at the usual hour of rest, and, drowsiness approaching, slept [33].

But the other, though she closed her eyes, enjoyed no sleep; her couch of leaves was deranged by repeated tossings of her limbs, and this was her thought:—'Surely the world of mortals is above all worlds, since therein are born such gems, the three-worlds' pride, laden with the company of all fine qualities[3]. Thus:—the moon is but a trickling drop

[1] This simile so common in Sanskrit poetry may be paralleled from Shakespeare 'Hamlet,' Act II. sc. ii. 465, 'So, as a painted tyrant, Pyrrhus stood,' and also Coleridge, 'Ancient Mariner,'

'As idle as a painted ship
Upon a painted ocean.'

[2] *Kuto'pi*=(1) 'somehow,' (2) 'from the earth.'

[3] Or 'heavy even for all necklaces.'

of his face's flood of beauty: his glances are beds of expanding lotuses, white, blue, and red: the sparklings of his gem-like lips are forest avenues of open *Bandhūkas*. To that body only the disembodied Kāma can add a charm. Happy the eyes, hearts, and young beauty of those women within whose vision he comes. In displaying him to me only for a moment my ill-deeds in former births have wrought their fruit. What resource is open to me now?' Amid such thoughts as these drowsiness coming over her, she at length lay still awhile, and falling asleep beheld (in a vision) that very youth with the long eyes. Through that second dream-meeting the lord of the crocodile banner, drawing his bow to the ear, dealt her a pitiless stroke. When she awoke thus smit by Kāma's bolt, then came unrest as if to learn her condition[1]. Thus was it with her:—from that hour, [34] even though unsmitten by the pollen-whitened wood-creepers, she felt a smart. Though her eyes might not be hurt by flower-dust wafted by gentle breezes, yet she would let fall a tear. Though not bedewed by Çoṇa spray scattered by myriad fanning *haṃsas*' wings, yet a moisture came upon her. Though not borne by pairs of rocking *Kādambas*[2], yet was she agitated by the tossing waves of the sylvan lotus pools. Though untouched by the smoke of parting sighs let fall by severed pairs of ruddy-geese, yet she wore a pallid hue. Though unstung by the honey-making tribes, all grey with flower-dust, yet she would feverishly start.

After the lapse of some nights Vikukṣi returning by the same route arrived at that place, and, having checked his attendants as before, approached with his umbrella-holder. Sarasvatī, who had observed his approach from afar, sprang joyfully up, and, gazing with straining neck like a woodland fawn, seemed to bathe the way-worn traveller with a glance that whitened the ten regions of space. When he had accepted a seat, Sāvitrī asked him affectionately 'My lord, is the young prince well?' He answered, 'Quite well, your highness, and he bears you both in remembrance: during the past days,

[1] I.e. as it were, to make a call.

[2] A goose with dark-grey wings.

however, he is somewhat thin in figure, and experiences as it were an inexplicable and causeless void. [35] Also there will arrive later[1] a lady named Mālatī, commissioned from him to inquire of you: she is a sigh of the prince.' Hearing this, Sāvitrī once more spoke:—'A magnanimous prince indeed to honour with his acquaintance[2] people scarcely known to him and seen only for an instant. His mind was, I suppose, accidentally caught by us for a moment as he passed, like a shawl by a wayside creeper. In your lord's son true nobility is not devoid of high birth. A listless world, truly, that it does not at any price purchase the hearts of the great so easily won to friendship. This is a pinnacle of nobility in the great, unattainable by others, whereby they win the whole world to their service.' Having spent some time in general[3] conversation Vikukṣi went away in the direction of his choice.

On the morrow as the adorable jewel of day arose with his thousand rays, illimitable in splendour, invading the starlight, veiling the darkness, eager to expand the red lotuses, Mālatī was seen to have crossed the Çoṇa and to be approaching with a small retinue of attendants[4]. [38] While still far away, she was looted as it were by Sarasvatī's wishes in her love for Dadhīca, hurried on by her eagerness, met by her longings, embraced by her yearning, welcomed into her heart, bathed in her tears of joy, anointed[5] by her smile, fanned by her sighs, arrayed in the light of her eyes, worshipped with (the flower offering of) her lotus face, made a friend by her hopes. So she drew near, and, alighting from her steed, saluted from a distance with bowed head: then having been embraced by the pair she modestly sate down. Being courteously addressed by them, she congratulated herself, and with hands humbly laid upon her head an-

[1] The Comm. explains *anvakṣam*=*pratyakṣam*='in person': but query?

[2] Or 'inquiries.'

[3] *Uccāvacaiḥ*: *prakṛitavastvasaṃsparçibhiḥ*, *vicitrair iti vā*. Comm.

[4] The long description of Mālatī will be found in the Appendix.

[5] Read *viliptā* with the Kashmir text.

nounced the respectful greeting wherewith Dadhīca had charged her; and in the course of various polite conversation she won the hearts of Sāvitrī and Sarasvatī by her urbanity of demeanour and courteous address.

When noon had passed in due course, and Sāvitrī was gone down to the Çoṇa to bathe, Mālatī sent away her attendants, and approaching Sarasvatī, who was lying on a couch of flowers, [39] said meaningly to her:—'Lady, I have something to communicate in private: so I wish you to bestow on me the favour of a moment's attention.' Sarasvatī, suspecting a message from Dadhīca, wondered what she was about to say. So concealing with a portion of her shawl of woven bark a heart which, as if the buds of curiosity were bursting forth, bristled with the rays from the nails of her left hand laid against her bosom; clinging to a neighbouring creeper (her hope of life, it seemed) which swayed with her incessant sighs, while her dangling ear-wreath suggested that her ear was running forth to listen; her blooming moonlike face flooding the world with an outpouring of beauty like a stream of passion; buoyed up by swarms of dusky bees attracted by the fragrance of her flowery couch, like embodied yearnings issuing forth blackened by the fire of Kāma's flame; slowly, slowly in the fever of love's dart she uprose from her couch of flowers, and drawing nigh to her ear the Mālatī reflected in her cheek, as if out of shame she would say 'Whisper it to me,' with honeyed voice she gravely said:—'Why do you speak thus to me, friend Mālatī? Who am I to grant attention as a favour? Even without asking[1], the charming and lovely[2] are masters of our bodies, our lives, our all. There is nothing that you are not to me, sister, friend, loved one, second self. Ordain what task, small or great, this poor body may perform. This compliant heart has no secrets from you. Deal as you please with your slave. Reveal, lovely lady, your meaning.'

'Lady,' the other replied, 'you do not need to be told the delightfulness of mundane things, the importunity of the

[1] *Aprārthito* 'without a request'; cf. *vidita* Kirātārj. I. 2.

[2] V. l. *ativelam* (= *atimātram*) for *atipeçalas* in Kashm. ed.

army of the senses, the intoxication of youthfulness, the restlessness of the mind. [40] The resistless power of Kāma is notorious. Therefore meet me not, I pray, with censure. My chatter is not due to folly, giddiness, or love of gossip. There is nothing which great devotion to a master does not make people attempt. From the very moment, princess, when the prince beheld you, love has been his spiritual guide[1], the moon his lord of life[2], the southern breeze his familiar[3], anguish has been in his secret counsels, pain the friend of his bosom[4], wakefulness his kinsman, yearnings his emissaries, sighs his vanguard[5], death his squire, disquiet his courier, fancies his aged advisers. How am I to speak? Should I say 'he is a match for your highness,' your heart will tell you that; 'of noble character,' that is beside the mark; 'a man of sense,' that is at variance with his state of mind; 'blessed by fortune,' that depends on you; 'constant in affection,' that implies experience; 'versed in rendering homage,' that is inappropriate to his princely rank; 'he is fain to be your slave till death,' a knave's plea; 'you shall be the mistress of his house,' a seductive tale; 'happy she who owns such a lord,' a partisan's story; [41] 'you are his death,' an unkind saying; 'you know not worth,' a reproach; 'you have often shown him favours in dreams,' unsupported by testimony; 'he pleads for his life,' a coward's act; 'go and visit him,' a command; 'though forbidden, he is coming perforce,' mere overbearingness. Therefore, when I have said that you are beyond the reach of words, the decision rests with you.'

So much said, she became silent. But Sarasvatī with eyes wide-open with love replied:—'I am unable to say many words. Here am I, lady of smiling speech, at your

[1] There is a pun on *guru*=(1) great, (2) teacher.

[2] I.e. as allaying his pain by its coolness. *Jīviteça* may, however, mean also (1) the god of death, as the moon serves to kindle his passion, and (2) *purohit* or spiritual guide: there is a complicated play on these three senses.

[3] Or 'a cause of sighing.'

[4] The word *paramasuhṛid* may also mean 'preëminently an enemy.'

[5] Or—punningly—'sighs go before his body.'

orders. Take charge of my life.' 'Your commands are the highest of favours,' replied Mālatī, beside herself with joy, and bowing passed on her galloping steed across the Çoṇa, and proceeded to Cyavana's hermitage to bring Dadhīca. But the other out of love for her friend made Sāvitrī also acquainted with the news. Her mind panting under its load of longing, she could scarcely pass the rest of the day which seemed an aeon. But when the adorable sun had sunk with all his radiance in the west, when the dusk was stilly descending, and the moon was issuing, like a lion from his cave, from the eastern quarter now gleaming as with a smile[1], then Sarasvatī sate herself down on the Çoṇa sands, white, delicate as China silk, rolling in waves, like a silken-soft bed. On her brow was a jewel, the imaged moonlight, as it were, of Dadhīca's toe-nails as in her dreams she fell in supplication at his feet. Reflected in the mirror of her cheek, the moon thus near to her ear seemed to be communicating Kāma's charge, 'Fair smiling one, here have I brought thy heart's darling.' As her hand fanned her moist cheek, its nails scattered a horizon of rays, like a bundle of moon-digits converted into a yak-tail fan. Above her heart, sighing[2] against her bosom, she had just strength to bear a young lotus stalk, like a rod let fall[3] in sport by Kāma across its portal to say 'Here none but Dadhīca may enter.' [42] Thus did she expect him, and this was the thought in her heart, 'Since I, even I, Sarasvatī, have been enslaved, like a low-caste woman, by this heart's son Kāma, what is to be expected of other poor excitable maidens?'

With Mālatī Dadhīca came bringing sweet perfumes like the month of honey, bearing like a *haṃsa* cooling lotus fibres, his face uplifted in deep joy like a peacock at a cloud[4], causing like the Malaya breeze a tremour upon a

[1] I.e. an *arch* smile at the meeting of the lovers.

[2] The Kashmir text, however, reads *stanayantī*, which will go with Sarasvatī.

[3] For *vetralatā* cf. Pañcatantra (Bomb. ed.), p. 16, l. 1.

[4] *Ghana*=(1) great, (2) cloud.

creeper-like form[1] all white with moist sandal: drawn on, as it seemed, by the lord of planets[2] with finger-like rays grasping his locks; wafted by the southern breeze potent in kindling love; borne on the billowy current of desire[3]. A throng of bees crowding towards his fragrance arrayed his willowy form as with a dark garment: the moon's image, gleaming within like the ear-shell[4] of love's raging elephant, whitened the convex of his cheek as with the coy aimless smile of a first union. Having arrived and greeted her with a voice which, broken like a *haṃsa's*, seemed interrupted by a tinkle of anklets from the loved one taken to his heart, he spent that fair night in the fashion enjoined by Kāma, taught by youth, [43] dictated by passion, and revealed by insight. Taking confidence, Sarasvatī made herself known to him, and with her he spent a full year brief as a single day.

Then by ordinance of destiny Sarasvatī conceived, and bare in good time a son graced by all auspicious signs. Upon him at the very hour of his birth she laid this blessing, 'By my favour all the Vedas with the mystic portions, all authoritative books, and all arts shall be fully and spontaneously manifested in him.' Then bearing Dadhīca in her heart as though to display him with the vaunt of an ideal spouse, she ascended by the Great Father's will with Sāvitrī to Brahmā's world. She having departed, Dadhīca also, pierced to the heart as by a lightning flash, went away sick with his loss to the woods to live as an ascetic: having appointed as his son's foster-mother a hermit's daughter named Akṣamālā, wife to Bhrātṛi, a Brāhman of the Bhṛigu race. She had borne a son at the very hour when Sarasvatī gave birth to hers. So the two children gradually grew up together, fed without favour at the same breast. The one was named Sārasvata simply[5], the other's name was Vatsa.

[1] I.e. Sarasvatī. The words may also mean "the creepers clinging to the sandal and grislea trees."

[2] The Moon.

[3] *Utkalikā*=(1) wave, (2) agitation.

[4] Because of its whiteness.

[5] I.e. 'Sarasvatī's son': *ākhyā* and *nāma* are here distinguished.

And between the two there existed an enviable affection like that of brothers.

Now Sārasvata, who through his mother's power was at the very outset of youth gifted with the full treasure of the sciences, conveyed it undiminished in the form of words to his dear confidant and loving twin-brother Vatsa. When Vatsa took a wife, he made for him in that same neighbourhood a mansion endearingly named The Pinnacle of Delight[1]: he himself, assuming the hermit's staff, black antelope skin, bark dress, rosary, girdle, and matted locks, went to join his father, the ascetic [44].

From Vatsa there proceeded a prolific stock like Ganges purifying, noised abroad through the growing fame of the school established by its founders, upheld on the Almighty's head, deep in the lore of all arts, honoured of great saints, potent to shake its foes, stretching far over the earth's surface, stumbling not in its going[2]. Wherefrom were born home-dwelling sages named Vātsyāyanas, devoted to Çrauta lore yet assuming not the false muttering of cranes, vowed to the 'Cock' rules of fasting yet free from the ways of cats, averse to worldly pretence, bare of all wily, deceitful, guileful or boastful intent, discarding hypocrisy, trampling on dishonesty, tranquil in nature, free from sudden change, reluctant in heart to reprove others, cleansed from darkness by detachment from the three colours[3], shaken clear of desire by deep thought, wavering not in soul, devoted to their followers, at rest from all the doubts of different schools, openers of all knotty points in the sense of books, poets, [45] eloquent, without envy, fond of charming speech, skilled in clever wit, versed in urbane ways, connoisseurs of dance, song and music, never surfeited with tradition, compassionate, pure through truth, honoured of the good, with hearts melting with a dew of

[1] This is probably the name of Bāṇa's home.

[2] The adjectives are all made by means of puns to apply both to the race and to the Ganges. This paragraph is full of untranslateable puns.

[3] *Varṇatraya* 'the triad of colours,' red, white, and black, is a synonym for the material world: cf. Çvetāçv. Upaniṣ., IV. 5. The pun is on *varṇatraya* = three castes and *andhas* = (1) darkness, (2) food. 'Their food pure through avoiding the three castes.'

tenderness to all beings; likewise endowed with all qualities yet unconquered by the quality of passion[1], possessed of patience, cheering their dependents[2], not cruel, girt with knowledge[3], not dull, masters of arts[4], free from faults, helpful[5], not inflaming others yet suns of brilliance, without heat yet sacrificers[6], without crooked ways, happy[7], no rigid Stoics, yet abodes of good deeds rewarded[8], unfailing in the performance of sacrifice, dexterous[9], guileless, superior to desire[10], preëminent among the twice born.

Now as this stock persisted mid the flux of things, the passing of aeons, the descent of the Kali age, the going of the years, the march of the days, and the lapse of time, [46] there was in due time born in the expansive Vātsyāyana clan, pressing on in unbroken succession, a certain twice-born man, Kuvera by name, devoted as the son of Vinatā to his guru[11]. He begat four sons Acyuta, Īçāna, Hara, and Pāçupata, propagating their race, like the four aeons, through the power of Vedic knowledge[12], like Nārāyaṇa's columnar arms gladdening the circles of the good[13]. Among them Pāçupata begat a single high-souled son, by name Arthapati, crest jewel of all the Brāhman schools, profound as the four oceans, and like a mountain keeping steadfast the law of

[1] Or—punningly—'by the armies of kings.'

[2] Or—punningly—'inheritors of earth, yet gone to the heavenly Nandana.'

[3] Or 'without swords yet Vidyādharas.' The Vidyādharas are always armed with swords.

[4] Or 'without coolness, yet moons.'

[5] Or 'teachers,' *tārakā: ācāryā*, Comm.: the word may also mean 'constellations,' forming a punning antithesis to *adoṣāḥ*, which may mean 'not belonging to evening.'

[6] Or 'fires.' [7] Or 'yet serpents.'

[8] Or 'without pillars, yet caravanserais of holiness.'

[9] Or 'yet Dakṣas.' Dakṣa's mythological sacrifice had been interrupted by Çiva.

[10] Or 'without serpents, yet Çivas.'

[11] =(1) parent, (2) teacher. The son of Vinatā is Garuḍa who stole the amṛita to purchase his mother's freedom.

[12] Or—of the aeons—'having a race sprung from Brahmā's creative power'=all beings.

[13] Or—of Nārāyaṇa's arms—'holding the discus and the sword.'

his race[1]. From him were born eleven pure sons, like the Rudras, with faces coated with a dew of the moon's ambrosia[2]; and their names were Bhṛigu, Haṃsa, Çuci, Kavi, Mahīdatta, Dharma, Jātavedas, Citrabhānu, Tryakṣa, Ahidatta, and Viçvarūpa. Of whom Citrabhānu was blessed with a son Bāṇa by a Brāhmaṇī woman named Rājadevī. The boy, while still a child, was deprived of his mother, who was taken away through the will of sovereign destiny. His father, however, conceiving a deep love for him acted a mother's part, and under his care the boy grew with ever increasing vigour in his own home.

But when, being now about fourteen years of age, he had passed through initiation and the associated rites, and had returned from his teacher's house[3], his father also, having performed in full the sacred duties proper to the twice-born as enjoined in Çruti and Smṛiti, departed ere he reached the allotted span to his rest[4]. After his father's decease Bāṇa in the anguish of a great sorrow, his heart all aflame by day and night, [47] passed some days, he knew not how, in his own house. When his sorrow gradually became less absorbing, he through indulgence in sundry youthful follies, due either to misconduct arising from independence, to the impetuosity prevalent in youth, or to the aversion of young manhood to steadiness, came into reproach[5]. He had friends and companions of his own years, and among them two brothers of low birth[6], Candrasena and Mātṛiṣena, a dear friend the vernacular[7] poet Īçāna, adherents Rudra and Nārāyaṇa, precep-

[1] Or—of the mountain—'with motionless ranges.'

[2] I.e. they were moonfaced. There may also be an allusion to the *Soma* juice.

[3] As a *snātaka*.

[4] *Adaçamīstha*, literally 'not in his tenth decade,' came to mean 'not having attained his allotted span,' because the Hindus regarded a hundred years as the natural life of man. The father of Bāṇa (who was 14 years old) cannot have been anywhere near this.

[5] *Itvaro babhūva* may however mean 'was wild.' The Comm. gives *gamanaçīla* as the equivalent of *itvara;* it means 'poor, mean' in the Divyāvadāna.

[6] *Pārāçavāu*=sons of a Brāhman and a Sūdra woman.

[7] *Bhāṣākavi* is explained by the comm. as a writer of songs or a vernacular poet.

tors Vāravāṇa and Vāsavāṇa, a descriptive poet Veṇībhārata, a Prākṛit poet the young noble Vāyuvikāra, two panegyrists Anaṅgavāṇa and Sūcīvāṇa, an ascetic widow[1] Cakravākikā, a snake-doctor Mayūraka, a betel-bearer Caṇḍaka, a young physician Mandāraka, a reader Sudṛiṣṭi, a goldsmith Cāmīkara, a supervisor Ṡindhuṣeṇa, a scribe Govindaka, a painter Vīravarman, a modeller[2] Kumāradatta, a drummer Jīmūta, two singers Somila and Grahāditya, a maid Kuraṅgikā, two pipers Madhukara and Pārāvata, a music-teacher Darduraka, a shampooer Keralikā, a dancer Tāṇḍavika, a dicer Ākhaṇḍala, a gamester Bhīmaka, a young actor Çikhaṇḍaka, a dancing girl Hariṇikā, a Pārāçara mendicant Sumati, a Jain monk Vīradeva, a story-teller Jayasena, a Çaiva devotee Vakraghoṇa, a magician Karāla, a treasure-seeker[3] Lohitākṣa, an assayer Vihaṅgama, a potter[4] Dāmodara, a juggler Cakorākṣa, a Brāhman mendicant Tāmracūḍa. [48] With these and others for his companions, pliant from youthfulness, smit with a passion for seeing other lands, despite the wealth sufficient for a Brāhman amassed by his father and grandfather, despite his hitherto uninterrupted pursuit of knowledge, he went forth from his home; and, being free from all restraint and seeming bewitched by early youth through a headstrong will, he brought himself into the derision of the great.

But gradually thereafter by observation of great courts charming the mind with their noble routine, by paying his respects to the schools of the wise brilliant with blameless knowledge, by attendance at the assemblies of able men deep in priceless discussions, by plunging into the circles of clever men dowered with profound natural wisdom, he regained the

[1] *Kātyāyanikā*: cf.

pañcāçadvarṣadeçīyāṃ vīrāṃ saṃsthitabhartṛikām |
vadanti kātyāyanikāṃ dhṛitakāṣāyavāsasām.||
Comm. and A. K. *Manuṣyavarga* 17.

[2] *Pustakṛit: lepyakāra* Comm.; the word may perhaps mean 'a scribe.'

[3] *Asuravivaravyasanī: pātālābhilāṣī.* Comm. Perhaps it means 'a miner or metallurgist.'

[4] *Dārdurika*, explained by Tārānāth as meaning 'potter,' is quoted by Pāṇini, IV. 4. 34.

sage attitude of mind customary among his race. After long years he returned once more to his own native soil, resort of Brāhmans, shelter of the Vātsyāyana line. There, welcomed, like a feast-day, by kinsmen respectfully announcing their relationship and renewing after long absence their kindly affection, he found himself in the midst of the friends of his youth enjoying almost the bliss of liberation[1].

Here ends the first chapter, termed 'the description of the Vātsyāyana race,' of the Harṣa-carita, composed by Çrī Bāṇa Bhaṭṭa.

[1] *Bālamitramaṇḍalasya madhyagato* may also, with reference to the liberated soul, mean 'in the centre of the mild sun's disc,' as the sun loses its power to burn in his presence.

CHAPTER II.

[49] It is with a king of profound wisdom for those who have no means of access to him as it is with a well for those who have no way of descending into it,—virtuous royal intercessors[1] secure the desired success; the day[2] plants within the susceptible lotus the beauty given by the sun; to help others, without regarding their virtues or faults, is the passion of the good.

There Bāṇa roamed about happily in the homes of his kindred seen after a long absence,—resonant as they were with the noise of continual recitation,—filled with young students attracted by the sacrifices, running about like so many fires with their long tawny braids of hair[3], and their foreheads white with sectarial marks made of ashes,—with the terraces in front of the doors green with little beds of soma plants all fresh from recent watering,—with the rice and panicum for the sacrificial cakes laid out to dry, scattered on the skins of the black antelope,—with the oblations of wild rice strewed by the young maidens,—with the fuel, leaves, and bundles of green *Kuça* grass brought by hundreds of pure disciples,—filled with heaps of cow-dung and fuel—with the covered terraces in their courts marked by the round hoofs of the cows as they

[1] The words will also mean "earthen pots furnished with a string."

[2] The day, as distinguished from the night, is the 'intercessor' between the lotus and the sun, as Kṛiṣṇa, the king's brother, is between Bāṇa and Çrī-Harṣa.

[3] Or, if taken with 'fires,' "betressed with stalks of tawny flames." Cf. Manu, ii. 219.

came in for the daily offerings, dropping the milk which was to be used for preparing the curds[1], [50]—with troops of ascetics busied in pounding the clay for making pots,—with the sacred limits purified by heaps of *udumbara* branches brought to make pegs[2] to mark out the altars for the three sacrificial fires,—with the ground white with lines of offerings to the Viçve Devāḥ,—with the sprays of the trees in the courts grey with the smoke of the oblations,—with the wanton calves sporting about, caressed by the young cowherds,—with the succession of animal sacrifices clearly suggested by the young spotted goats playing about,—all peaceful through the cessation of the labours of the Brāhman teachers, while busy repetitions were now commenced by the parrots and mainas,—like so many hermitages for the incarnate Three Vedas.

While he stayed there, Time in his character of Summer, with his smile white with the jasmines in full flower, yawned and swallowed up the two flowery months[3]. At first he was gentle and showed compassion to the thirsty young gardens, as if they were the young children left behind by the spring when it was conquered and had passed away; and at its first rising by its warmth the hot season [51] unloosed[4] all the imprisoned blossoms throughout the earth. The tresses of the fair [damp after bathing] were seized by the god of love[5] as if they were chowries used at the coronation of the Spring, the King of Seasons [and so still wet with the waters of installation]; and the Sun made his expedition against the North as if in wrath for the lotus beds which the winter frosts had burned.

As the forehead-burning sun grew hot, the moons of the women's foreheads undertook vows of paying homage to him,

[1] Curds composed the Vaiçvadeva oblation.

[2] Used in measuring the altar, see Kātyāy. *Sūt.* v. 3. 14.

[3] Caitra and Vaiçākha, i.e. from the middle of March to that of May. Grīṣma is from the middle of May to that of July. Mahākāla also contains a punning reference to Çiva in his character as the destroyer.

[4] As a King at his accession sets prisoners free.

[5] Ragh. xvi. 50.

—being decorated with sandal-lines on their foreheads as sectarial marks, and wearing their curls as the ragged garments of ascetics, and bearing rosaries with the pearly drops of perspiration for beads. The women themselves slept away the day, grey with sandal-wood applications, like the night-lotuses unable to bear the sight of the sun; their eyes, heavy with sleep, could not bear the light of their jewels, far less the cruel sunshine. In the sultry season the moonlight nights grew less and less, like the rivers, which cheered by the diminishing distance the parted pairs of cakravākas on their banks [52]. The fierce heat of the sun made people long not only to drink water perfumed with the strong scent of the trumpet-flower, but even to drink up the very wind.

But as the season's childhood passed away and the sun's rays became hotter, the lakes grew dry, the streams sank lower, the waterfalls ebbed away, the din of the crickets increased, every thing was deafened by the continued cooing of the distressed doves. Then the other birds grew audacious, the wind swept away the refuse, the shrubs grew less dense[1], the hard clusters of the grislea tomentosa were licked by the young lions in their blind thirst for blood, the sides of the mountains were wet with the water spouted from the fainting elephant-herds, and the bees were dumb, as they lay in the dark patches of the dried ichor of the heat-distressed elephants. The season appeared with its borders painted red with the blushing *Mandāra* flowers, while the splitting crystal rocks were marked by the horns of the buffaloes as they were bewildered in the doubt whether what they saw was a flowing stream of water,—the dry creepers rustled in the sultry heat, the scratching wild cocks were frightened at the straw-conflagrations in the heated dust, the porcupines took shelter in their holes, [53] while the pools were dried down to their muddy bottoms which were discoloured by the fishes as they lay rolling on their backs, disturbed[2] by the troops of ospreys hovering in the *arjuna* trees on the banks; and the

[1] From the falling of the leaves.

[2] *Jvara.* The Schol. takes *Kūṭa* as the bird's cry.

world lighted its forest conflagrations like a solemn lustration ceremony, and the nights fell into a consumption[1] as the days lengthened.

The winds raged madly, leaping up in every direction in the waste places and openly carrying off masses of the roofs of the watering-sheds,—rubbing against the rough stony places as if they were itching with the irritating prickings of the ripe stinging bushes of *Mucuna pruritus*,—gathering a material outline and scattering powder as they went, and bearing the sharp shoots of the *mucukunda* as their teeth,—moistened by the drops in the mouths of the noisy flying grasshoppers,—plunging into the false waters of the mirage as it trembled as with waves in the heat of the young sun,—hurrying through the desolate tracks rustling with the dry *çamī*-trees,—actors in the wild miracle-play[2] with its passionate circular dances[3] and the uproar of the hurrying hither and thither of the dust whirlwinds, [54]—blackened with the ashes of the sites of old forest conflagrations and gathering up the scattered peacocks' feathers as if they had learned the ways of wandering mendicants[4],—carrying bunches of the rattling dry seeds of old *karañja* trees as if they had marching drums,—bursting out with the panting snorts of the buffaloes faint with the heat,—followed as by their children by the long lines of swift deer springing up,—frowning with their curls of smoke-like chaff, rising as from burning threshing-floors,—spreading the waves of hell by their hot mists,—shaggy as with hair by the threads of the bursting silk-cotton pods,—covered with dry leaves as with a cutaneous eruption, [55]—bearing the long lines of grass like a sick man's exposed veins,—shaking the points of the barley-awns as if they were a beard,—taking the shed quills of the porcupines for their teeth, and the flames of fire for their tongues,—whirling up the snakes' cast-off skins as their crests,—practis-

[1] Cf. Taitt. Saṃhitā ii. 3. 5; ii. 5. 6.

[2] For the *ārabhaṭī* cf. Sāhitya D. 420.

[3] Read *rāserasa*.

[4] The Digambara Jainas carry peacocks' tails in their hands to sweep insects from their path. *Sarva-Darç. Saṃgraha* transl. p. 63.

ing on the hot lotus-juices as a preparation for the future task of swallowing the liquids of the whole world,—alarming the three worlds by the shrill sound of rattling the dry bamboo-thickets as if they were the drums to proclaim the imminent drying up of the entire watery element. Their path was variegated with the scattered feathers of the darting blue jays,—they seemed coloured by the live coals and sparks of the bursting red *guñjā*-berries, as if they had caught the varied hues from the scorching torch of the sun's rays; waking up as they wandered the wild sounds of the mountain caves, —skilled in preparing a magic potion to reduce the world to dust,—propitiating the forest-fires with showers of the coral-tree's flowers as with offerings of blood,—with their course bestarred with burning sand, and bedewed with melted bitumen from the heated rocks; [56] and scented, as they blew, with the strong smell of the insects in the hollows of the trees, which were baked[1] in the fragments of the sparrows' eggs which had exploded as they grew hot in the forest-conflagration.

Dreadful forest-conflagrations appeared on every side,—raging as if fanned to fury by a thousand bellows, like exhalations blowing from the cavern-like jaws of old dragons,—sometimes like deer[2] quietly eating up the grass at their will,—sometimes like tawny-coloured ichneumons creeping in the holes at the bottom of the trees,—sometimes like followers of the Muni Kapila, wearing matted locks,—sometimes like hawks destroying the nests of the birds,—sometimes like women's lower lips red with melted lac,—sometimes like arrows, gaining their speed by the wings of the birds which they have overtaken,—sometimes like those who attain *nirvāṇa*, burning up all the causes which produced them[3],—sometimes like lovers, veiled in garments[4] scented with flowers,—

[1] This refers to a particular method of preparing drugs, the various substances being wrapped up in leaves, covered with clay, and roasted in the fire.

[2] The word for 'deer' (*hariṇaḥ*) might mean 'yellow' and so *babhru* and *kapila* in the two following similes.

[3] Or 'the causes of birth.'

[4] Or 'clouds.'

sometimes as if languid with indigestion, heavy with *fumes*, [57]—sometimes with an insatiable craving desiring to devour the whole world,—sometimes like very old men, leaning on the top of a bamboo,—sometimes like a consumptive patient, indulging in a long course of bitumen,—sometimes fat as feasting on every kind of food—sometimes burning fragrant gums like the worshippers of Rudra,—sometimes standing on the bare stems, with the thorny *madana* trees[1] burned entirely, roots and branches and flowers,—actors in the wild dance with their quivering flame-locks outspread,—worshipping the Sun with their opened flame-hands, which shower down the dry bursting grains of parched wild-rice and make a way through the dried tanks,—longing without disgust for the smell of the raw flesh of the fullgrown tortoises as they are suddenly offered up as in sacrifice, and consuming even their own smoke lest it should rise up and become clouds[2]—with quantities of massed insects crackling in the dry grass like oblations of mustard seed,—with the white shells in the dried lakes breaking into pieces through the heat like the skins of leprous patients,—raining beeswax in the woods from the bee-hives full of melting honey, as if they were covered with sweat,—with their curls of flames now all dying away in the salt wastes as if they were bald, [58]—and again, swallowing apparently mouthfuls of rocks amidst crags which seemed built up of the fragments of the blazing sun-crystals.

One day during that terrible hot season as he was in his house, after having eaten the afternoon meal, Candrasena, his half-brother by a Çūdra mother, entered, saying,—"A renowned courier is waiting at the door, sent to you by Kṛiṣṇa, the brother of Çrīharṣa, the king of kings, the lord of the four oceans, whose toenails are burnished by the crest gems of all other monarchs, the leader of all emperors." He replied, "Introduce him without delay."

Then he beheld the messenger entering as he was

[1] This can also mean "standing like Çiva, with Kāma bearing his flowery arrows consumed by his blazing eye."

[2] Which might bring rain to extinguish them.

brought before him,—his legs tired and heavy with the long journey, with his tunic girt up tightly by a mud-stained strip of cloth, the knot hanging loose and fastened up by a ragged clout swinging behind him, and having his head wrapped with a bundle of letters, which had a deep division pressed into it by a very thick thread that bound it; and he said to him, while he was yet some way off, "Is all well with my honoured friend Kṛiṣṇa, who is the disinterested friend of all the world?" He answered, "All is well"; and then making his obeisance he sat down at some distance and said, after resting awhile, "This letter has been sent by our honoured lord," and he unloosed it and gave it. Bāṇa took it respectfully and read it to himself. [59] '"When they have once learned the news from Mekhalaka, the wise will avoid all delay as hindering success"; this is the real essence of the writing,—all else is mere rhetorical compliment[1].' Having mastered the contents of the letter and sent away his attendants, he asked for the message. Mekhalaka replied, "My lord thus addresses thee in thy wisdom, 'Your honour knows that the belonging to one gotra, or to one caste, or the being brought up together or the dwelling in one place or the constantly seeing each other, or the hearing of each other's mutual affection, or the conferring of benefits when absent, or a similarity of disposition can all be causes of affection; but without any cause my heart is tenderly affected with a firm love towards thee, even though thou art not seen by me and as though thou wert a relation near at hand when thou art really afar off, just as the moon feels towards the lotus-bed, however distant it may be. In thy absence the king was on various occasions prejudiced against thee by the malevolent; but it was not a true report. There are none so situated, but, even if they are good, they will have friends, neutrals, and enemies[2]. Some unworthy remark was uttered concerning thee by some envious wretch through thy mind being not wholly averse to the levity of childhood, and others caught it up and repeated it. The minds of the unreflecting toss about, rolling to and

[1] Cf. the Persian phrase *Ziyāda ci bar-ṭarāzad.* [2] *Manu*, vii. 158.

fro like water. What now shall the lord of the earth do, when he comes to a settled decision after hearing many different suggestions? Though thou wast far away, yet thou wast immediately represented by us who sought to know the real truth. The sovereign has been reminded with regard to thee that 'every one's youth in the opening of life is usually guilty of some levities,' and he at once assented to the excuse. Therefore [60] your highness must repair to the palace without delay. I cannot approve thy habits, living as thou dost thus away from the king amidst thine own friends like a tree without fruit away from the sun's beams. Nor shouldst thou shrink from the toil of court-attendance or feel any fear of waiting upon him; for although it may be true enough, 'Alas! he who is unskilled in waiting upon a king is like Kāma,—he cannot speak out his request, although the opportunity is come exactly as he had wished,—he gives pain (to his patron) by hundreds of ill-timed petitions for favours,—and by his folly he throws away his livelihood in a moment[1];'—yet these other common kings are one thing, and *our* ambrosial lord is quite another, who puts to shame such ancient heroes as Nṛiga, Nala, Niṣadha, Nahuṣa, Ambarīṣa, Daçaratha, Dilīpa, Nābhāga, Bharata, Bhagīratha, and Yayāti. His eyes are not stained by the deadly poison of pride; his voice is not choked by the convulsive effects of the baneful drug of conceit; his postures do not lose their natural dignity through any sudden epileptic fit of forgetfulness caused by the heat of arrogance; his changes of feeling are not exaggerated by the fevered outbursts of ungovernable self-will; his gait is not agitated by the unnatural movements of an access of self-conceit; his voice is not rendered harsh by the words being uttered under a tetanus of hauteur which distorts his lips. Thus his idea of jewels attaches to men of pure virtues, [61] not to bits of rock,—his taste delights in

[1] These lines must be read with a series of puns, when taken as referring to Kāma. "Although his realm and power are sprung from fancy, Kāma cannot be called 'corporeal' (*dehī*),—he gives pain to lovers by his hundreds of arrows—and by his folly he sacrifices his life in a moment consumed by Çiva's anger." Saṃkalpaja is one of the names of Kāma.

pearl-like qualities, not in heaps of ornaments,—his judgement as to proper means is versed in deeds of bounty, not in the ichor-flowing temples of poor worms of elephants[1],—his highest love is for preeminent glory, not for the withering stubble of this life,—his magnificence is devoted to adorning the different quarters of the earth whose tribute he seizes, not the dolls which he calls his wives,—his notion of bosom friendship belongs to his well-strung bow, not to the courtiers who live on the crumbs of his board. His natural instinct is to help his friends, sovereignty means to him helping his dependants, learning at once suggests helping the learned and success helping his kinsfolk, power means helping the unfortunate and wealth helping the brāhmans; his heart's main occupation is to remember benefits and his life's sole employment is to assist virtue, his body's one use is to carry out the dictates of courage, and the earth's to be an arena for his sword, attendant kings are wanted to amuse him, and enemies to help his majesty to shew itself. It could have been by no common merits in former births that he attained this glorious preeminence so that the shadow of his feet diffuses an all-excelling ambrosia of happiness round him."

Having heard this, he said to Candrasena, "Refresh the messenger with food and clothing, and then let him rest" [62]. When he was gone and the day had come to a close, and the afternoon sunshine, crimson like a young crow's beak, was fading away as if drunk up by the cups of the closely joined red lotuses, and when the sun, as the speed of his horses was relaxed,—pale-pink like a garland of China roses,—seemed to limp as if he stumbled on the western mountain, as though his feet had been pierced by the (fancied) thorns of the lotus-beds,—he offered his evening prayers and retired to his couch, as the early night was hurrying on in the east, her long locks of scattered darkness seeming to hang dangling in the air, and her face as it were dark with sorrow for the moon's absence. He pondered by himself, "What shall I do?

[1] Elephants are one of the component parts of an army (*sādhana*); of course there is also a pun on *dāna*.

I have indeed been misunderstood by the king, and this advice has been given by my disinterested kinsman Kṛiṣṇa; but all service is hateful, and attendance is full of evils, and a court is full of dangers. My ancestors never had any love for it, I have no hereditary connection with it,—nor is mine the consideration from remembering former benefits, nor the affection caused by service rendered when a child, nor family dignity, nor the kindness of old acquaintance, nor the allurement of mutually imparting information, nor the desire of more knowledge, nor the respect paid to one's fine appearance, nor practice in all the turns of voice fit for inferiors, nor the cleverness needed in the circles of the learned, nor the skill to win friends by the expenditure of wealth, nor long intercourse with royal favourites. Still I must certainly go. Purārāti, the venerable guru of the world, will do everything that is proper when I am away." Thus having considered, he made up his mind for the journey.

The next day, having risen and bathed betimes, and put on a dress of white silk and seized his rosary and repeatedly recited the hymns and sacred texts fit for one starting on a journey,—after washing the image with milk[1], he offered worship to Çiva, with lighted lamps, ointments, oblations, banners, perfumes, incense and sweet flowers [63]. Then, having offered a libation with profound reverence to the holy fire[2], whose right flame was kindled by a profuse pouring of ghi, and whose fiery crest was noisily crackling with the splitting husks of the restless mustard seeds, which had been previously offered, he distributed wealth according to his means to the brāhmans, and walked solemnly round a sacred cow which faced the east, himself decked with white unguents, and wearing white garlands and white garments, and having his ears adorned with *giri-karṇikā* flowers, fastened with the ends of *dūrvā*-grass, and covered with yellow *rocanā* paint,—and having white mustard put on his topknot. All the rites necessary at starting on a journey were

[1] Cf. Bk. v. (Text, p. 171. 2.)

[2] The rare Vedic word *āçuçukṣaṇi* here used for 'fire' is also used in the old Bengali poem *Caṇḍī*.

performed for him as by a mother by his father's younger sister Mālatī, clad in white garments and with her heart overflowing with tenderness, as if she were the impersonate goddess Sarasvatī[1]; he was greeted with blessings by the aged women of the family, applauded by the old female attendants, dismissed with good wishes by the gurus whose feet he worshipped, kissed on the head by the elders whom he himself saluted, while the birds by their omens increased his eagerness for starting and the astrologers wished their utmost to secure favourable constellations. So in a favourable moment,—looking upon a full water-jar that was set in the court-yard which was daubed with brown cow-dung,—with a mango-spray placed on its mouth, itself white with five finger-breadths of flour[2], and with its neck encircled by a garland of white flowers;—having paid his homage to the family deities and being followed by his own brāhmans with their hands holding flowers and fruits and muttering the *apratiratha* hymn[3],—he went out from the village of Prītikūṭa, setting his right foot first.

On the first day, having slowly passed through a grove sacred to Caṇḍikā which was parched and waterless from the hot season, and ugly with leafless trees,—with figures of the goddess carved on the trees at the entrance, which received the homage of passing travellers [64],—though dried up, yet seeming to be sprouting with the thousands of red tongues which hung lolling from the mouths of the thirsty wild beasts,—all astir with the swarms of bees flying out of the masses of honeycomb as they were licked by the monkeys and bears,—and bristling with the hundreds of new shoots of stout asparagus which had sprung up luxuriantly from the burned soil[4],—he arrived at last at the village Mallakūṭa.

[1] Called here *Mahāçvetā*.

[2] The Comm. seems to explain *piṣṭapañcāṅgulam* (cf. text, p. 157. 7) as flour daubed on with the five fingers moistened with goat's-milk (*ājakāktābhiḥ*), but cf. Morris' note on *pañcaṅgulika* in the Pali Text Soc. Journ. for 1884.

[3] *Ṛigv.* 10. 103.

[4] After the burning of forests plants often spring up whose seeds had been lying dormant. (*Balfour's Bot.*)

There he stayed happily, hospitably received by his brother and his friend Jagatpati who was just like his own heart. The next day, having crossed the holy Bhāgīrathī, he passed the night in a forest-village named Yaṣṭigṛihaka[1], and the next he arrived at the royal camp, which was pitched near Maṇitāra along the Ajiravatī river; and he stopped near the royal residence.

Having bathed and eaten his meal and rested, when only one watch of three hours remained of the day, and when the king had dined, he proceeded leisurely with Mekhalaka to the royal gate, one by one observing the many camps of the renowned subject kings. Here the royal gate was all dark with crowds of elephants,—some brought to carry turbans of honour, others to bear drums, some newly bound, others acquired as tribute or as presents, some sent by the rangers of the elephants' district, or brought in the excitement of a first visit to the court or sent at the time of an embassy or presented by the lord of a wild settlement or demanded for the spectacle of a mimic battle, or given or taken by force, or let loose, or set ready for a watch, or collected to conquer all continents like so many mountains to make a bridge over the ocean,—all gay with banners, cloths, kettledrums, conchs, chowries, and unguents, like so many ready-made festival-days for the royal ceremonies when the moon enters the asterism Pushya [65]. The place seemed all in waves with the plunging horses as they leaped up to the sky in anger against the horses of the sun's chariot, with their chowries and ornaments serving as wings, and challenged Indra's horse to a contest by their joyous neigh, and mocked the whole race of deer as too laggard of foot, with the foam curling round the corners of their mouths like a scornful laugh, and set the Royal Prosperity herself a-dancing as the drum of the ground was struck by their ceaselessly prancing hoofs[2].

In another part it was tawny with troops of camels sent

[1] Bombay ed. Yashṭigrahaka.

[2] The Schol. would also take it as meaning "striking *the earth* with their hoofs."

or being sent as presents or brought back in return for others which had been sent, tawny like monkeys' cheeks,—like pieces of evening-glow spangled with stars, for their mouths were ornamented with lines of cowries which were like so many marks left in counting the number of leagues which they had travelled,—or like red rice-fields covered with red lotuses, for their ears were gay with red chowries; or like old *karañja* forests with hundreds of dry pods cracking, for they were decked with strings of ever-jingling golden ornaments; having long tufts of hair and variegated threads of wool of five colours hanging near their ears; all tawny-red as monkeys' cheeks.

In another part it was all white with its masses of white umbrellas, like autumnal clouds white through having just emptied themselves of their water-stores, or like trees of paradise whose circles of shade are annihilated by the splendour of their masses of pearls, or like the lotuses on Nārāyaṇa's navel[1] with Garuḍa's (jewelled) wings resting close to them, or like tracts of the Milky Ocean with huge masses of coral shining in them, or like the surface of the serpent Çeṣa's hoods with large rubies sparkling upon it, or like islands in the White Ganges covered with flamingoes,—overpowering the summer-brilliance, and mocking the splendour of the sun, and drinking up the sunshine,—they turned the earth into a moon, [66] time into a world of white lotuses, the day into moonlight, and the sky into a mass of foam, and they seemed to create a thousand moonlights out of due time and to laugh to scorn all the pomp of Indra.

In another part it was waving with thousands of stirring chowries bright like moonbeams, which seemed to spread a firmament of white lotus-fibres, and to make an autumn in every direction with forests of *kāça* grass[2] blossoming everywhere, and to abolish the rule of the demon of ill-luck[3],

[1] Viṣṇu is called Padmanābha. Garuḍapakṣa may also be a kind of jewel; the white umbrellas were adorned with gems.

[2] Saccharum spontaneum, see Wilson's Hindu *Dr.* ii. p. 196, note.

[3] Or "every haunt of the demon of the iron age."

dark as the disgrace of a coward king, and to turn the day into continual vicissitudes of going and returning by their uplifting and lowering, and seemed to steal away the world as its eight regions were seen for a moment and then lost.

It seemed like a flock of white geese from the shell-amulets in the elephants' ears, or a forest of heavenly trees from the elephants' banners, or a grove of ruby trees from the umbrellas of peacocks' feathers, or the stream of the heavenly Ganges from the muslin dresses, or the Milky Ocean from the linen robes, or a grove of plantains from the flashing emeralds;—it created as it were a second day by the morning-rays of the rubies, and made a new sky by the sapphires, and caused an unprecedented night by the dark-violet of the *mahānīla* stones. A thousand Yamunās seemed to be flowing from the radiance of the emeralds, while the flashes of the rubies gleamed like charcoal.

[67] The camp was filled on every side with conquered hostile vassal-chiefs,—some who could not find admission hung down their heads and seemed in their shame to sink into their own bodies through the reflections of their faces which fell on their toe-nails,—others seemed to present chowries in obsequious service under the form of the rays issuing from their nails, which were thrown back from the ground which was scratched by their bare fingers,—others with the flashing sapphires hanging on their breasts seemed to be carrying sword-blades suspended from their necks to propitiate their lord's anger,—others with their faces darkened by the swarms of bees which flocked attracted by their perfumed breath were as if they wore their beards long as in mourning for their lost prosperity,—others with circles of bees flying up round their crests as if their topknots were flying away afraid of the coming mortification of paying homage,—honoured even in being conquered, and destitute of every other refuge,—continually asking the servants of the different domestic porters who at intervals made their exits and their entrances, and whose track was followed by thousands of various suppliants,—"Good sir, will it be to-day? will the great lord give an audience in the hall

after he has dined? or will he come out into the outer court?" and thus spending the day in the hope of an audience.

Other kings too were there, come from the desire of seeing his glory, natives of various countries, who were waiting for the time when he would be visible. There were also seated by themselves Jains, Ārhatas, Pāçupatas, mendicants of the school of Parāçarya, Brāhman students, natives of every land, and savages from every forest that fringes the ocean-shore, and ambassadors from every foreign country. It seemed like a creation-ground where the Prajāpatis practised their skill, or a fourth world made out of the choicest parts of the other three; its glory could not be described in hundreds of Mahābhāratas,—it must have been put together in a thousand golden ages, [68] and its perfection constructed with millions of svargas, and it seemed watched over by crores of tutelary royal deities.

In his astonishment he thought to himself, "Surely such a vast multitude of living beings as this must have involved to the creating Principles a destruction of the elements or a lack of atoms or a failure of time or a cessation of vital power or an exhaustion of possible forms!" But Mekhalaka, being recognised from afar by the doorkeepers, asked him to wait a while, and himself pressed forward unrepelled and entered.

Then in a moment he came out, followed by a tall man fair like a karṇikāra flower, clothed in a clean jacket, with his waist tightly bound by a girdle ornamented with a quantity of flashing rubies,—with his chest broad like a rock of Mount Himālaya, and having his shoulder rising over it like the hump of Çiva's bull,—and carrying on his breast a string of pearls like a noose to tame the whole restless race of deer,—and gleaming with two jewelled ear-rings at his ear, as if they were the sun and moon brought to be asked whether even a king of the solar or lunar race were such as our king?—while the sunbeams seemed to give place to him through respect for his office, as though they were rebuked before the stream of beauty which flowed from his face. He greeted Bāṇa from afar with his long eye as if it were a wreath of full-blossomed lotuses taken up as an offering[1], —set in the very centre of stern discipline and yet, with his topknot bent down to the ground, lifting his white turban as a token of respect, [69] and grasping in his left hand his sword, its handle rough with the pearls which thickly studded it, and in his right his burnished golden staff of office like a lightning-flash suddenly become motionless. Having come out, Mekhalaka said to him, "This is the chief of all the doorkeepers, the king's special favourite Pāriyātra; let him who pursues success treat him with suitable ceremony." The doorkeeper, having come up and saluted him, addressed him respectfully in a gentle voice, "Approach and enter, his highness is willing to see you." Then Bāṇa entered, as he directed, saying, "I am indeed happy that he thinks me worthy of this honour."

He next beheld a stable filled with the king's favourite horses from Vanāyu, Āraṭṭa, Kamboja, Bharadvāja, Sindh, and Persia,—red, dark, white, bay, chestnut, dappled like partridges, marked with the five auspicious kinds of marks[2], with eyes spotted with white, or marked with light yellow spots in groups like the Pleiads; with long thin jaws and short ears, and round delicate well-proportioned throats, [70] with long upraised curved necks like sacrificial posts, with their shoulders stout and robust at the joints, their chests full and projecting, their legs thin and straight, and their round hoofs hard like masses of iron; their round bellies seemed solid, as if they had no entrails within them, lest they should be broken by their excessive swiftness, and their broad flanks were divided by a long depression[3], with the hairs like new shoots swaying about in the wind[4]. They were with difficulty restrained by the ropes fixed tightly in the ground on both sides, and they seemed to grow longer as they struggled with one foot thrust out of the ropes' confinement, and the studs on their necks were ornamented with cords of many

[1] Cf. p. 25, l. 27.

[2] Sc. on the chest, back, face and flanks.

[3] *Droṇī* is doubtful,—there is a reading *udyacchroṇī*.

[4] *Jagatī* seems to be used for *jagat* in this rare sense.

strings,—their eyes were closed, and they kept moving their mouths, which were flecked with bits of foam dark with the juice of *dūrvā* grass, while the skin itched and twitched about and was bitten for a moment and then let go by the teeth. Some stood, lazily moving their tails, with one side of their loins drooping as they rested on one hoof, seeming to ponder in sleep, and slowly uttering interrupted neighs, while the ground was marked by their hoofs, whose foreparts rattled with the noise of their foot-rests as they struck upon them; others sought for food, having their longing excited by the stray morsels of fodder scattered about, [71] while the pupils of their eyes trembled for fear at the yells of the angry Caṇḍālas who guarded them. They seemed to have a lustration-fire always near to protect them, from their bodies being yellow with a saffron unguent rubbed on them, while an awning was spread over them and the tutelary deity (Govinda) was worshipped before them. As he looked, his mind was filled with curious wonder, and he entered a little further within, and saw on his left hand an elephant-stable indistinct owing to the distance, but regaling the nostrils with an odour as of groves of *vakula* trees[1] in full bloom which diffused itself far and wide, while the stable was filled with streams of ichor covered with bees, and its outskirts were surrounded by a grove of plantain-trees[2], and its height seemed to crowd the very sky.

He asked "What does the king do here?" The other replied, "This is his majesty's favourite elephant, his external heart, his very self in another birth[3], his vital airs gone outside from him, his friend in battle and in sport, rightly named Darpaçāta[4], a lord of elephants—this is his special pavilion." He replied, "O my friend, if he is called Darpaçāta and he has no faults, I may surely see this lord of elephants,—will you take me to him, for I am overcome by curiosity?" "Be it so," he answered, "draw near by all

[1] From the *mada* or ichor exuding from the elephants' temples.

[2] *Kadalī* also means 'a flag carried by an elephant.'

[3] Or 'veiled by a new nature.'

[4] 'Keen (or perhaps attenuated and so lacking) in pride.'

means, what harm is there in it? have a good look at the lord of elephants."

[72] So he went forward in that direction, and there while he was still at a distance he saw the elephant Darpaçāta surrounded by the troops of *cātaka* birds uttering their loud notes in the sky as they were excited by the deep sound issuing from his throat (which suggested clouds), and the domestic peacocks which made the ground resound with their cries, —filling the surrounding space with the spirituous scent of the ichor which rivalled the full-blown *kadamba* flowers,—like a rainy season out of its time wearing an embodied form,— throwing off the fourth period of life by an outburst of red spots on his skin like a lake covered with lotuses brown with thick drops of honey,—chanting as it were a tune for his auspicious entrance upon the fifth period with his shell-ornaments as they mingled with the deep sound of his flapping ears,— seeming as if for fear of bursting the earth he tried to lighten his weight by swinging his long huge body with sportive oscillations on his three feet as they kept varying in constant motion, as though he were rubbing his body against the walls of the world,—challenging the world-bearing elephants of the various regions as he threw up his trunk in defiance, and seeming to be cleaving the pillar of the world with a saw armed with thick sharp teeth. It was as though the world could not contain him and he was striving to force a passage out, while his drivers tried to shew him every service which could alleviate the hot season, some[1] like clouds with long-accumulated stores, hurrying up with fresh juicy shoots and creepers, others like lakes whose waters are variegated with heaps of Vallisneria plants and lotus fibres scattered on them. [73] He threatened to block up the whole world with all its mountain-ranges, seas, continents and forests, with his huge bar of a trunk, which was all wavy with thin lines of wrinkles running round it as if they were marks to reckon up the number of past victories which he had won in battle, while it was held aloft as if he scented the ichor of some rival

[1] Read *leśakaiḥ*.

elephant approaching,—one of his tusks had its root wet with spray from a thick piece of plaintain covered with leaves which was enclosed in the trunk, the other seemed to have dropped its bough and was as it were all horripilated with the joy of battle from a quantity of lotus fibres which hung from it in play. He appeared to vomit whole beds of lotuses which he had eaten in his gambols in the lake, through the bright colour of the two tusks together, and spread his own glory through the four quarters of space; and he seemed to laugh to scorn the lions who vaunted their rough play with some poor scarecrows of elephants whom they had worsted, while he appropriated for himself a silken veil which might have been taken direct from the heavenly tree. When he lifted up in play his huge trunk, he seemed to drop a shower of red lotuses which he had eaten, or to vomit a quantity of fresh shoots, as he then displayed his palate which was soft to the touch like red silk. His bright tawny eyes seemed to emit a stream of honey which he had drunk up with the mouthfuls of lotuses, while his cheeks poured out under the guise of ichor a rich mixture of perfumes as if he had been eating groves of the *pārijāta* tree of heaven, together with mangoes, *campakas, lavalīs,* cloves, *kakkolas,* cardamoms, and *sahakāras,* and perfumed with abundance of camphor. He seemed to be busy, night and day, bestowing all the woods on the other elephants by royal inscriptions of donation, made vocal with the swarms of bees which hummed round them as if reading them, and scratched by the half-cut branches of red sugar-cane as by a graver, and which seemed by a mistake to stay on hand instead of being dispersed abroad[1]; [74] he was constantly cooled by a trickling garland of ornaments cut out of the moongem[2] in the shape of the constellations, and he carried his head high as if it had been crowned with the tiara of universal empire

[1] This sentence is very obscure; *hasta-sthiti* seems to imply a pun, as *hasta* means 'hand' or 'trunk'; the trunk is as it were marked all over with lines which the bees seem to be reading aloud. There is also the usual pun in *dāna* as meaning "patches of ichor," and in *vibhrama* as 'mistake' and 'haste.'

[2] Or perhaps 'ice.'

over all his compeers; he stood as though he were loyally fanning the Guardian deity of the royal family who lay pillowed on his tusks, with his huge ears, which, as they flapped, seemed alternately to conceal and reveal the wide world; while his tail waved like some flyflapper marked with the signs of elephant-empire and handed down through a long succession of hereditary rulers[1]. He seemed to pour out again from his mouth the rivers which he had drunk up in his triumphal progress of conquest, in the form of the clear cold water which he spouted forth; and he displayed his sensitiveness to insult by loud trumpetings which followed various movements of his body as he heard the drums borne by other elephants, while all his limbs had been motionless for a moment as he listened attentively. He seemed to pity himself for not being in the thick of the fray, and as if ashamed of the humiliation of bearing a driver he poured out streams of ichor and scratched the ground with the tip of his trunk; his eyes were a third closed as with the languor of intoxication, when his driver shouted angrily, as he scornfully took up and dropped the mouthfuls of food, and finally took them slowly and reluctantly, [75] while the juice issued from his mouth discoloured, like a stream of ichor, by the dark juice of the *tamāla* boughs which he had eaten. He moved restlessly with pride, he snorted with repressed energy, he swelled with intoxication, he staggered with youth, he flowed freely with ichor, he leaped about with conscious strength, he was drunk with arrogance, he seemed to be ever seeking the highest place with ambition, he gasped with excitement, he affected all with his gracefulness, he rained influence on every side by his beauty.

His nails were smooth, his hair was rough,—he was reverend in face but a gentle disciple in deportment; soft as to his head, but firm in his friendships; his neck was short but his life was long; he was stinted in his belly but lavishly bounteous in ichor; a very Balarāma in his wild

[1] *Āyatavaṃça* can also suggest a pun as meaning 'the backbone.'

exploits, but like a highborn wife in his devotedness; a Jina in patience, a shower of fire in his storms of anger; he was Garuḍa in his power to lift *nāgas*[1], he was Nārada in his love of quarrels[2], a thunderbolt without rain in his sudden attacks, a Makara in his power to disturb armies[3], a serpent in the might of his teeth, Varuṇa in the noose which he held in his hand, he was Yama's net in entangling his enemies, he was Time in his buttings[4], Rāhu in his grip[5], Mars in his crooked movements, a circling torch in his rapid rounds. He was to valour, a very mountain of the jewel which gives all desires; to chivalrous feeling, a palace-home with his tusks for two pillars of pearl; [76] to magnanimity, a heavenly chariot, moving at will, and gay with ornaments, chowries, and bells; to anger, a shower-bath of scented water, dark with a constant raincloud of ichor; to ambition, a temple with a golden image[6] within; to pride, a pleasure-hill with streams running down its sides; to arrogance, a diamond house with an arch of ivory; to royalty, a moving hill-fort with its high frontal-globes as so many towers; to the earth, an iron wall indented with thousands of arrows[7]; to the king[8], a tree of heaven, resonant with hundreds of bees. Thus he was a music-hall for the dancing of his flapping ears, a drinking-saloon for the swarms of bees, a gynæceum for the display of paint and decorations[9], a festival of Kāma for the sportive gambols of intoxication, a faultless evening for the sight of all the constellations[10]; a

[1] i.e. 'elephants' or 'snakes.'

[2] Nārada is expressly called *kalahapriya* and *kalikāraka*. Several instances of his mischief-making propensities occur in the Viṣṇu Purāṇa.

[3] *Vāhinī* is 'a river' as well as 'an army.'

[4] *Pariṇati* also means 'power to ripen.'

[5] Or 'in his seizure of the sun.'

[6] *Pratimā* also means 'the part of an elephant's head between the tusks.'

[7] Or 'with loopholes from whence to discharge arrows.'

[8] Bhūnandana can also mean "the heavenly garden of the earth."

[9] *Çringāra* means "love" and "the marks with red lead on an elephant's head and trunk."

[10] *Nakṣatra* has been used before as an elephant's ornament.

rainy season out of season, for the overflowing rivers of ichor; a deceptive autumn for the perfume of the *saptaparṇa* trees[1], an unprecedented cold-season for the showers of dew, and a fictitious cloud for the trumpeting thunders.

As he wondered, thinking to himself, "Surely in his creation the mountains were used up as atoms, how else could this astonishing majesty have been produced? It is indeed a marvel,—a Vindhya with tusks, the primeval Boar with a trunk!"—the doorkeeper addressed him; "See! when his enemies, wandering in the forests, would vainly try[2] by a hundred wishes to paint again their old glory gone without leaving a rack behind, and when their minds are bewildered with devising means to express their imaginations,—[77] this lord of elephants, if he comes by chance into their recollection as they listlessly muse in despondency, cannot endure as rivals even the world-supporting elephants in the Mānasa lake[3].—But come, you will have another opportunity of seeing him; you shall now see my lord himself!"

On hearing these words he with an effort drew away his eyes which had fallen on the elephant's ichor-bedewed cheek and were half closed as if intoxicated with the sweet odour; and, following the path indicated by the doorkeeper, he passed through three courts crowded with subject-kings, and in the fourth he saw King Harṣa, in an open space in front of a pavilion where he used to give audience after eating, surrounded at a distance by his attendants in a line, all six feet in height[4], fair like *karṇikāra* flowers, armed and of old families[5], like so many golden pillars,—with his special favourites seated near him. He was sitting on a throne made of a stone clear like a pearl, washed with sandalwood water, and bright as the moon with its feet[6] of ivory

[1] Which is like that of the ichor.
[2] The Kashmir edition rightly reads *ālikhatām*.
[3] Or 'even the elephants of hope in their minds.'
[4] Or 'their bodies tall through exercise.'
[5] Or of the pillars, 'shaped by tools and firmly set.'
[6] Or 'rays.'

and its surface cool to the touch like snow-water,—he rested the weight of his body on his arm which was placed on the end of the seat, and he seemed to be sporting with his subject-kings under the far-shining canopy of the brightness of his body with the rays of his jewels diffused round, as if it were in a lake delightful in the hot season, the water of which was tangled with clusters of the long soft lotus-roots; and he seemed made as it were out of the pure atoms of light. [78] He was embraced by the goddess of the Royal Prosperity, who took him in her arms and, seizing him by all the royal marks on all his limbs, forced him, however reluctant, to mount the throne,—and this though he had taken a vow of austerity and did not swerve from his vow, hard like grasping the edge of a sword[1]; clinging closely to duty through fear of stumbling in the uneven path of kings, and attended with all her heart by Truth who had been abandoned by all other kings, but had obtained his promise of protection,—and waited on reverentially by the reflected images of a fair handmaid standing near, which fell on his toe-nails, as if they were the ten directions of space impersonate[2]. With his long glances which penetrated space he seemed to examine what the Regents of the different quarters had done or left undone, while the sun seemed to seek his permission to rise, as its beams rested on the back of his footstool supported by jewelled feet,—the day made its reverential march round him, while a clear space was kept in the centre, marked out by the splendour emitted from his ornaments; he burned with vexation when even the mountains did not bow before him, and so displayed the ocean of his beauty which was white like sandal-wood, boiling as it were into foam through the heat of his heroic passion,—in his isolated sovereignty feeling indignant that his own image should be repeated even in the reflections on the crest jewels of the prostrate kings round his feet, and keeping his Royal Glory continually sighing under the guise of the wind of his chowries as she sat fuming with vexed pride; [79] he was embraced by the Goddess Çrī who came

[1] Cf. Raghuv. xiii. 67.

[2] As reflected in the ten nails.

to him after spoiling all the four oceans of their beauty[1]; though he gave away thousands of rainbows from the coruscations of his ornaments and sent them as a present to Indra, yet he still in his seeming penury[2] rained ambrosia in his interviews with other monarchs; in poetical contests he poured out a nectar of his own which he had not received from any foreign source; he ever shewed his heart in his confidential intercourse even when it was not sought; when he shewed favour, he seemed to place Glory, though herself immoveable, in various positions by his patronage; in the parleys of heroes he seemed listening to the whispered kindly counsels of the Goddess of battles with his cheek horripilated in joy; during the recital of the past conflicts of heroes, he ever turned his eye like a shower of soft cleansing oil on the loved sword; in easy jests flashing from his bright teeth his clear meaning to the circle of kings standing awed by his majesty: abiding in the hearts of all the world and yet never leaving his own proper place; in his greatness, he was beyond the sphere of all good qualities, out of the range of ordinary successes, outside of common benefactions, beyond the possibility of blessing, out of the reach of desires, far removed from fortune, not within the scope of comparisons, out of the influence of fate, and beyond the past experience of prosperity. He displayed an avatāra of all the gods united in one, as he had the lost delicate feet of Aruṇa[3], the slow-moving thighs of Buddha, the brawny forearm of the Thunderer (Indra), the shoulder of Justice[4], the round lip of the sun, the mild look of Avalokita[5], the face of the moon and the hair of Kṛiṣṇa. [80] His left foot was playfully placed on a large costly footstool made of sapphires, girt round with a band of

[1] Çrī only rose from *one* ocean when she became Viṣṇu's queen.

[2] *Parityaktam* may be also taken as neuter with *madhu*.

[3] The charioteer of the Sun, who was born without feet. Taking the proper names as adjectives, it is to be read, "he has delicately pink feet, slow gracefully-moving thighs, his forearm hard as the thunderbolt, a bull's neck, a bright round lip, a mild aspect, a moon-face and black hair."

[4] Represented as a bull.

[5] A Bodhisattva who is especially worshipped in Northern Buddhism.

rubies,—as if it were the (dark) head of Kali the demon of the iron age,—while the surface of the ground was dyed by the rays which fell on it; like the youthful Kṛiṣṇa when he planted his foot on the circle of hoods of the serpent Kāliya, he dignified the earth by the spreading rays of his toe-nails, white like fine linen, as with the tiara of his chief queen[1]. His feet were very red as with wrath at unsubmissive kings, and they shed a very bright ruby-light on the crowded crests of the prostrate monarchs, and caused a sunset of all the fierce luminaries of war and poured streams of honey from the flowers of the crest garlands of the local kings, and were never even for one moment unattended, as by the heads of slain enemies, by swarms of bees which fluttered bewildered at the sweet odour of the chaplets on the heads of all the feudal chiefs; and they formed as it were sylvan summer-houses of full-blown red lotuses for the Goddess Çrī to shelter in as she acted as his shampooer, and bore signs which told of his sovereignty over the four oceans in their auspicious marks, such as the lotus, the shell, the fish and the makara. His two thighs were like two ruby pillars, set to bear the weight of the earth which rested on his heart, like two sandal-trees with their roots shining with the rays from the crest-jewels of the serpents clustered round them, or like two streams from the ocean of beauty overflowing and all covered with foam, or like two huge tusks of a world-bearing elephant, bent through being used to block up a yawning makara's mouth[2]. He shone, like the mountain Mandara with Vāsuki's skin[3] at the churning of the ocean, with his lower garment which was radiant with shot silk-threads, washed in pure water, clinging closely to his loins, ornamented with the rays of the jewels of his girdle, and white like a mass of ambrosial foam,—while he appeared girt with his thin upper garment spangled with worked stars like the round world with its surrounding ether cloudless and full

[1] Cf. Bombay ed. p. 186, 8. [2] For the pun see note *supr.* p. 18.

[3] Each of these epithets applies to Vāsuki's skin as well as to the king's garment; and so too in the next sentence they similarly apply to Kailāsa as well as to the king's chest.

of stars. [81] He shone with his broad chest, like Kailāsa with a cliff of crystal,—able to bear the shock of various armies, too sturdy to be confined within the limits of its garment[1], and made smooth in spite of its hardness by the thousands of elephants' tusks which had collided against it. His neck was encircled by a necklace of pearls like the serpent Çeṣa, now sleeping peacefully in the sense of relief at depositing the burden of the whole earth on his stalwart arm, or like the dividing-line which draws the boundary between the respective empires of Çrī and Sarasvatī over his bosom and face. His breast was wrapped in a fold of rays from the pearls in his necklace as if it were a strip of cloth put on to signify the solemn conferring as a special gift of all the property gained during one's whole life[2]; he was like a jewel mountain, with its outstretched wings of jewels, spread on both sides,—with the red rays of the bracelets as if they were the paths for the passage of the glory produced by his arm or the continued streams of honey from the lotuses in the ears of Çrī as she lay on the pillow of his arm, or as if they were other arms newly budding forth in rivalry of Viṣṇu's four arms. He at once destroyed the greatness of the four regions of space and their rulers by his two long arms, which were as the bolts to blockade the path[3] through the world-encircling Lokāloka, and as the rock-walls built outside the moats of the four oceans, and as a cage of adamant to confine all illustrious kings, and as a jewelled triumphal arch for the festal entrance of the world's goddess of Victory. The redness of his lip bedewed all the regions of space like the exudation of a branch of the heavenly tree, and the lip itself seemed as if it were the Kaustubha gem, taking its place as a feature of his face in its desire to kiss its sister Lakṣmī[4] who sat enthroned there. He displayed at intervals a sudden flash of illumination to the Goddess of Empire who was somewhat dull and bewildered by nature, through the

[1] Or 'the shock of rivers' and 'the limits of the sky' (*ambara*).
[2] The Comm. does not explain the ceremony which this refers to.
[3] Cf. Wilson's Viṣṇu Pur. vol. ii. p. 206.
[4] Both being produced at the churning of the ocean.

gleaming flashes of his teeth as he laughed at the sportive sallies of his companions; (when he smiled) he seemed to be sending away the lotuses which had come to him in uncertainty whether it was his face or the moon—and was dismissing the autumnal moonlight which had entered under the illusion that the flash of his line of bright teeth was a bed of lotuses; [82] and he made a new anniversary of the churning the ocean by the odour which exhaled from his mouth perfumed by the mingled scent of wine, ambrosia, and *pārijāta* flowers, which filled all the regions of space,—while the perfume of his breath was continually inhaled by his overhanging nose which rose like a bud on his expanded lotus-face. With the brightness of his milk-white eye he deluged the regions of space as with a full tide of the milky ocean at the rising of his unparalleled moon-face,—and the chowrie-woman, as reflected in his stainless cheeks, seemed to be Sarasvatī who inhabited his mouth taking bodily shape; while his broad forehead was reddened by the pink hue of his crest-ornament, as if it were the lac dye of Lakṣmī's feet which had clung to it, when he sought by prostration to appease her jealousy at the preference shewn to Sarasvatī. He was listening, like one skilled in music to lute-players, to the tribes of bees in his ear-rings, which with restless feet played a tiny lyre consisting of the end of his ear-ring jewel with the web of its rosy rays for strings; while his locks were encircled by a wreath of white jasmine flowers mimicking Durgā's wreath of sculls, and serving as a halo round his moon-face, like a circle of moonlight from the nails of the Goddess of Empire, which had remained behind as she grasped his hair in amorous play. He was consecrated by the light of the pearls in his top-knot and the dark rays of the emeralds, as they crossed in their intermingling, as if the braid-like streams of the united Yamunā and Ganges had come of their own accord from Prayāga.

His imperial splendour was however eclipsed by the women, as their foreheads became blackened by the darkness produced through the ornamental *tilaka* of black agallochum being melted by the drops of perspiration, as if it were a dark mark produced by their repeated prostrations at his feet to incline him to grant their coaxing requests,—[83] propped up[1], as they were, by their flashing pearl-necklaces which were like so many waves rising from the tossed Mānasa lake[2],—seeming in jealousy to rebuke Çrī herself by the action of their creeper-like eyebrows, tremulous with a playful motion,—dragging him captive as with bonds by their long sweet-scented sighs which seemed made of the Malaya wind,—with their great jar-like bosoms, encircled with bands of large *Vakula* flowers, drawing from him every drop of contentment with his own proper spouse,—violently dragging him into their hearts, by the attraction of the rays of the trembling jewels of the necklaces which were set in motion by the trembling of their bosoms,—embracing him, as with many outstretched arms, with the rays of their far-flashing ornaments,—keeping their minds back, as it were, which had started off too impetuously, with their open hands which served as a covering over their mouths which wore an additional grace from a languid yawn,—skilfully moving their eyes which were half-closed as fainting at the arrows of Kāma and had their corners contracted on account of the pollen of the flowers in their ears, shaken by the bees which flew about blinded by intoxication,—striking the lotuses in their own ears with the sidelong glances of their eyes shot from under the play of their frowns through their mutual jealousy,—carrying the king reflected in their soft cheeks, as if he had been drunk up by their eyes whose lashes were motionless with the flood of joy[3] born of their unblinking gaze,—creating for love's assistance new moon-rises by their involuntary smiles through the playfulness of desire,—and seeming as in anger to break ever so many of Kāma's useless bows in the form of the rays of the curved nails as the joints of their fingers gave a loud crack when their twined hands, as they gesticulated, came into close contact in the rapid bendings of their limbs. He lay smiling, while he languidly struck on the head with the bow of

[1] Cf. *fultam*, Pers. i. 78.

[2] Or 'like so many longing regrets rising in the mind.'

[3] The Kashmir ed. reads *rāçi-*.

a lute the shampooing attendant, as his lotus feet dropped from her spray-like hands which were trembling in her perspiring emotion; [84] while he taught the Goddess of Empire as well as the lute (both equally dear) while each had its *koṇa*[1] firmly grasped in his hand. Single as he lay there, he was viewed in very different lights by different spectators,—riches called him cold, all faults turned from him as inaccessible, the senses felt awed at his love of self-control, the genius of the iron age said 'he is beyond my reach,' all vices pronounced him as passionless, dishonour looked on him as timid; Love said, 'the workings of his mind are hard to be understood'; Sarasvatī complained that 'he is uxorious'[2], other men's wives that 'he is impotent'; ascetics said that 'he is a seer of the highest order,' harlots that 'he is a deceiver'; his friends thought that 'he is easily led by others'; Brāhmans that 'he is our ready servant'; and his enemies' soldiers that 'he has faithful allies.' More truly the lord of Vāhinī[3] than Çantanu[4], more illustrious for victory[5] than Bhīṣma, more delighting in the bow[6] than Droṇa, more unerring with the arrow[7] than Açvatthāman, dearer to Mitra[8] than Karṇa, more forbearing[9] than Yudhiṣṭhira, possessing the might of more elephants than Bhīma, more worthy of figuring in the war of the Mahābhārata than Arjuna. He was as it were the cause of the Golden Age, the source of the creation of the Gods, the native land of pride, [85] the home of compassion, the close neighbour of Puruṣottama[10], the mine-mountain of valour, the assembly-

[1] *Koṇa* seems to mean here the bow of the lute and also 'an intermediate direction of the compass' for the empire.

[2] As devoted to his lawful spouse, Empire?

[3] *Vāhinī* means an army as well as the Ganges.

[4] Çantanu was the father of Bhīṣma by the goddess Gaṅgā, Viṣṇu Pur. iv. 20.

[5] Bhīṣma conquered his senses when he resigned the kingdom to his half-brother's children.

[6] Or 'more averse to desire.'

[7] Or 'more certain to help suppliants.'

[8] His friends or the Sun; Karṇa was the son of the Sun.

[9] Or 'possessing more land.'

[10] Kṛiṣṇa or 'the best of men.'

room for all sciences to Sarasvatī, an anniversary of the churning of the Ocean for ambrosia to Lakṣmī, an exhibition of power to Dexterity, a common meetingplace of the proprieties, a valuation of her treasures to Beauty, final perfection to the creation of the atoms of form, an expiation of all past evil deeds to Empire, a challenge against all opposing power to Kāma, a means for displaying Indra to all men as 'the city-stormer,' a visible return of ideal justice, the seraglio of the fine arts all together, the ultimate authority for defining good fortune, the final bath which completes the rites of installation to all monarchs,—the grave and gracious, the awe-inspiring and affable, at the same moment a holiday and a holy day, the universal Monarch.

Having seen him,—feeling, as it were, at once welcomed and checked, full of desire and yet satisfied, with his face horripilated with awe, and with tears of joy falling from his eyes, he stood at a distance smiling in wonder and pondered, "This then is the Emperor Çrī Harṣa, that union of separate glories,—noble in birth and of well-chosen name,—the lord of the field bounded by the four oceans,—the enjoyer of all the fruits of Brahmā's pillar, the world,—the surpasser of all the victories won by all the kings of ancient times. Through him the earth does indeed possess a true King! His youthful exploits, unlike Kṛiṣṇa's, transgress not right[1]; [86] his freaks of power cause no offence to the man of refinement[2] as did those of Çiva; his boasts lead to no destruction of families as did those of Indra to that of the cowpens[3]; unlike Yama, he is not too fond of wielding the rod of punishment; unlike Varuṇa, his treasure-houses are not guarded by thousands of pitiless sea-monsters[4]; unlike Kuvera, seeking an interview with him is never fruitless; unlike Jina, the sight of him is never without solid result[5];

[1] *Vṛiṣa* may also mean a demon slain by Kṛiṣṇa, cf. Viṣṇu P., V. xiv.

[2] Or 'Dakṣa,' Çiva's father-in-law.

[3] Alluding to Indra's name *gotrabhid.*

[4] Or 'sword-bearers.'

[5] Or 'his *darçana* (system) has *arthavāda.*' Should we read *arthāpatti*, as the Jainas do not accept this as a *pramāṇa*?

unlike the Moon, his glories do not wane. Wonderful is his royalty, surpassing the gods! His liberality cannot find range enough in suppliants, nor his knowledge in doctrines to be learned; his poetical skill finds words fail, as his valour lacks opportunities to exercise it; his energy wants scope and his fame sighs for a wider horizon, his kindly nature seeks in vain more hearts to win, his virtues exhaust the powers of number, and all the fine arts[1] are too narrow a field for his genius.

Under this monarch are found only the cloths worn by devotees in meditation, and not forged documents[2]; the royal figures of sculptors and not the vulgar disputes with kings; only bees quarrel in collecting dews (*dues*)[3]; the only *feet* ever cut off are those in metre; only chessboards teach the positions of the four 'members[4],' there is no cutting off the four principal limbs of condemned criminals; only snakes hate Garuḍa the king of birds (*dvija-guru*), no one hates Brāhmans or gurus; and the followers of the Mīmāṃsā alone have to ponder problems in administering justice (*adhikaraṇa*), while they examine the several *adhikaraṇas* or 'cases for discussion' in their system."

[87] So approaching, wearing the sacred thread, he uttered his good wishes.

Then on the north not far from the royal palace the attendant on the elephant chanted this sweet couplet in the *aparavaktra* metre;

"O young elephant, dismiss thy playful restlessness, follow the rules of good behaviour, with bent head; the heavy hook, crooked like a lion's claws, held aloft, does not spare thee[5]."

But when the king heard it and saw him, he asked, filling the sky with his voice deep like the roar of a lion in a

[1] I.e. the 64 *kalās*.

[2] This is a double-meaning of the phrase *yoga-paṭṭakāḥ*; and so in the other sentences.

[3] *Lit.* 'in collecting ichor' or 'in giving and taking.'

[4] Sc. *caturaṅga* 'the four members of an army,' or Chess. The phrase may also mean the cutting off of the four principal limbs.

[5] The lines can be also taken as a tacit rebuke to the luxurious Bāṇa.

mountain cave, "Is that Bāṇa?" The doorkeeper replied, "As my Lord commands; it is he." "I will not see him yet, as he has not as yet offered his tribute of respect," so saying, he turned the long brilliance of his eye, whose pupil trembled as it inclined to the corner of the eye, as if he was shaking a curtain variegated across with white and dark silk, and said to his favourite, the son of the king of Mālwa, who was sitting behind, "He is a thorough *petit-maître*." But when the other paused for a moment in silence at this unexplained speech of the king and the courtiers were all dumb, Bāṇa replied, "Why, my lord, do you thus address me, as if you did not know my character and did not believe me, as if you depended on others for guidance and did not understand the ways of the world yourself? The nature and talk of people will always be wilful and various; but the great ought to see things as they are. You surely will not regard me with prejudice as if I had no special claims. I am a Brāhman born in the family of the Soma-drinking Vātsyāyanas. Every ceremony was duly performed, as its time came, beginning with the investiture with the sacred cord; [88] I have thoroughly studied the Veda with its six aṅgas, and as far as I was able I have heard lectures on the çāstras, and from my marriage I have been a diligent householder; what signs have I of being a *petit-maître*[1]? My youth indeed was not without those follies which are not directly inconsistent with either world,—so far I will not deny; and my heart on this point will confess a feeling of repentance. But now-a-days, when your highness,—calm in mind like Buddha himself, one who carries out all the rules for the castes and orders like Manu, and bears the rod of punishment as visibly as Yama,—governs the whole earth girdled by the seven oceans, and bearing all the continents as its garland,—who would venture without fear even to act in his own mind the character of indecorum, that bosom-friend of open profligacy? I will not dwell on human beings,—in consequence of your power even the bees drink honey[2] in fear, even the ruddy-geese are

[1] Or 'Kāma is a petit-maître, not I.'

[2] *Madhu* means 'wine' as well as 'honey.'

ashamed of their too great fondness,—the very monkeys are alarmed when they play their wanton tricks, and even all the destructive animals eat flesh with compassion. Your highness will in time know me thoroughly by yourself, for it is the nature of the wise that their minds never act perversely." Having said this, he was silent.

The king also, after simply saying, "So we have heard," was silent; but he did not welcome him with any signs of favour such as friendly conversation, inviting him to sit down, etc.; he only revealed his inward pleasure by a gracious glance which seemed to bedew him with a shower of ambrosia; and as the setting sun was verging to the west, [89] he dismissed his courtiers and entered his private apartments. Bāṇa also went out and retired to his place of abode. The day was now calm and its fierce blaze soft like polished brass, and the sun[1], the diadem of the western mountain's crest, as he left the sky, was letting fall his rays like the sprays of the *Nicula* tree[2]; the deserted cow-stations in the forests had their patches of tender grass covered with families of deer lazily ruminating; the river-banks resounded plaintively with the cooing of the melancholy female ruddy-geese; in the pleasure-groves near the house all the waterpots were being turned over to fill the basins near the trees, while the troops of chattering sparrows were sitting on the boughs which formed their home; the companies of hungry calves were drinking their mothers' flowing udders, after they had returned from wandering during the day; the sun's round goblet for drinking the evening libation of the western ocean was sinking covered with a red glow as if it were plunged into a stream of mineral veins in the western mountain; the religious mendicants were intent on worshipping the shrines, having washed their feet and hands in the outpour of their water-pots; the fire, with the sacred grass spread round it, was blazing up, with its hands purified by the sacrificial vessels; the devout sacrificers were duly offering their libations; the trees of the groves stood with their monkeys resting from all their tricks,

[1] Read in the Bombay ed. *maricimati*.

[2] A tree with scarlet myrtle-like flowers in long pendent racemes.

and with the nests of the crows crowded with their inmates fast asleep[1]; the owls, settled in their huts in the hollow trunks of old trees, were preparing to go out on an expedition; a thicker host of stars was indenting the expanse of the sky, like a quantity of water-drops scattered at the time of the evening worship by the thousand hands of the sages; the crest of night floated over the sky like a mountaineer-woman's topknot; the young *avatār* of evening, dark like Çiva's neck, was devouring all that remained of the daylight; the lines of the lamps shone out as if they were the ray-fingers of the sun which had entered into the earthly fire at night[2] and had come forth to point in scorn at the darkness; the gates seemed to announce their closure by the creaking of the folding leaves; [90] the children were beginning to long to go to sleep, having enjoyed a good lying in bed while listening to the long stories of the old nurse; the dreadful mouth of early night was beginning to yawn, with its darkness as black as ink or an old buffalo, and waking up 'the good people[3].' Kāma with his twanging bow-string was raining a continual succession of arrows and stealing the intellect of all the world, the ladies had their loins jingling with the girdles of many woven threads tied by their tire-women, while romantic heroines started on their wanderings in the empty roads, following the guidance of love; the pleasant chatter of the geese in the ponds became rare, as it was dulled by the tinkling of the anklets of the women, and the notes of the cranes, as these grew longer as they became deeper asleep[4], melted the hearts of separated lovers; and a number of lamps were scattered about like the seeds beginning to shoot of the coming day.

He reflected to himself, "King Harṣa is very gracious, since he is still fond of me, though he is vexed at the rumours which have naturally spread about my many youth-

[1] The Comm. explains *vidrāṇa* as *alasa*, cf. p. 90, l. 9, 230, 13, and 235, 16.

[2] Taitt. Brāhmaṇa ii. 1, 2, 9; Raghuv. iv. 1.

[3] The Yakṣas or benevolent goblins who attend Kuvera are so called.

[4] *Vidrāṇa.*

ful follies; if I had been really under his displeasure, he would not have honoured me with an audience. He wishes me to be virtuous; for lords teach proper behaviour to their dependents even without words by granting them an appropriate reception. Shame on me, thus blinded in my mind by my own faults, and crushed by neglect,—that I venture to indulge in various fancies concerning this most excellent monarch. Verily I will endeavour so to act that he may recognise me in time in my real character."

Having made this resolve, he went out the next day from the royal camp and remained for a while in the houses of his friends and relations, until the king of himself learned his true character and became favourably inclined to him. Then he reentered again to visit the royal abode; [91] and in the course of a very few days he was received by his gracious majesty into the highest degree of honour springing from kindness, of affection, and of confidence, and shared with him in his wealth, his hours of unbending, and his state dignity.

Here ends the second chapter—entitled The Visit to the King—of the Harṣa-Carita composed by Çrī Bāṇa Bhaṭṭa.

CHAPTER III.

[92] Raining affection on their country[1], thronged by many devoted people[2],
Even as fine seasons are kings born through the merits of their subjects.
To serve the good, to behold the goddess of glory, to tread the heavens,
Whose heart is not eager?—aye and to hear the fortunes of heroes.

On a certain occasion Bāṇa left the king's presence and went to that Brāhman settlement to revisit his kin. It was the beginning of autumn, when the clouds are thinned, when the *cātaka* is distressed, when the *kādamba* duck gives voice,—the season deadly to frogs, robbing the peacock of its pride. Then the caravans of *haṃsas* are welcomed back[3], the sky is like a whetted sword, the sun brilliant, the moon at her clearest, tender the array of stars. The rainbow of Indra fades, the girdling lightning is at rest, Viṣṇu's sleep is invaded[4]; the waters run hued like lapis lazuli, the clouds rolling light as mists leave Indra unemployed. Then closes the *Nīpa*, the *Kuṭaja* has no flower; budless is the plantain,

[1] Or of the seasons—'bringing moisture by their rain.'

[2] Or 'with people rich in rice.'

[3] The wild geese fly to the hills when the inundations cover the plains at the beginning of the rainy season, and they return in the autumn.

[4] Cf. Wilson, 'Hindu Theatre,' II. 197.

soft the red lotus, the blue lotus exudes honey; the water-lily is a joy, the nights are cool with the *Çephālikā*, the jasmine [93] becomes fragrant; the ten regions are all ablaze with opening night lotuses, grey are the winds with *Saptacchada* pollen, lovely clustering *Bandhūkas* form an unexpected evening glow. The horses have undergone lustration, the elephants are wild, the herds of oxen intoxicated with ferocity. The range of mud diminishes, young sand isles bud forth by the river banks. The wild rice is parched to ripeness, the pollen is formed in the *Priyaṅgu* blossoms, the cucumber's skin is hardened, and the reed grass[1] smiles with flowers.

Gratified beyond measure at the news of Bāṇa's favour with the king, his kinsmen came forth to meet him with congratulations. In due course he experienced the great joy of finding himself among his numerous relatives, greeting some, greeted by others, kissed by some, kissing others, embraced by some, embracing others, welcomed with a blessing by some, blessing others. The elders being seated, he took a seat brought by his excited attendants. At the receipt of the flower offering and other hospitable attentions his delight was still further increased, and it was with a joyous heart that he made his inquiries:—"Have you been happy all this time? Does the sacrifice proceed without hindrance, gratifying the Brāhman groups by its faultless performance? Do the fires devour oblations with ritual duly and without flaw performed? Do the boys pursue their studies at the proper time? Is there the same unbroken daily application to the Veda? The old earnestness in the practice of the art of sacrifice? Are there the same classes in grammar exposition, showing respect by days not idly spent in a series of emulous discussions? Is there the old logic society, [94] regardless of all other occupations? The same excessive delight in the Mīmāṃsā, dulling all pleasure in other authoritative books? Are there the same poetic addresses, raining down an ambrosia of ever-new phrases?"

[1] Cf. Wilson, 'Hindu Theatre,' II. 196 n.

They replied:—"Son, the affairs of us people devoted to contentment, whose intellectual pastimes are always at command, and whose only companion is the sacrificial fire, are of little importance, so long as the earth is happily protected by our monarch's arm, swaying the whole world and long as the body of the king of serpents. We are in any case happy, but especially now that you, having cast aside indolence, occupy a cane seat beside our sovereign lord. All the ceremonies proper to Brāhmans are fully carried out as far as our powers and means permit and in due season."

Mid such conversations as these, court news, remembrances of past boyish sports, and stories of the men of old he amused himself with them for some time; at length rising at noon, he complied with the usual observances. After dinner his kinsmen gathered round him. Soon the reader Sudṛiṣṭi was observed approaching, wearing a pair of silken Pauṇḍra cloths pale as the outer corner of the peacock's eye: his sectarial lines were painted in *gorocanā* and clay from a sacred pool blessed at the end of his bath; his hair was made sleek with oil and myrobolan, a thick bunch of flowers, kissing his short topknot, added a touch of spruceness, the glow of his lips had been heightened by several applications of betel, and a brilliance imparted to his eyes by the use of a stick of collyrium: he had just dined [95] and his dress was decorous and respectable. He seated himself on a chair not far away, and, after waiting a moment, set down in front of him a desk made of reed stalks, and laid upon it a manuscript from which he had removed the tie, but which still seemed encircled by the rays of his nails like soft lotus fibres. Next he assigned a place to a bee and a dove, which he set down close behind him. Finally, having turned over the intervening leaves marked by the end of the morning chapter[1], he took a small light block[2] of a few leaves, and read with a chant the Purāṇa uttered by Vāyu, the rays of his teeth seeming to cleanse the ink-stained syllables, and to

[1] Which had been already read.

[2] Literally 'small door-panel,' from the shape.

worship the volume with showers of white flowers, and his honeyed intonations[1], like the anklets of a Sarasvatī brought near his mouth, charming the hearts of his hearers.

While Sudṛiṣṭi was thus reading with a chant delightful to the ear, the minstrel Sūcīvāṇa, who was not far from him, accompanied the modulation of the chant by reciting in a voice loud and sweet this *āryā* couplet[2]:—

'Itself sung by sages, itself widespread[3], embracing the world, cleansing from sin,
'Methinks this Purāṇa differs not from the achievements of Harṣa!
'Following the law of heredity[4], free from discord, noised abroad by its deeds[5], including all India under its sway,
'Issuing from a Çrīkaṇṭha[6], this chant resembles the sovereignty of Harṣa!'

[96] Hearing this Bāṇa's cousins, who had previously arranged together, looked meaningly at each other, while a smile's ambrosia whitened the convex of their cheeks[7]. There were four of them brothers, Gaṇapati, Adhipati, Tārāpati, and Çyāmala, and their aspect was, like Brahmā's four faces, made pure by the study of the Veda[8], their looks, like the four methods[9], endearing from the employment of conciliation; men of mild manners, and culture, holding the

[1] The Comm. explains *gamakāḥ* as 'points of transition from note to note'; the Vācaspatya Dict. says *svaro yo mūrchanām eti gamakaḥ sa ihocyate | Kampitaḥ sphurito līno bhinnaḥ sthavira eva ca || āhatāndolitau ceti gamakāḥ sapta kīrtitāḥ.* |

[2] The couplet is replete with puns.

[3] Or 'surpassing Pṛithu,' the primæval king.

[4] Or 'sound of the flute.'

[5] Or 'with clear rhythm.' *Bharatamārgabhajanaguru* contains a punning ref. to (1) Bharata, the divine sage of music, (2) the Bharatavarṣa, 'India.'

[6] I.e. 'an honoured throat'; Çrīkaṇṭha is the name of Harṣa's ancestral kingdom.

[7] This paragraph is full of untranslateable puns.

[8] Each Veda being promulgated by a special mouth, see Viṣṇu Pur. I. v.

[9] For the four Methods of Policy cf. Manu 7. 109: the compound may also mean 'with their commencement endearing from the employment of conciliation' as the first Method, or 'with mouths endearing from repeating the Sāma-Veda.'

status of preceptors, expounders of Nyāya, deep in the study of able works, receiving only good words[1] both in the world and in grammar, versed in the acts of all monarchs and sages of old, inspired in mind by the Mahā-Bhārata, acquainted with all legends, great in wisdom and poetry, full of eagerness to know stories of heroes, thirsting[2] for no elixir but that of listening to well-turned phrases, foremost in years, speech, distinction, asceticism, the conference, the festival, in person, and in sacrifice.

At a signal from the others the youngest of them with eyes long as lotus petals, Çyāmala by name, much loved by Bāṇa and disposer almost of his soul, respectfully spoke, [97] bathing the heavens with the light of his teeth[3]:—"Friend Bāṇa, the king of the twiceborn[4] ravished his preceptor's wife. Purūravas was severed from his beloved Āyus through greed for a Brāhman's gold. Nahuṣa, lusting after another's wife, became a great snake[5]. Yayāti took upon himself to win a Brāhmaṇī woman's hand and fell[6]. Sudyumna actually became a woman[7]. [98] Somaka's cruelty in murdering Jantu[8] is notorious. Through infatuation for the bow Māndhātṛi went with his sons and grandsons to hell. Even while an ascetic, Purukutsa wrought a deed of shame upon the daughter of Mekala[9]. Kuvalayāçva, through resorting to the world of snakes, avoided not the Nāga-girl Açvatarā[10]. Pṛithu, that fine

[1] I.e. 'they are called good,' and as grammarians 'they receive only good words.'

[2] *-avitṛiṣṇa* = 'free from all thirst (=desire) except etc.'

[3] In this speech Bāṇa mentions the various stains on the honour of all ancient heroes,—only Harṣa is spotless. Some of the accusations however rest only on plays of words.

[4] The moon carried off Tārā the wife of Vṛihaspati. In the next sentence *Āyus* may also be translated 'life.'

[5] Or 'rake,' cf. Mah. III. clxxxi. [6] Mah. I. lxxxi.-lxxxiv.

[7] Or 'follower of women,' cf. Viṣṇu Pur. IV. i.

[8] He offered his only son Jantu in sacrifice to obtain a hundred sons, Mah. III. cxxvii. The word *jantu* also means 'living creatures.'

[9] Narmadā. For a legend of some connection between this king and the river Narmadā see Viṣṇu Pur. IV. iii.

[10] This refers to some legend of this king having been drowned while bathing after hunting. *Bhujaṅga*, 'snake' and 'rake,' contains a pun.

first of men, did violence to Pṛithivī. In Nṛiga's becoming a chameleon[1] a confusion of castes was seen. By Saudāsa the earth was not protected, but confounded[2]. Nala, unable to control his passion for dicing[3], [99] was overcome by Kali. Saṃvaraṇa had a weakness for Mitra's daughter[4]. Daçaratha came by his death through overfondness for his beloved Rāma[5]. Kārtavīrya was slain[6] for persecuting cows and Brāhmans. Marutta, though he performed the Bahusuvarṇa sacrifice, involving vast expenditure, was not highly honoured by gods and Brāhmans[7]. Çantanu, separated through infatuation from his (loved) river[8], wept all alone in the forest. [100] Pāṇḍu in the midst of the woods lost his life, like a fish, in the heat of passion[9]. Yudhiṣṭhira, downcast through fear of his guru[10], diverged from truth in the battle-front. Thus no reign has been stainless except that of this Harṣa, king of kings, sovereign of all continents. Concerning him indeed many marvels are reported:—In him we see[11] how a 'Subduer of Hosts' has set at rest the moving partisan kings[12]. In him

[1] Mah. XIII. vi.; there is a pun here, as it may also mean "a confusion of *colours*."

[2] Mah. I. clxxviii. *Narakṣitā* may go with Saudāsa in the sense of 'murderer.'

[3] Or 'without control over heart and senses.'

[4] Mah. I. clxxi. By a pun the author implies 'a weakness for his *friend's* daughter.'

[5] Or 'for beloved women.'

[6] By Jāmadagnya.

[7] Marutta wished to offer a great sacrifice, but Vṛihaspati, the priest of the gods, refused to officiate, and he had to submit to many indignities before he could secure the services of the Brāhman Saṃvartaka at Benares, see Mah. XIV. vi. vii.

[8] For the legend of Çantanu's love for the goddess Gaṅgā see Mah. I. xcvi.–xcix. *Vāhinī* beside 'river' may also mean 'army.'

[9] Mah. I. cxxv.

[10] Droṇa, see Mah. VII. cxci. The truthful Yudhiṣṭhira is once persuaded to prevaricate, when in order to stop Droṇa in his career of victory he tells him that Açvatthāman has been killed, meaning an elephant of that name and not Droṇa's son. Droṇa had said that his pupil Yudhiṣṭhira would never tell a lie even for the sovereignty of the three worlds.

[11] He proceeds to shew by a series of plays on words how Harṣa fulfils the feats of mythological heroes.

[12] Or 'a Balajit (Indra) has fixed fast the winged mountains.'

a 'Lord of People' has displayed forbearance towards all other rulers[1]. In him a 'Best of Men' has won fame by pounding a king of Sindh[2]. In him a 'Man of Might' has loosened a king[3] from a circling trunk and abandoned an elephant[4]. In him a 'Lord' has anointed a young prince[5]. [101] In him a 'Master' has signalized his power by laying low his enemy[6] at one stroke. In him a 'Man-lion' has manifested his might by cutting down his enemy with his own hand[7]. In him a 'Supreme Lord' has taken tribute from an inaccessible land of snowy mountains[8]. In him a 'World's Lord' has stationed the world's guardians at the entrance to the regions, and the treasure of all the earth has been distributed among the first of the people[9]. These and the like great undertakings do we see, resembling those of the first age of gold. Therefore we are eager to hear from the beginning onwards in the order of his lineage the fortunes of this auspiciously named hero, rich in the merit won by noble deeds. It is long since we first desired to hear. As the magnet attracts hard and sapless iron, so do the qualities of the great even the hard and tasteless minds of insignificant people: much more those of others naturally tasteful and susceptible. Who could be without curiosity regarding his story, a second Mahā-Bhārata? Pray relate it, your highness! Let our Bhṛigu race become even more pure by the purificatory

1 Or 'a Prajāpati has set the earth upon the hoods of the serpent Çeṣa.'

2 Or 'a Puruṣottama has obtained Lakṣmī by churning the ocean.'

3 The king's name was Çrikumāra or Kumāra Gupta. Harṣa rescued him when encircled in the trunk of a mad elephant, which he then let loose in the woods. The words may also mean 'a Bali has set free the encircled mountain and loosened a great serpent (= Vāsuki).'

4 The great elephant's name was Darpaçāta.

5 Ref. to the god of war, Kumāra, and to Harṣa's young son.

6 There is a pun on Arāti, 'king of the demons,' slain by Kumāra.

7 There is an involved ref. to the story of the Dwarf Avatar of Viṣṇu.

8 There is a punning ref. to Çiva's taking Durgā to wife.

9 I.e. the Brāhmans. The words also refer to Viṣṇu apportioning the earth to the other deities as its regents and dividing its treasures among the early kings.

hearing of the deeds of the royal sage[1]." So much said he became silent.

"Sir," replied Bāṇa with a smile, "your remarks accord not with fitness. I consider the demands of your curiosity impracticable. People absorbed in their own objects are commonly void of discrimination between the possible and impossible. Attracted by the virtues of others and confused, I suppose, by passion for hearing stories of friends, the minds even of the great lose their discernment. Consider, sir! On the one hand you have a mere student's wit of an atom's capacity, on the other his majesty's story [102] commensurate with the whole edifice of Brahmā[2]; on the one hand a few sounds with circumscribed letters and the five modes of word-formation, on the other virtues beyond calculation. Beyond the comprehension of the omniscient, beyond the capacity of the god of speech, beyond the strength of the goddess of eloquence, how much more is he beyond such as I! What man could possibly even in a hundred of men's lives depict his story in full? If, however, you care for a part, I am ready. In what way may a feeble tongue possessed of a few grains of letters be of service? Your highnesses are the audience, the fortunes of Harṣa the theme: what more can be said? The day, however, is near its close. The adorable sun, bright with matted locks of ruddy rays trailing behind, is sinking in the mass of the evening glow, like the Bhṛigu Rāma in the great pool of all Kurukṣetra's[3] blood. To-morrow I will narrate the story." "So be it," they all assented, and rising soon after, he proceeded to the Çoṇa for his twilight worship.

Then, with heat soft as a Mālwa woman's wine-flushed cheek, the day folded itself up. Red exceedingly, as if through toying with the lotus beds, the sun kissing the dusk declined: following the track of whose chariot horses, the

[1] Or—reading *rājarṣivaṃçacaritaçravaṇena*—'hearing of the fortunes of this royal sage's house.'

[2] I.e. the world.

[3] *Samantapañcaka* = 'the whole land of the five lakes,'—alluding to Paraçu-Rāma's slaughter of the Kṣatriyas.

darkness sped like Yama's buffalo along the firmament. In due course the bark dresses hanging upon the hut-roofs of the house ascetics were gathered in along with their patches of red blaze[1]. The heavens were gladdened by the smoke of the Agnihotra rite, stealing away the taint of the Kali age. The sacrificers preserved a rigid silence: the women strolled around in the restlessness of recreation time. Bundles of green panicum and rice were being strewn about for the sacrificial cows after milking; the Vāitāna fires were being lighted, the braided ascetics, hairy with black antelope skins, were seated on their clean mats, [103] the students mumbled their tasks, the meditating *yogis* squatted in the Brahma posture, innumerable scholars ran about with sounds of clapping, while, by leave of their wearied old teacher, a concourse of dolts, dandies, and boys performed their twilight task[2] by blunderingly belching out the disconnected lines of their books.

As the evening was now established in the sky and the lamps called stars were peeping forth, Bāṇa proceeded to the house, and sate down in the same company with his loved kinsmen. The first watch having been so spent, he betook himself to a bed in the house of Gaṇapati. With all the others, however, who in spite of closed eyes obtained no sleep, waiting like lotus beds for the sunrise, curiosity made the night wear but heavily away.

Awaking at the fourth watch of the night, the same bard as before sang a couple of verses:—

'Stretching out his foot behind, elongating his body upwards to full length by bending his spine,
'With bowed neck leaning his mouth upon his breast, tossing his dust-grey mane,
'His projecting nostrils restlessly moving through desire for fodder, the steed,
'Now risen from his bed, gently whinnying paws the earth with his hoof.
'With bent back and loins brought near his mouth, curving his neck sideways,
'His curls matted about his ears, the horse with his hoof rubs the corner of his eye,

[1] Cf. Çakuntala 32.

[2] Should we read *saṃdhyāṃsam*?

'Inflamed by irritation in sleep, while small bits of chaff cling to his moving eyelashes,
'And his eye is uneasily smitten[1] by his tossing hoar-frost-scattering forehead-tuft.'

[104] Hearing this, Bāṇa dispelled his slumbers, and having arisen, washed his face, worshipped the holy twilight, took his betel at sunrise, and sought the same place as before. Meanwhile all his kinsmen collected and sat down in a circle round him. Having learnt their object through the former discussion, he began to relate to them the fortunes of Harsha:—

"Listen. There is a certain region named Çrīkaṇṭha, peopled by the good, a heaven of Indra, as it were, descended upon earth, where the laws of caste usage are for ever unconfused and the order of the Kṛita age prevails. Owing to the number of its land lotuses the ploughs, whose shares uproot the fibres as they scar the acres, excite a tumult of bees, singing, as it were, the excellencies of the good soil. Unbroken lines of *Puṇḍra* sugar-cane enclosures seem besprinkled by the clouds that drink the Milky Sea[2]. On every side its marches are packed with corn heaps, like extemporized mountains, distributed among the threshing floors[3]. Throughout it is adorned with rice crops extending beyond their fields, where the ground bristles with cumin beds watered by the pots of the Persian wheel. Upon its lordly uplands are wheat crops variegated with *Rājamāṣa* patches ripe to bursting and yellow with the split bean pods. Attended by singing herdsmen mounted on buffalos, pursued by sparrows greedy for swarms of flies, gay with the tinkle of bells bound to their necks, roaming herds of cows make white its forests, revelling on *Vāṣpachedya*[4] grass and dropping milk as if the Milky Sea had been drunk by the bull of Çiva

[1] Should we read *āhanyamānām*?

[2] By reason of their sweetness, Comm.

[3] But v. Comm. *khaladhānadhāmabhiḥ ·khalapālāiḥ* 'by the owners of the threshing floors.'

[4] Lit. 'To be cut with tears': the name denotes the excessive tenderness of the grass (cf. Pāṇ. ii. 1. 33).

and then divided up by him into many portions through fear of indigestion. Like eyes let fall by Indra[1] when blinded by the smoke of its divers burnt sacrifices, thousands of spotted antelopes dot the districts. [105] Regions, pale with the dust of *Ketakī* beds emitting white pollen, gleam like the approaches of Çiva's City when made grey by the sprinklings of the Pramathas. Pot-herbs and plantains blacken the soil around the villages. At every step are groups of young camels. The exits are made attractive by vine-arbours and pomegranate orchards; arbours, ablaze with *Pīlu* sprays, besmeared with the juice of hand-pressed citron leaves, having flower bunches formed of spontaneously gathered saffron filaments, and travellers blissfully sleeping after drinking the juice of fresh fruit, very hostels, as it were, with wood-nymphs dispensing ambrosia: orchards, where the fruit, ripe to bursting, seems coloured by the beaks of the parrots attacking the seeds, and the flowers are tinged by the cheeks of climbing monkey tribes. There are lovely groves where woodrangers taste the cocoa-nut juice, where travelling folk plunder the date-trees, monkeys lick sweet-scented date juice, and partridges tear the *Āruka* to pieces with their beaks. Not barren are the sylvan hollows of forest pools, refuge of myriad travellers, encircled with avenues of tall *Arjuna* trees and turbid at the edges through the descent of herds of kine. Troops of camels and flocks of sheep form in hordes under the guardianship of camel boys. Wandering droves of mares, besmeared with the sap of crushed saffron beds, where they roll as if to seduce the steeds of the sun's chariot, visit the land, roaming like the deer of the Maruts[2] at will, with snorting nostrils and uplifted heads drinking in the air, as it were to beget speed in the young lying in their wombs.

Seen like wild geese amid the dusk of ever-smoking sacrifices, the reeds are white upon the earth. The land's vast resources sound through the animate world like peacocks wild at the sound of drums in concert. Good

[1] The god of the Thousand Eyes.

[2] The Maruts are borne in their chariots by deer.

men, in conduct[1] spotless as the moon's rays, adorn it like pearls. [106] It has the attraction of all-welcoming hosts, like huge trees whose rich fruit is plundered by hundreds of voyagers. Great men are its bulwarks, clad, like the feet of the Himālaya, with the hair of deer bearing the fragrance of civet. Graced is it with ponds like Viṣṇu's navel, where fine birds[2] are seated upon lotuses with tall stalks. Its regions are filled with wide ranches[3], which, like the turmoil of the churning of the Milky Ocean, wash the lands with torrents of churned milk. Such is the land of Çrīkaṇṭha.

There did false doctrines fade away, as if washed out by a rain of tears due to the smoke of the Triple Fire. Sinful ways vanished, as if consumed by the burning of the bricks for altars. Demerit was scotched, as if cleft by the axes which fashioned sacrificial posts. Caste confusion ceased, as if cleansed by a rain from the smoke clouds of oblation fires. Sin fled, as if gored by the horns of the many thousands of presented oxen. Disasters were cut away, as if excised by numerous axes chiselling stone for temples. Calamities sped afar, as if routed by the tumult of munificent rites. Disease was dissipated, as if consumed by myriad blazing sacrificial kitchens. Sudden death came not near, as if alarmed by the sharp beat of holy drums struck at bulls' wedlocks[4]. [107] Plagues departed, as if deafened by the never-ceasing noise of hymns. Overwhelmed, as it were, by the rule of law, mishap did not arise.

In such a country is a certain district called Sthāṇvīçvara, blessed, like the world's first youth, with sweet fragrance of lovely flowers in divers pleasances; bedecked, like the road

[1] The Sanskrit has a play on the double sense of *vṛittam* = (1) conduct, (2) round and of *gunin* = (1) worthy, (2) strung on a cord.

[2] *Dvijottama* = (1) best of birds, (2) Brahmā, (3) Brāhman, there being an allusion to the story that Brahmā reclines on a lotus springing from Viṣṇu's navel.

[3] Beside 'wide ranches' *mahāghoṣa* may denote 'mighty rumblings.'

[4] For the letting loose of bulls cf. Wilson, H. D. I. p. 20 n. and reff. ap. B. and R.

to Dharma's gynæceum, with many myriads of buffalos[1] stained from rolling in saffron; whitened at its borders, like a part of the celestial realm, with yak-tail flappers shaken by the winds; blazing to all the ends of heaven, like the encampment of the Kṛita age, with thousands of flaming sacrificial fires; allaying all inauspicious signs, like the Brahma-world's first descent, by the meditation of Brahmarṣis seated in the posture of thought; thronged, like a rival[2] to the Northern Kurus, with hundreds of great rivers[3] uproarious with tumult; surpassing Tripura, as it were, in having all its people unacquainted with the devastating might of Çiva's arrow; bright, like a replica of the moon world, with rows of white houses plastered with stucco[4]; like a claimant to the name of Kuvera's City, oppressing the world with clanking ornaments of wine-flushed beauties.

Sages entitled it a hermitage, courtesans a lover's retreat, actors a concert hall, foes the city of death, seekers of wealth the land of the philosopher's stone, [108] sons of the sword the soil of heroes, aspirants to knowledge the preceptor's home, singers the Gandharvas' city, scientists the Great Artificer's temple, merchants the land of profit, bards the gaming-house, good men the gathering of the virtuous, refugees the cage of adamant, libertines the Rogue's Meet, wayfarers the reward of their good deeds, treasure-seekers the mine, quietists the Buddhist monastery, lovers the Apsaras' City, troubadours the festival congress, Brāhmans the stream of wealth.

There are women like elephants in gait[5], yet noble-minded; virgins, yet attached to worldly pomp[6]; dark, yet possessed of rubies[7]; their faces are brilliant with white teeth, yet is their breath perfumed with the fragrance of

[1] There is a pun on *mahiṣī*, which means 'a crowned queen' as well as 'a buffalo.' The paragraph contains many other puns.

[2] The Bombay text reads *vipakṣa* 'rival' for *vikṣepa* ('threat'?).

[3] Or—punningly—'armies.'

[4] Or—punningly—'ambrosia.'

[5] Or—punningly—'visiting vile outcasts.'

[6] Or—punningly—'past child bearing.'

[7] Or 'dark as night yet bright with red lotuses.'

wine[1]; their bodies are like crystal, yet their limbs are soft as acacia flowers; they are unattainable by paramours, yet robed in bodices[2]; wide are their beautiful hips, yet are they possessed of thin waists[3]; lovely[4] are they, yet honeyed in speech; they trip not, yet have a bright and captivating beauty[5]; they are without curiosity[6], yet wedded.

[109] Their eyes are a natural *muṇḍamālā* wreath, the garlands of lotus leaves are a mere burden. The images of their curls in the convex of their cheeks are ear-pendants that give no trouble; *Tamāla* shoots are a superfluity. The talk of their dear ones forms happy ear-ornaments; rings and the like are but affectation. Their cheeks alone give a perpetual sunshine; for pomp only have they jewelled lamps by night. Tribes of bees attracted by their breath are their beauteous veils, the duty of noble women their hair-nets. Their voices alone are their sweet lutes, harp-playing is but an irrelevant accomplishment. Laughs are their exceeding fragrant perfumes; needless is camphor powder. The gleam of their lips is a more brilliant cosmetic; saffron unguent is a worthless blot upon their loveliness. Their arms are the softest of playfully smiting wands; purposeless are lotus stalks. Drops of the sweat of youthful warmth are their artful bosom ornaments, necklaces but a burden. Their laps are broad squares of crystal slabs for their lovers; jewelled couches in their mansions a needless means of repose. Bees clinging in greed for such lotuses are their resonant foot-ornaments; useless are anklets of sapphire. Domestic *kalahaṃsas*, summoned by the tinkle of their anklets, are the unfailing companions of their walks; attendants are but the accidents of greatness.

In that country there arose a monarch named Puṣpabhūti,

1 Or 'with faces pure as Brāhmans, yet &c.', wine-drinking being forbidden to Brāhmans.

2 Or—punningly—'libidinous.'

3 Or—punningly—'far-famed as wives (Or 'having brilliant retinues'), yet reckoned among the poor.'

4 Or—punningly—'tart in speech.'

5 Or—punningly—'they are flushed with wine.'

6 Or—punningly—'the marriage thread.'

having, like Indra incarnate, a bow supporting all castes[1], Meru-like in the attribute of a golden nature, Mandara-like in attracting glory[2], ocean-like in observing proper bounds[3], ether-like in the noising abroad of his fame[4], moon-like in his receptivity for arts[5], Veda-like in truthful[6] speech, earth-like in [110] supporting all mankind, wind-like in sweeping away the bad passions of all kings[7], a Guru in speech, a Pṛithu in breast, a Viçāla[8] in intellect, a Janaka in asceticism, a Suyātra in splendour, a Sumantra in secret council, a Budha in station, an Arjuna in brilliance, a Bhīṣma with the bow, a Niṣadha in frame, a Çatrughna in battle, a Çūra in vanquishing armies of heroes[9], a Dakṣa in fecundity; framed in fine as it seemed of the compounded splendour of all the primaeval kings.

This king, jealous of the saying "this earth was made a cow by Pṛithu," made the earth his queen[10]. Now the minds of the great are naturally wilful and follow their own lights. Wherefore from boyhood upwards he, untaught by any man, entertained a great, almost inborn, devotion towards Çiva the adorable, readily won by faith, upholder of the universe, creator of creatures, annihilator of existence. From all other gods he turned away. Not even in dreams did he take food without worshipping him whose emblem is the bull. Devoted to the Lord of Beings, the increate, ageless, guru of the immortals, the foe of the Demons' City, the lord of countless Hosts, spouse of the Daughter of the Mountains, him before whose feet all worlds bow, he thought the three spheres void of all other deities. The dispositions of his subjects also were conformable to their monarch's mind.

1 Or 'of all colours.'
2 Or 'Lakṣmī.'
3 Or 'rectitude.'
4 Or 'manifesting sound,' which is the property of *ākāça*.
5 Or 'assemblage of digits.'
6 Or 'increate.'
7 Or 'all earthly dust.'
8 The name of a Bodhisattva, Comm.
9 Or perhaps 'in conquering Çūrasena.'
10 *Mahiṣī* may also mean 'a buffalo-cow.'

Thus:—house by house the holy lord of the Cleaving Axe was worshipped: the winds blowing in those pure districts were fragrant with much resin melted in the sacrificial pits, they dropped a rain of dew from the milk used for bathing[1], they whirled along petals of Bel twig chaplets. [111] It was with gifts and presents customary in Çiva's worship that the king was honoured by citizens, dependants, councillors, and neighbouring sovereigns, whom his arm's might had conquered and made tributary. Thus:—they gratified his heart with huge Çiva bulls[2] white as Kailāsa's peaks, and ringed about their horn-tips with gold-leaf creepers; with golden ewers, with oblation vessels, censers, flowered cloths, lamps on jewelled stands, Brāhmanical threads, and *mukhakoças*[3] inlaid with bits of precious gems. His queens also complied with his desire, voluntarily undertaking the threshing of the scattered rice, deepening the glow of their hands by staining the temples with unguents, occupying all their attendants in stringing flowers. Now this monarch so devoted to Çiva heard men speak of a certain great Çaiva saint named Bhairavācārya, almost a second overthrower of Dakṣa's sacrifice[4], who belonged to the Deckan, but whose powers, made famous by his excellence in multifarious sciences, were, like his many thousands of disciples, spread abroad over the whole sphere of humanity. Harmony in character conciliates good will even towards unknown persons; and so, immediately on hearing of this saint Bhairavācārya, the king conceived towards him, though far away, a deep affection as towards a second Çiva, and desired even with longing by all means to see his face.

One day, as the failing light was kissing the western hill, the portress approached the king, who was in the harem, and said: 'Your majesty, a recluse stands at the door and declares that he has come by order of Bhairavācārya.'

[1] I.e. bathing the god's image.

[2] I.e. bulls let loose in honour of Çiva.

[3] It is difficult to see what this word means: the Comm. says *mukhayuktāḥ koçā mukhakoçā ye liṅgopari dīyante.* Perhaps it is a covering for wrapping the image of the liṅga.

[4] The real overthrower of Dakṣa's sacrifice was Çiva himself.

'Where is he,' the king with profound respect inquired, 'conduct him here, introduce him.' The chamberlain did so, and soon the king saw the ascetic enter, a tall fellow [112] with arms extending to his knees, emaciated by a mendicant's life yet from the stoutness of the bones in his limbs appearing fat, broad in the head, his forehead undulating with deep wrinkles, fleshless hollows beneath his eyes, which were round and ruddy as wine drops, his nose slightly curved, one ear very pendulous, the rows of his prominent teeth distinct as seeds in a gourd, his lip loose as a horse's, his jaw elongated by a hanging chin. A red ascetic's scarf hanging from his shoulder formed his *vaikakṣaka* wrap; his upper robe, consisting of a tattered rag knotted above his heart and stained with red chalk, seemed to betoken the knotted passions of his heart, which he had rent in pieces[1]. In one hand he grasped his bamboo stool. His left held a yoke pole resting on his shoulder, where its motionless point of support was tied with a complicated fastening of hair rope; to this were attached his dirt-scraper and sieve of bamboo bark, his loin cloth at the end, his alms bowl contained in its receptacle, namely a cavity of *Kharjūra* wood, his waterpot fixed in a triangular support made of three sticks, his slippers disposed outside, and a bundle of manuscript bound by a string of stout cord.

As he drew near, the king welcomed him with the usual courtesies, and when he was seated, asked where Bhairavācārya was. Charmed with the king's gracious speech, the mendicant stated that he was staying near the city in a deserted house contiguous with the woods on the Sarasvatī's banks; and he further added 'His reverence honours your sovereign majesty with his blessing.' With which words he drew from his pack and presented five jewelled silver lotuses sent by Bhairavācārya, which overlaid the harem with a glow of light.

[113] The king, shrinking, as politeness dictated, from slighting a friend's gift, but also unwilling to be guilty of too hasty acceptance, paused a moment wavering, but at length,

[1] We have here a pun on *rāga*—'mortal passion' and also 'red colour.'

yielding to his great nobleness, he took the gifts and said:— 'Our devotion to Çiva, the source of all fruitful results, produces fruits inaccessible indeed to desire, seeing that we find such favour with his reverence, the guru of the world. To-morrow I will see his reverence.' With these words he dismissed the ascetic, profoundly delighted at his news.

The next day he rose early, mounted his horse, and with his white umbrella held above him, and a pair of white chowries waving, proceeded accompanied by only a few nobles to see Bhairavācārya, like the moon visiting the sun. Having advanced some distance, he saw one of Bhairavācārya's own disciples approaching, and inquired where his reverence was staying. 'In a Bel-tree plantation,' the man replied, 'north of yon old temple to the Mothers.' So he proceeded to the place, dismounted, and entered the plantation.

In the midst of a great throng of recluses [116] he beheld Bhairavācārya[1], who on seeing him at a distance moved like the ocean seeing the moon, and, after his disciples had first risen, rose and went forward to meet the king. Having presented a gift of Bel fruit, he pronounced a benediction in tones deep as the roar of Ganges' flood when it was vomited forth from Jahnu's ear.

The king, whose eyes, expanding their white in pleasure, seemed to repay the lotuses many-fold, and whose brilliant crest-jewel, declining upon his forehead, seemed to put forth a third eye as a manifestation of Çiva's favour[2], repeated his salutation by a bow from a distance; while from his ear-wreath, as he bent down, bees flew away like departing sins all uprooted by Çiva worship. 'Approach, be seated here,' said the teacher, pointing to his own tiger-skin. 'Your reverence,' the king respectfully replied in a voice flowing like a river of honey and rich with the passionate throbbing utterance of lovesick *haṃsas*, 'you ought not to make me suffer for the faults of other princes. It is surely the bad manners of that inglorious glory which all kings regard, or else the mean pride of wealth, which makes the teacher deal so with me.

[1] For the description of Bhairavācārya v. Appendix.

[2] Çiva himself has a third eye in his forehead.

I am no object for ceremoniousness. Enough of formality: however far removed, in will I am your reverence's disciple. A teacher's seat should be like himself respected, not desecrated. Let your highness only sit here.' So much said, he seated himself on a rug brought by his attendants. Bhairavācārya likewise, complying graciously with the king's not to be resisted words, reoccupied as before his tiger skin. All being seated, the nobles and retinue and also the students, he made the customary offering of flowers and the like. In due course captivated by the king's charm of manner, [117] he began to speak, displaying teeth glittering like devotion to Çiva made visible, and stainless as a piece of moonlight:—'My son, your exceeding condescension of itself proclaims the majesty of your virtues. You are a vessel for universal good-fortune. Your undertakings harmonize with your greatness. I from birth upwards have never had regard to riches. This poor person of mine therefore is not sold to wealth, that fuel to the fire of the whole round of vice. My life is sustained by alms. A few hard-won syllables of knowledge are mine. I have some small store of merit acquired by humble service of the holy Master Çiva. Be pleased to appropriate whatever of this deserves to be of service. Like flowers, the minds of the good can be bound by very slight ties[1]. Moreover good men approved by the wise, like good words, at the first hearing produce a flash even in profound minds. I was being borne away on the foam-white currents, as it were, of a curiosity plunging into hidden depths[2], when your nobility drew me back by its array of virtues[3].'

'Your reverence,' replied the king, 'let the bodies of the good be ever so devoted, their owners alone can be our friends[4]. The mere sight of you has done me infinite good. By his mere coming the teacher has placed me in an enviable position.' After some time spent in these and various discourses he went home.

[1] Or 'virtues.'

[2] I.e. 'of knowledge': the metaphor is from a river vanishing underground.

[3] Or 'cords.'

[4] I.e. I do not need your services, but yourself.

Another day Bhairavācārya on his part went to see the king, who placed himself, his harem, his court, and his treasury at the ascetic's disposal. But the sage with a smile replied:—'What have we children of the woods to do, your majesty, with power? Wisdom withers sure enough, like a creeper, under the blaze of wealth. The brightness which shines in us is like that of the firefly [118], which scorches no other being. Only your majesty's peers are vessels for fortune.' Then after staying some time he departed.

The mendicant as before presented five silver lotuses on each occasion. One day however he entered with something wrapt in white rags, and, having sat down as before, after a pause spoke:—'Most fortunate king, his reverence informs your majesty that he has a Brāhman disciple named Pātālasvāmin, who from the hand of a Brahmarākṣasa[1] took a great sword called Aṭṭahāsa. Pray accept of this, a weapon befitting your majesty's arm.' With these words he removed the covering of rags, and drew forth from the sheath a sword, like the autumn sky converted to a scimitar, Kālindī's stream solidified to rival Viṣṇu's sword, the Kāliya snake in its anger against Kṛiṣṇa become a weapon, a bit of the black cloud of doomsday fallen from the heaven foreshadowing a rainfall[2] to dissolve the world; resembling the smile of Hate[3] displaying a circle of great teeth, or Hari's stout arm with the fist[4] tightly clenched; formed as it were of deadly poison capable of taking the lives of all the world; composed of steel heated by the fiery wrath of fate; in its exceeding sharpness humming as with rage at the mere touch of the air; seeming, as its image fell upon the jewelled pavement of the hall, to cleave its very self in twain: jagged in edge with rays, like hairs left upon it after decapitating foes; mincing the day, whose light was cut in pieces by an inlay of radiance flickering like the lightning's frequent flash; a side-glance,

[1] Manu XII. 60.

[2] There is a punning reference to the notion of 'sword-edge water.'

[3] Hiṃsā wife of Adharma.

[4] *Muṣṭi* may also mean 'hilt.' There is also a reference to a demon of that name.

as it were, of the night of doom, death's ear-lotus, the triumphal shout [119] of pitilessness, the ornament of arrogance, the family friend of wrath, the body of pride, the comrade of valour, the child of death, the path of approaching glory, the road of departing fame.

The king took it in his hand, and gazing at it for a while, seemed, as it reflected his image, to be giving the weapon a loving embrace[1]. At length he gave his message:—'Inform his reverence that, though too practised in the art of scorning the acceptance of other people's property, my mind is unable in his case to commit the impropriety of going counter to his words.' Pleased at the acceptance, the mendicant answered, 'Fortune attend your majesty: I now take leave of you,' and so departed. The king, naturally of a warlike humour, felt that by aid of that sword the earth lay in the hollow of his hand.

The days passing, Bhairavācārya on one occasion made a secret petition to the king:—'The dispositions of the great, your majesty, are careless of their own interests, versed in serving others. To such as your majesty seeing petitioners is a festival, solicitation is to confer a favour, the acceptance of gifts by others a boon. You are the centre of all men's wishes. Wherefore I now address you:—Listen; by a crore of muttered prayers have I, in garlands, clothes, and unguents all of black as enjoined in the Kalpa, performed in the great cemetery the exordium of the potent rite called Mahākālahṛidaya. Its completion ends with the laying of a goblin. Without companions this is unattainable. You are capable of achieving this. Should you undertake the task, there will be three other assistants: one the friend of my boyhood, Ṭīṭibha, the mendicant who visits your majesty; the second Pātālasvāmin; the third a Drāviḍian disciple of mine, Karṇatāla by name. If you approve, let this arm of yours, long as a sky elephant's trunk, take Aṭṭahāsa and for one night become the bolt of one quarter of the heavens.'

To this speech the king, delighted, like one in darkness

[1] We might, however, translate "embracing it with his hand which remained motionless as if painted."

[120] who sees a light, at the opportunity of conferring a favour, replied:—'I am highly honoured, your reverence; I consider myself favoured by a charge to be shared with your disciples.' Overjoyed at the king's words, Bhairavācārya proceeded to make an appointment;—'Your honour, armed with your sword, will find us in the empty house near the great cemetery here at this hour on the approaching fourteenth night of the dark fortnight.'

The days having passed and the fourteenth having arrived, the king after initiation in the Çaiva ritual fasted. The sword Aṭṭahāsa he perfumed and honoured with scents, frankincense, and wreaths. The day came to a close. A ruddy hue spread over the heaven, as though some one had performed a Bali ceremony with sprinkled blood to ensure the success of the rite. The sun's rays hung down like vampires' tongues greedy for the scattered blood. As though out of attachment to the king he too wished to become a warder of the sky, the sun had occupied the western quarter; like goblins seemed the lengthening shadows of the trees. The encircling darkness started up like hell-haunting fiends to stay the rite. In the firmament the starry clusters gathered close, as if to look upon a horrid act. Thus at the dead of night, in the soundless stillness of a sleeping world, the king, eluding his court and harem, a dagger gleaming in his left hand, Aṭṭahāsa drawn in his right, cloaked from head to foot in the spreading radiance of his sword like a dark blue silken robe assumed to escape detection, set forth alone from the city, and reached the appointed spot; royal majesty attending unbidden, [121] and success dragged, as it were, by the hair behind in the shape of braids of bees attracted by his fragrance.

Then the three, Ṭiṭibha, Karṇatāla, and Pātālasvāmin, came up and announced themselves, armed like Droṇa's son, Kṛipa, and Kṛitavarman in the Night Assault, bathed, garlanded, and strangely attired. About their topknots of flowers ranged murmuring bees, which formed as it were a magic hair tie. On their heads they wore turban wraps with large Svastika knots fastened in the centre of their foreheads, and resembling huge mystic seals. Their cheeks were lit with the light of dazzling earrings pendant from the cavity of one ear, while their mouths were as it were drinking up the gloom of night in the wish to weaken its roaming goblins. Jewelled rings dangling from the other ear anointed them with sparkling lustre like a spell-charmed *gorocanā* pigment. Brandishing sharp swords, wherein their images were reflected, they seemed offering human sacrifices to ensure the success of the rite, while the long-continued flashes of the steel lined the darkness, as if they would cleave the night in three with a view to guarding their several quarters of the horizon. Their bucklers, bearing crescents and scintillating starlike groups of silver globules, might be compared to bits of darkness sheared by the hard sword's edge and forming a second and artificial night. They wore thick new cloths girt with golden chain-belts, and daggers were fastened to their waists.

'Who goes there?' demanded the king of the three. They severally announced their names, and with them at his heels he proceeded [122] to the silent, deep, and awful graveyard, where all was in readiness and pounded resin, flaming in magic lamps, filled the heavens with incense and smoke, as if the night were fleeing away with its gloom half-burned by a scattered mustard charm[1].

In the centre of a great circle of ashes white as lotus pollen Bhairavācārya could be seen, a form all aglow with light, like the autumn sun enveloped in a broad halo or Mandara in the whirlpool of the churned Ocean of Milk. Seated on the breast of a corpse which lay supine anointed with red sandal and arrayed in garlands, clothes and ornaments all of red, himself with a black turban, black unguents, black amulet, and black garments, he had begun a fire rite in the corpse's mouth, where a flame was burning. As he offered some black sesamum seeds, it seemed as though in eagerness to become a Vidyādhara he were annihilating the atoms of defilement which caused his mortal condition. The gleam of

[1] The luminous smoke is compared to the half-burnt night fleeing away into the sky.

his nails falling on the oblation appeared to cleanse the flames of the pollution due to contact with the dead man's mouth, while his smoke-inflamed eye flung as it were an offering of blood upon the devouring blaze. His mouth, showing the tips of white teeth as he slightly opened his lips in his muttering, seemed to display in bodily shape the lines of the syllables of his charms. The lamps near him were imaged in the sweat of his sacrificial exertions, as if he were burning his whole body to ensure success. From his shoulder hung a Brāhmanical thread of many strands, encircling his form, like a multiple Vidyārāja charm.

Having approached, the king saluted, and being welcomed set about his own task. [123] Pātālasvāmin chose Indra's quarter, Karṇatāla that of Kuvera, the mendicant that of Pracetas, while the king himself adorned that marked by Triçaṅku's light[1].

The warders of the regions having taken their stations, Bhairavācārya confidently entered the cage composed of their arms, and proceeded with his awful work. The opposing fiends having after fruitless resistance and much uproar been allayed, suddenly at the very instant of midnight the earth was rent open to the north and not far from the magic circle, displaying a fissure like the jaws of the mighty boar of doomsday. Forthwith, like a copper post torn up by the sky elephants, there ascended out of the chasm a spirit dark as a blue lotus, with shoulders thick and square as the Great Boar's, a fiend, as it were, risen from the womb of earth or the demon Bali springing up from the cloven hell. The gleam of a *Mālatī* wreath amid locks of crisp curled hair, sleek, dark and growing thickly, produced the effect of a sapphire temple crowned with the blaze of a jewelled lamp. A throbbing voice and an eye naturally red suggested one drunk with the vapours of youth. A necklace tossed about his throat. Ever and anon he smeared shoulders comparable to the sky elephants' frontal globe with clay crushed in his clenched hand. Irregularly bespotted with moist sandal

[1] Triçaṅku is suspended in the southern heavens, see Rāmāy. I. 60.

paste, he resembled a tract of autumn sky speckled with bits of very white cloud. Above a petticoat white as the *Ketakī* petal his flank was drawn tight by a scarf, the long white cotton fringe of which, carelessly left loose, hung to the ground just as if it were the serpent Çeṣa supporting him from behind. His stout thick thighs [124] planted slow paces as if he feared to break through the earth: yet they could scarce support his mountain-like form with its burden of overmastering pride. Again and again he doubled his left arm athwart his breast, raised the right cross-wise, bent his leg, and furiously slapped his arms[1] with such a noise as though he would raise a storm to hinder the rite and maim the animate world of one sense. 'Ho, my would-be paramour of Vidyādharīs,' he sneeringly shouted in tones awful as the echo of Narasiṃha's roar, 'whence this conceit of knowledge or blind reliance on your helpers, that without making an oblation to me you aspire—fool that you are—to success? What madness is this? Has no mention come to your ears after all this time of me, the Nāga Çrīkaṇṭha, after whom this region, whereof I am lord, is named? Against my will what power have the very planets to move in the heavens? What a miserable unkingly king is this, who accepts favours from such Çaiva outcasts as you! Receive now along with this wretched monarch the reward of your misconduct.' When he had said thus much, the three, Ṭīṭibha and the rest, rushed upon him; but with furious buffets he dashed them, armour, swords and all, to the ground.

Never before had the king heard himself reviled. His limbs, albeit unwounded, poured forth a stream of furious sweat, water of the sword-edge, as it were, drunk in many a battle. His hair bristled like an array of arrow heads shot out in hundreds to lighten him for the fray. Even Aṭṭahāsa, mirroring the constellations, seemed to proclaim his unbending spirit by a contemptuous smile showing clearly a row of white teeth. As his hands moved restlessly in the

[1] An Indian challenge to combat.

act of tightening his girdle, their horizon-like gleam of nails [125] seemed a demon-quelling charm circle, blocking the wide heaven to guard against escape. Scornfully he cried, 'Ho, serpent, crow, are you not ashamed to demand an oblation in the presence of such a royal flamingo as I? But what avail these taunts? Valour dwells in the arm, not in the voice. Take to your weapon. Not thus are you my match. My arm is untaught to smite the weaponless.' With still greater disdain the Nāga replied:—'Approach, what care I for swords? With my two arms will I crush your pride,' and so slapped his arms. Ashamed to vanquish a weaponless foe with weapons, the king, flinging away sword and buckler, girt up his loins outside his cloak for a fight with fists. So they fought till their furious slapping had bedewed them with a rain of blood from lacerated arms, which falling like stone pillars almost converted the whole world into sound. Soon the king smote the serpent to the earth, and having seized him by the hair, had drawn Aṭṭahāsa to strike off his head, when amid the wreath on his shoulder he detected the sacred thread. Forbearing his weapon, 'Villain,' he cried, 'this then is the seed of your career of ill-doing, this is whence you proceed without fear in your wicked courses,' and so let him go. Straightway as in a moment he beheld a great brightness; a perfume as of lotus beds opening in autumn smote upon his nostrils; instantaneously he heard a tinkle of anklets, and guided his glance in pursuit of the sound.

In the centre of the sword resting in his hand, like a lightning flash in the womb of a black cloud, he beheld a woman whose radiance seemed to swallow up the night. Her hands were like red lotuses. Like seaside coral beds clinging to her feet trailed the web-like rosy glow of her soft toes. [126] Disguised as her white toe-nails she bore along the splintered moon-disk, as if for fear her lotus hands should close[1]. Clasped anklets lay about her ankles, as though in her coming she had burst from a prison of thick linked chains. Out of a dazzling white silken robe, embroidered

[1] The night-lotus would close in the absence of the moon.

with hundreds of divers flowers and birds, and gently rippled by the motion of the breeze, her form rose up as from an ocean's waters. The *tribali* clasped her waist like the threefold Ganges pleased at her birth from the deep[1]. Her round bust with its prominent bosoms was like the sky displaying the sky-elephants' frontal bones, and across her bosom, like the dew on the trunk of Airāvata in his time of rut, lay a necklace with lustrous pearls like stars of autumn. Swayed like white chowries by her soft, soft breathing, the light of the necklace seemed to fan her. Her hands bore a naturally rosy tint, as if they had caught a vermilion tinge from slapping the forehead of a rut-blinded scent elephant[2]. Her flashing ear-ring shone like the second[3] half of Hara's crest the moon, curved to a circle. Clinging about her ear was an ornament of *Açoka* shoots like a cluster of the Kaustubha's brightness. Her forehead lacked not a great sectarial line dark as elephant's ichor, like an unseen umbrella's circular shadow[4]. Moon-white sandal, like the glory of the kings of old, brightened her form from hair-parting to feet. Flowery wreaths, dangling from her throat and kissing the ground, flowed over her like rivers finding their repose in ocean[5]. Limbs soft as lotus fibres voicelessly proclaimed her lotus birth.

'Who art thou, lady?' cried the king unappalled, 'and wherefore hast thou come within my sight?' 'Hero,' she said, almost overpowering him with an unabashedness at variance with her sex, 'know me to be that deer whose pleasure haunt is Nārāyaṇa's breast, the banner-pennon of Pṛithu, Bharata, Bhagīratha and the other kings of old, [127] the gay doll upon the victory columns of heroes' arms, the flamingo wantoning

[1] Lakṣmī rose from the deep at the churning of the ocean.

[2] Lakṣmī's elephant is referred to. The *gandhadvipa* is a particularly powerful kind of elephant.

[3] Çiva wears a *crescent* moon —this was the second or *absent* half.

[4] The umbrella being a sign of sovereignty. *Mada* is described as dark like *Tamāla* shoots in Kādambarī p. 243 l.; *tamāla-pallava-rasa-çyāmena madajalena.*

[5] I.e. as if they were the rivers which had flowed into the ocean from which she had risen at its churning.

with yearning to sport upon the waves of battle's bloodshed stream, the peacock of the thickets of kings' white umbrellas, even Çrī, the lioness whose caprice is to roam in the forest of sharp scimitar edges, the lotus bed of the pools of sword-edge water. I am ravished by this thy valorous spirit. Crave of me a boon: I will give thee thy heart's desire.'

Heroes are unwearied in serving others. So the king bowed to her, and heedless of his own advantage, besought the success of Bhairavācārya. Highly gratified, the goddess, anointing the king with her wide-open eyes like a milk ocean thrown over him, replied 'So be it,' and added, 'Because of this magnanimity of thine and because of thy superlative devotion to the holy Lord Çiva thou, like a third added to the Sun and Moon, shalt be the founder of a mighty line of kings persisting unbroken upon earth, daily increasing in greatness, full of matchless heroes elate with purity, high-fortune, truth, munificence, and fortitude. Wherein shall arise an emperor named Harṣa, governor like Hariçcandra of all the continents, world-conquering like a second Māndhātṛi, whose chowrie this hand, spontaneously abandoning the lotus, shall grasp.' So saying she vanished.

The heart of the king was beyond measure gratified to hear this. Bhairavācārya himself, having by the words of the goddess and the full performance of the rite instantly acquired the hair-lock, diadem, earring, necklace, armlet, girdle, hammer, and sword, became a Vidyādhara. Addressing the king he said:—'The wishes, O king, of indolent feeble-minded people embrace not remote objects: but the favours of the good are of their very nature far-reaching. [128] To bestow this boon, unimagined even in dreams, who except your majesty had power? A man of light qualities is lifted up like a scale by the acquisition of a mere particle of success. Having been served by your virtues and having attained my purpose through none other than you, I am inspired by the immodesty of an infatuated heart. And so it is my wish to win remembrance by endeavouring in whatever way I can to afford you some grain of assistance.' The stout hearts of the wise, however, are proof against reciprocation of favours, and the king therefore refused, saying, 'By your reverence's success my task is finished; let your reverence proceed to a station according with your wish.'

After this reply from the king, Bhairavācārya, now on the point of departure, warmly embraced Ṭīṭibha and the others, and regarding the king with a tearful eye like a blue lotus-bed streaming with frosty dew, "Friend," he resumed, "should I say 'I am going,' that were a poor token of affection[1]; if I say 'my life is yours,' 'tis superfluous; 'make this poor body your own' would imply the creation of an unreal distinction; 'you have purchased me bit by bit,' the bits fall short of your kindnesses; 'you are my kinsman' would place a distance between us; 'my heart remains with you' would want evidence; 'a success which severs us is torment' would not find credence; 'your kindness was unmerited' a mere reiteration; 'keep me in remembrance' a command. At least in all talk of ingrates and all narrations of ignoble people let me be remembered as one remorselessly bent on his own advantage." So speaking, he mounted to the sky, lashing the constellations with pearls that started from a necklace burst in his speed, and passed in an orbit cleaving the planet clusters to a station fitting his good-fortune. Çrīkaṇṭha also spoke; 'Deign, O king, whenever necessary to favour with your commands one bought by your valour and taught discretion,' [129] and so with the consent of the king entered again the same fissure in the earth.

By this the night was nearly spent. Fragrant with the breath of opening day-lotus beds, frosty as if with sweat from the sport of ravishing shawls from the bosoms of forest nymphs, the sylvan breeze had begun to blow, attracting the bees by its perfume, lulling the night-lotuses to sleep, chilled

[1] या and गम् are roots of ill-omen, which must not be used in conversation. When Macaulay talks of the Lucknow people singing songs in Hastings' honour

'*Hāthī par hauda ghore par zīn*
'*Jaldī jāo jaldī jāo Warren Hastīn.*'

'Howdah on elephant, saddle on horse
'Ride on in triumph W. H.'

they *meant* "Go to hell, go to hell quickly, W. H."

by the night's ending, and interspersed with rime. Scorched as it were by the sighs of ruddy-geese in the anguish of their severance, the night subsided into the western ocean. The lotus beds peeped forth, as if curious to view the bodily presence of Lakṣmī. As the birds awoke, the forest, quivering in all its creepers beneath the soft breeze, rained down showers of hoar-frost, like bunches of flowers. With their noisy imprisoned bees the closing night-lotuses hummed like auspicious horns to awake the beauty of the day-lotuses. The stars, buds of the creepers of night, clustered together in the western sky, as if wafted on by the panting breath of the rising sun's chariot-horses. Occupying Mandara's peak, the Seven Sages became grey, as if coated with pollen from thickets of heavenly creepers rocked by the gentle breeze. The Starry Deer as it sank seemed like a fallen goad[1] of the gods' elephant.

Taking Ṭīṭibha and the others, the king, whose limbs were befouled by the give and take of battle with the demon, bathed in the pure water of a sylvan pool. He then entered the city, and next day gratified all three with unguents, food, and clothing immediately after his own person[2].

After the lapse of a few days the mendicant, despite the king's remonstrances, departed to the woods. Pātālasvāmin [130] and Karṇatāla, men of a warlike spirit, remained in the king's service. Elevated to a fortune beyond their wildest dreams, drawing their swords in the midst of the royal guard, occupying the front rank in the battle, now and then on occasion of story-telling appointed to narrate various actions of Bhairavācārya and incidents of their own childhood[3], they arrived at old age by the king's side.

Here ends the third Chapter—entitled The Exposition of The King's Ancestry—of the Harṣa-Carita composed by Çrī Bāṇa Bhaṭṭa.

[1] A reference to the shape of the constellation, i.e. Capricorn, Comm.

[2] According to the Comm. he first makes the ascetic's friends bathe and then bathes himself.

[3] *Çaiçavavṛittāntāḥ* seems to be here used much in the same way as the Welsh *Mabinogion*, which originally meant 'amusements of youth' but came to be the name for the collection of Welsh heroic legends.

CHAPTER IV.

[131] No alliance[1] wish they even in dreams, they make no joining of hands[2];
By the sole power of their name do the great become liege lords of the wedded earth!
Like thetusk set at a wide interval[3] in the capacious mouth of the elephant-headed god, so in a royal house though populous
There arises but one like to Prithu, causing all monarchs[4] to shake!

From[5] this Puṣpabhūti there issued a line of kings, as from Viṣṇu a lotus whose calix the best of the twice-born voluntarily occupied[6], as from the ocean a treasure of jewels attended by Lakṣmī[7], as from the orient mount a troop of planets including Jupiter, Mercury, Venus, the Moon, the Sun, and Mars[8], as from the might of Sagara a sea capable of supporting a commerce of greatness, as from Çūra a Hari race boasting a Durjaya and a Bala[9]. In which line were

[1] Or—punningly—'strategy.'

[2] Or 'grasping of taxes.'

[3] There is a pun on *pratimā* = (1) likeness, (2) the space between the tusks in an elephant's mouth. Gaṇeça has only one tusk.

[4] Or 'mountains.'

[5] Only a small part of the puns in this paragraph is susceptible of translation. The words for Viṣṇu ('lotus-eyed'), ocean ('collection of jewels'), Orient Mount ('source of greatness'), might of Sagara ('one mighty as Sagara'), Çūra ('hero') may all apply to Puṣpabhūti, the others similarly to the race.

[6] Or 'whose treasures were grasped at will by the best of the twice-born (= Brāhmans).' Brahmā is the best of the twice-born.

[7] Or 'attended by splendour.'

[8] Or 'including teachers, wise men, poets, artists, men of might, and kings.'

[9] Or 'boasting invincible might.' Durjaya and Bala are Viṣṇu and Bala-Rāma.

born kings free from the stain of violating Dharma, [132] as living beings came from the commencement of the golden age; dominating the world by their splendour, like the rays from the source of light; thronging the regions with their armies in array, like the hills sprung from Brahmā; strong to support the world, like the sky elephants born from Brahmā's hand; rising in might to guard[1] the oceans, like clouds from the season of rain; bestowing the fruits of desire, like trees of Paradise from the Heavenly Garden; embracing all beings, like the variations of existence sprung from Viṣṇu.

The line so proceeding, there was born in course of time a king of kings named Prabhākaravardhana[2], famed far and wide under a second name Pratāpaçīla, a lion to the Huṇa deer, a burning fever to the king of the Indus land, a troubler of the sleep of Gujarat, a bilious plague to that scent-elephant the lord of Gāndhāra, a looter to the lawlessness of the Lāṭs, an axe to the creeper of Mālwa's glory. From his members of royalty the coronation water purged no foulness but filthy lucre[3]. Even an enemy's life, that coward's darling, when kept like a straw in the mouth of battle[4], filled him with shame. It was torture to him to be accompanied in battle even by his image in the sword-blade which his hand bore, torture that even his bow bent to the foe in conflict. A proud man, he was vexed by his proud ambitions. Steadfast he kept his royal majesty, as if pinned by the implanted[5] arrow-points of countless foes. [133] Levelling on every side hills and hollows, clumps and forests, trees and grass, thickets and anthills, mountains and caves, the broad paths of his armies seemed to portion out the earth for the support of his dependants. By deterring all enemies his own prowess

[1] Or 'drink.'

[2] On the Sōnpat seal (Corpus Inscr. Ind. III. pp. 231-2) Harṣa mentions his father under this name.

[3] Meaning that at his coronation his ministers distributed money.

[4] To carry a straw in the mouth was a sign of surrender: cf Acworth's 'Maratha Ballads,' p. 43:

'And 'twixt the teeth a straw is fit
For curs who arm but to submit.'

[5] There is a play on *antargata*, which, taken with 'foes,' means 'dead.'

annoyed him as much as that of others, leaving his passion for battle ungratified. In the seraglios of slain rivals his valour was, as it were, materialized in the form of the five elements, fire in the women's hearts, water in the hollows of their eyes, wind in their sighs, earth upon their forms, ether in the vacant solitude[1]. As in a mirror, his glory was matched in those gems among ministers who attended him[2]. Once more:—his greatness was made to glow by the fire of his valour, his success was digested by the heat of his courage, the growth of his race was fostered like a bamboo by the water of the sword's edge, his valorous deeds were proclaimed by the mouths of the wounds which his steel dealt, his grasping of tribute[3] by the callosity of the bow string. A furious onslaught he counted a present, war a favour, the approach of battle a festival, a foe the discovery of a treasure, a host of enemies the acme of prosperity, a challenge to conflict a boon, a sudden onset an ovation, the fall of sword strokes a shower of wealth. Beneath his rule the golden age seemed to bud forth in close packed lines of sacrificial posts, the evil time to flee in the smoke of sacrifices meandering over the sky, heaven to descend in stuccoed[4] shrines, Dharma to blossom in white pennons waving over temple minarets, the villages to bring forth a progeny of beautiful arbours erected on their outskirts for meetings, alms' houses, inns, and women's marquees[5], [134] Mount Meru to crumble in a wealth of utensils all of gold, a very cornucopia to bear fruit in bowls of riches lavished upon Brāhmans.

This king had a queen, Yaçovatī[6] by name, noble as Çaṅkara's Pārvatī, but remaining Satī in another incarnation[7], holding the heart fast like Viṣṇu's Lakṣmī, with sparkling

1 Or 'their vacant hearts.'

2 His ministers were gems reflecting his greatness.

3 Or—punningly—'his hand's grasp.'

4 *Sudhā*=(1) stucco, (2) ambrosia.

5 *Prāgvaṃçaḥ*=*patnīçālā* is a hut erected on the sacrificial ground for the sacrificer's family.

6 The Sōnpat seal has Yaço*m*atī.

7 I.e. she was *satī*=(1) noble, (2) *çobhanā* 'blonde,' whereas Pārvatī's other incarnation was *çyāmā* 'brunette.'

glancing eyes[1] like the moon's Rohiṇī, mother of all her people like Prajāpati's Buddhi, descended from towering kings[2] like the ocean's Ganges, deft in compliance to his will[3] like the *haṃsa*-king's Haṃsī, with an adoring world at her feet[4] like Dharma's Triad, never abandoning his side night or day like Vasiṣṭha's Arundhatī. She was endowed with the gait of a *haṃsa*, the voice of a cuckoo, the answering love of a ruddy-goose, the full bosoms[5] of the rainy season, the laugh of wine, the manifold worth of a treasure, the rich gifts of a golden shower, the enfolded charms of a lotus, the fruitfulness of a flower, the adorableness of the twilight, the moon's freedom from heat, a mirror's responsiveness to all creatures, Samudra's[6] intuition of character, the Supreme Spirit's universal penetration, the scriptures' stainless principles. She was honey in converse, ambrosia to those who sought delight[7], rain to her servants, beatitude to her friends, bamboo-like to her elders. The pride was she of the family of smiles, the penance purity of womanhood, the fulfilment of Kāma's ordinances, [135] the Eureka[8] of loveliness, the ovation of passion, the fruition of beauty's wishes, the special providence of charm, the genesis of affection's ancestry, love's boon-winning, grace's perfect creation, youth's majesty, intelligence's cloudless rain[9], glory's lustration, goodness' bloom of beauty, Dharma's heart's delight, Prajāpati's creation of the atoms of bliss: the quietude of quiescence, the decorousness of decorum, the nobility of high birth, the temperateness of temperance, the stand of steadfastness, the witchery of grace. Such was the queen, the centre of all

1 Or—punningly—'stars.'

2 Or 'mountains.'

3 Or 'visiting Mānasa.'

4 Or 'schools': the Triad is the three Vedas.

5 Or 'clouds.'

6 He is the inventor of palmistry: a literal rendering would be 'In knowledge of the characters of others she was the essence of Samudra's book.'

7 Or—reading *triṣyatsu*—'to the thirsty.'

8 *Vyutthānabuddhir* = the resultant thought of a yogin's meditation.

9 'Cloudless rain' is a synonym for 'a marvel.' Comm.

creatures' love, confidence, duty, and felicity, who upon the king's bosom shone like Lakṣmī on the bosom of Hell's Vanquisher.

The king was by natural proclivity a devotee of the sun[1]. Day by day at sunrise he bathed, arrayed himself in white silk, wrapt his head in a white cloth, and kneeling eastwards upon the ground in a circle smeared with saffron paste, presented for an offering a bunch of red lotuses set in a pure vessel of ruby and tinged, like his own heart, with the sun's hue[2]. Solemnly at dawn, at midday, and at eve he muttered a prayer for offspring, humbly with earnest heart repeating a hymn having the sun as its centre[3].

The heavenly will can be won to favour its worshippers. So it happened that on the occasion of one hot season the king slept on his palace roof white with stucco spotless as the moon-light; and the queen lay on a second couch at his side. [136] The night was near its close, and the lord of stars was declining with faded radiance, robbed of his beauty by the approach of dawn. A cool frosty dew was falling, like the moon's sweat evoked by his delight as his finger tips[4] touched the lotus beds. Smit by the breath of intoxicated sleeping beauties, the seraglio lamps staggered as if drunk. The king slept. The stars mirrored in his white nails seemed to be stroking his feet. His limbs were carelessly extended, as if consigned to the queens of the quarters. The beauty of his lips[5] fanned him with wine-perfumed breath like the wind of her own lotus-like hand acting as a fan. In the clear surface of his cheek the imaged moon shone like a topknot of white flowers displaced by the clutching of hair in amorous dalliance.

Suddenly with a cry 'Help, my lord! help' the queen leapt up, a tremour swaying her willowy form, and her tinkling anklets seeming to call out to her attendants.

[1] On the Sōnpat seal Harṣa attaches the epithet *paramādityabhaktaḥ* to his father, brother, and other members of the family.

[2] There is a pun on *anurakta* = (1) devoted, (2) reddened.

[3] Cf. Weber Ind. Stud. IX. 91.

[4] I.e. 'rays.'

[5] I.e. the personified beauty of his face.

Instantly, scorched as it were in both ears by a cry for help such as never in all the world he had heard, much less in his queen's mouth, the king awoke from sleep. With a right hand that trembled with rage he drew from beside his head a sword whose glittering edge drew a line like a prolongation of his ear-wreath across the night. His left hand swept aside his robe of fine muslin, as if it were the intervening ether. Loosened by his hand's furious movement, his golden bracelet flashed upon the heavens, as if his heart were roaming in search of the cause of alarm. He brought his left foot furiously down with a stamp that shook the palace. His necklace, which had fallen in front of him, having come within range of his sword edge, shone like a severed portion of the moonlight. Inflamed with rage and sleep, as if stained with betel from Lakṣmī's kisses, his eyes cast a glow upon the whole circle of the heavens, [137] while a dark trident-shaped frown seemed to bring night back again, as he leapt up hastily crying, 'Fear not, my queen, fear not'. When however on casting his glance in every direction he saw nothing, he inquired of the queen the cause of her fright.

By this the women of the night watch had run up like family goddesses, and the servants who slept near were all awake. So now that the alarm which had made her heart tremble had subsided, the queen replied:—'I know now, my lord. I saw in a dream two shining youths issue from the sun's disk, filling the heavens as with radiance of morning, and turning the whole world as it were into lightning. They wore crowns, earrings, armlets, and cuirasses: swords were in their hands: they were bathed in blood cochineal red. All the world bowed before them with upturned faces and hands joined reverently at their foreheads. Accompanied by one maid like a moon incarnate, who issued from the ray Suṣumṇa, they lighted upon the earth, and while I screamed, cut open my womb with a sword and essayed to enter. My heart quaked, and I awoke with a cry to my lord.'

At that juncture the morning horn rang out at the porch,

like the first utterance of the king's glory proclaiming the vision's fulfilment. Briskly sounded the tom-toms, as if to announce a coming exaltation. The daybreak drum boomed, as if pleased to be struck with the stick. 'Victory! Victory!' pealed the loud voices of those who recited well-omened calls from sleep. In the stable yard of the favourite horses the slowly rising marshal chanted a Vaktrā and an Aparavaktrā verse, as before the sweetly neighing steeds he scattered emerald grass a-drip with frosty water:—

[138] 'By misshapen trees a treasure, by flashing light a fine jewel,
'By an omen the approach of luck is clearly in the world revealed!
'As the dawn, his harbinger, announces the sun, as the speeding blast the rain's approach,
'Even so the appearance of a previous vision foretells good, yea and evil hap to men!'

At these words the king's heart was filled with delight. 'Queen,' said he, 'you are dejected at the hour of joy. Your parents' prayers are answered. Our wishes are fulfilled. Our family goddesses have accepted you. In his graciousness the holy god of the radiant crown[1] will grant you joy, and that soon, by the gift of three noble children.' So much said, he descended and performed the customary ceremonies. Yaçovatī also was cheered by her husband's words.

After the lapse of a short period of time his majesty Rājyavardhana came first of three to being in the queen's womb. Even as he lay in the womb his glory shed a pallor over his mother. Oppressed as it were by the weight of his virtues, she could not support her frame. As if satisfied with the ambrosia of his outpouring loveliness, she became averse to food. Languid with the slowly growing burden of her child, she yet insisted on being conveyed with the support of friendly hands to salute her parents, who would have stayed her. In her lassitude she could be seen, like a doll-figure, propped against the nearest walls and trunks of trees. She could not lift her feet, which seemed checked by bees

[1] I.e. the Sun.

greedily settling upon such lotuses. Slow, slow was her gait, as if she were conducted by domestic *haṃsas* clinging in greed for lotus threads to the rays of her toe-nails. Seeking a support, she would put forth a lotus hand even towards forms reflected in jewelled walls, much more then towards her women friends. She longed to clasp even the rays of gemmed pillars, much more the house-creepers. Her household duties she had scarce strength to command, not to speak of performing them. Needless to say that her feet were wearied by the burden of her anklets,—even her imagination failed to mount the palace. She could not support even her limbs, much less her ornaments. [139] The very idea of climbing play hills made her bosom tremulously heave. When she should have risen in welcome, her child, as if through pride, kept her motionless with slender hands in vain applied to the points of her knees. All day long her downcast glance was turned in joy upon her zone, her lotus face brought near her bosom as if longing to see her child had drawn it inwards. With her child in her womb, and her husband in her heart, she bore as it were a double majesty. Resigning her form to her friends' bosoms, she set her feet on the laps of her handmaids, on the heads of her co-wives. When the tenth month arrived, she brought forth my lord Rājyavardhana, a prince composed as it were of lightning atoms to quell the cabals of all kings[1]; capable of supporting the whole world's weight, as if endowed with the mechanism of Çeṣa's hood; heart-shaker of all kings[2], as if constructed with the limbs of sky elephants. His birth was a birth of joy to the people, who became as it were dancing incarnate. For one month, which seemed a day, the king held a great festival, innumerable blown horns noisily sounding, hundreds of beaten tom-toms merrily booming, a world filled to overflowing with the burden of deep-rumbling drums, the hearts of all mankind ravished in a madness of delight.

[1] Or—punningly—'to clip the wings of all mountains,' referring to a feat of Indra.

[2] Or 'mountains.'

A second period having elapsed, in the month[1] of plantains, when the bud is on the *Kadamba* tree, the barley blades grow in clusters, the red-lotus stands erect, the *cātaka's* heart expands, and the dwellers in Mānasa are dumb, in that month Harṣa came to being at once in the heart and womb of Yaçovatī, even as Kriṣṇa in Devakī. Gradually once more her willowy form, arrayed as it were in all her child's pure worth, assumed a pallid hue. As pregnancy came on, her cup-like bosoms grew dark in their tender nipples, as if stamped for an emperor to drain. Like a river of milk let into her face for her bosom's supply, her eye, long, moist[2] and white, assumed a sweeter expression. Slow grew her gait beneath the load, as it were, of a frame weighed down by the whole array of auspicious marks. As she moved tardily about, [140] the earth, clasping her lotus feet mirrored in the spotless mosaic, seemed to pay her a prelude of worship. All day long as she lay on her couch, the reflection of figures embroidered in the awning rested on her cheek's clear round[3], like a Lakṣmī awaiting the child's birth. In the night time, when she had mounted the roof, the moon's disk imaged in her round bosom, when bared of her shawl in the pangs of pregnancy, appeared like a white umbrella mysteriously held above her child. Even the chowrie women on the painted walls waved their chowries while she slept in her apartment. In her dreams all the four sky-elephants seemed to consecrate her, bearing water in folded lotus leaves held by their trunks. When she awoke, the puppet servants in the chamber on the roof raised not once alone the cry of 'Victory!' If she called to her maids, incorporeal voices went forth, crying 'Say your commands.' Even in play she would suffer no violation of her will[4]. Moreover a wish grew upon her to bathe even in the united waters of the four great

1 *Nabhas* = the month Çrāvaṇa, i.e. July—August. The plantain flowers all the year, but especially in the rains.

2 There is a pun in *snigdha* = (1) charming, (2) viscous.

3 Cf. Daçakumāracarita I. p. 73 (Bomb.) l. 12.

4 This and the following contain allusions to the superstition that the mother's mind echoes the thoughts of her child: hence the reference to the four oceans — the limits of Harṣa's empire, &c.

oceans. It was her heart's desire to roam round sand isles in creeper arbours by the sea shore. Even on occasions of urgency her brow would capriciously move. Despite the jewelled mirrors close to her hand she was bent on seeing her face in a drawn sword's blade. Supplanting the lute, the bow's twang, ill-suiting a woman, was pleasing in her ear. Her eye was gratified by lions in their cages. Even in saluting her parents she scarce could bend her apparently stiffened head. Her friends, never for an instant leaving her side, brightened the house, as in anticipation of the approaching birth festival, with eyes wide-open in joy, as though strewing on every side a ceaseless protective charm in the shape of a rain of blooming lotus petals, white, red and blue. Great physicians holding various herbs[1] sat in their proper places, supporting her as the mountains support the earth. In the knots of her necklace-cord were fixed fine jewels, [141] like the hearts of the oceans come with Lakṣmī.

At length in the month Jyaiṣṭha, on the twelfth day of the dark fortnight, the Pleiads being in the ascendant, just after the twilight time, when the young night had begun to climb, a sudden cry of women arose in the harem. Hurriedly issuing forth, Suyātrā, daughter of Yaçovatī's nurse and herself dearly beloved, fell at the king's feet, crying 'Good news! your majesty, you are blessed with the birth of a second son,' and carried off the customary festal spoil[2].

At that very instant approached the astrologer Tāraka, a man very highly esteemed by the king. Hundreds and hundreds of times he had shown supernatural insight by announcing facts beyond the ken of man, a calculator, deeply read in

[1] *Vividhoṣadhidharās* applies also to the mountains. So also *praçastaratnāni* in seqq. has a twofold application.

[2] For *pūrṇapātra* the Comm. quotes

ānandado hi sauhardād etya vastrādikam balāt |
ajñnato haraty eva pūrṇapātraṃ tu tat smṛitam ||

The Vācaspatya quotation is clearer, if we read *eva* in the second line.

harṣād utsavakāle yad alaṅkārāṃçukādikam |
ākṛiṣya gṛihyate pūrṇapātram pūrṇakaṃ eva tat ||

all the treatises on astronomy, extolled and liked among all astrologers, endowed with knowledge of the three times, and a Maga[1]. 'Give ear, O king!' he cried; 'it was on a day like this, free from the taint of all evil conjunctions such as malignant aspects of the sun and moon, at a moment like the present, when all the planets were similarly at their apexes, that Māndhātṛi came to birth. Since then in all the intervening time no second has in the whole world been born at a conjuncture so fit for an universal emperor's birth. [142] The son now born to your majesty shall be coryphaeus of the Seven Emperors[2], bearer of the Seven Imperial Signs[3] and the Great Jewels[4], lord of the Seven Oceans, performer of all sacrifices of Seven Forms[5], the peer of him of the Seven Steeds[6].'

Instantly unblown horns rang out spontaneously loud and sweet. Unbeaten boomed the consecration drum deep as the roar of oceans in turmoil. Unstruck the auspicious tabors pealed. Like a timbrel proclaiming security to all the world, the tabor's echo thrilled through the aerial spaces. Tossing their manes, the horses neighed with joy, while their muzzles were graced by wisps of green *Dūrvā* sprays which they haughtily took. Sportively uplifting their trunks as if dancing, the elephants trumpeted in sounds grateful to the ear. Soon a heavenly breeze, fragrant with perfumes of wine, blew like a sigh of Lakṣmī letting fall the disc[7]. In the courts of the sacrificers the unfed Vaitāna fires blazed up with flames curving to the right to foretell the coming luck. From the earth uprose great treasures, enclosed in cups bedecked with

1 For the Bhojakas or Magas see Wilson's Viṣṇu P. (Hall's ed.), vol. v. p. 382.

2 These are Bharata, Arjuna, Māndhātṛi, Bhagīratha, Yudhisṭhira, Sagara, Nahuṣa.

3 The signs are peculiar formations in hands, feet, &c.

4 The six great jewels are enumerated in the verse

maṇyaçvakaricakrāṇi varā strī pariṇāyakaḥ |
ṣaḍ etāni tu ratnāni kīrtitāni manīṣibhiḥ ||

5 Ṛig. V. x. 124. 1 (Sāyaṇa), and Weber *Ind. Stud.* IX. 120.

6 = the Sun.

7 The weapon of her husband, Viṣṇu.

chains of gold. In the shape of echoes from the beaten tabors the regents of the sky seemed joyfully to give forth a clamour of congratulation to the heavens. At that moment white-clad Brāhmans approached with the Veda on their lips[1], like the Prajāpatis of the golden age, to foster the new-born life. Like Dharma incarnate came the family priest with lustral water and fruits ready in his hand. Like immemorial customs the arriving elders of the family could be seen. Away ran disorderly crowds of freed prisoners, their faces hairy with long matted beards, their bodies black with many a miry smirch, like the kindred of a waning Kali age. Like camp lines of a now departed wickedness [143] seemed the rows of shops, given up to general pillage[2]. In a great throng of boys danced the old nurses, encircled, like the young mother's tutelary deities incarnate, in a troop of dwarfs and deaf people with laughing upturned faces[3]. So proceeded the great birth festival, the order of the royal household gone, the pretence of chamberlains laid low, the macebearers robbed of their maces, entrance to the harem in no wise criminal, master and servants reduced to a level, young and old confounded, learned and unlearned on one footing, drunk and sober not to be distinguished, noble maidens and harlots equally merry, the whole population of the capital set a-dancing.

From the morrow onwards the wives of the neighbouring kings could be observed in thousands approaching the palace from every side. Amazonian nations they seemed, pouring onwards, wide-opened mines, Kṛiṣṇa's mistresses on the march, families of Apsarases lighted upon the earth. After them followed servants bearing garlands in wide baskets, with bath powder sprinkled upon the flowers; dishes laden with bits of camphor, clear as crystal granules; jewelled caskets of saffron scents; ivory boxes, studded with rows of sandal-hued Areca nuts and tufted with slim *Khadira* fibres dripping mango oil;

[1] *Brahmamukhās* has two senses, (1) as in text, (2) 'headed by Brahmā.' There are other puns in addition.

[2] Cf. Carlyle, Frederic, II. 195.

[3] *Jātamātṛidevatā mārjārānanā bahuputraparivārā sūtikāgṛihe sthāpyate.* Comm. 'the tutelary deity of a new mother, with a cat's face and surrounded by a crowd of children, is set up in the lying-in chamber.'

vermilion and powder boxes red and pink, with murmuring bees sipping *Pārijāta* perfumes; betel trees with bundles of nuts[1] hanging from the young slips. As they danced, the quarters of the heavens rang with jewelled anklets clashing as their feet knocked together[2].

[144] Thus the festal jubilation gradually blossomed forth. Here young people, of ancient noble houses and unused to dancing, showed by frolics their love for the king. There drunken slave women allured the favourites, while the monarch himself looked on with a secret smile. In one place respectable old feudatories were, much to his amusement, clasping the necks of the intoxicated bawds of the capital in a furious dance. In another place naughty slave boys, set on by a glance from the sovereign, betrayed in songs the secret amours of the ministers of state. Elsewhere wanton water-girls raised a laugh by embracing aged ascetics. Elsewhere again in the eagerness of ardent rivalry throngs of slaves carried on a war of foul language. In another place chamberlains knowing nothing of dancing were, to the entertainment of the maids, violently forced to dance by the king's women. The festival showed mountains of flower heaps, rum-booths like shower-baths, Nandana forests of *Pārijāta* scent, a hoar-frost of camphor dust, a booming of drums like Çiva's laugh[3], a hubbub like the ocean-churning, vortexes of dancing rings, a horripilation of rays from jewelled ornaments, a very tiara of sandal forehead marks, a never ceasing propagation of echoes, an endless efflorescence of tokens of favour.

Young men frolicked in thousands, prancing, like Kāmboja steeds, with garlands of *Keçaras*[4] hanging upon their shoulders, leaping with dancing eyes like spotted antelopes[5],

[1] Read *-vīṭikāvīṭakāṃçca*. *Vīṭikā* is explained by B. and R. as 'cut areca nuts in cube form covered with roots and folded in a betel leaf.'

[2] Read *caraṇakuṭṭana-* in place of *caraṇāni kuṭṭana-*.

[3] Literally 'possessing a Çiva (*Aṭṭahāsa* "the God of the loud laugh") in its booming drums.'

[4] Or—punningly—'manes.'

[5] Their eyes are compared to the spots of the antelope.

rending the earth with furious stamps, as did the sons of Sagara with spades. Scarce could the earth sustain the tramp of troubadours dancing to time. Smash went the pearls in the ornaments of the young princes slapping each other in their play. [145] Minium dust crimsoned the shell of Brahmā's egg[1] in every part, as with the blood of a reproduced Hiraṇya-Garbha foetus. The heavens gleamed with clouds of perfume powder, as if Mandākinī had disclosed a thousand sand isles. Yellowed with scattered scent dust, the daylight glowed, as though Brahmā's lotus, ground by the rocking world, had stained it with clouds of pollen from its filaments. Men tripped over heaps of pearls that fell from necklaces broken in collisions.

In this place and in that harlot-women danced to the accompaniment of instrumental music. Tambourines were slowly, slowly thumped; reeds sweetly piped, cymbals tinkled, string drums were belaboured, the low gourd lute sang, gently boomed the *kāhalas* with their brazen sounding boxes, while all the time a subdued clapping proceeded. Even the clank of jingling anklets kept time pace by pace, as if intelligent, with the clapping. Whispering softly, like cuckoos, in low passionate tones, they sang the words of vulgar mimes, ambrosia to their lovers' ears. Wreaths were about their brows, and chaplets round their ears, upon their foreheads sandal marks. With upraised creeper-like arms, vocal with rows of bracelets, they seemed to embrace the very sun. Like Kashmir colts, they leapt all aglow with saffron stains[2]. Great garlands of amaranth hung down upon their round hips, as if they were ablaze with passion's flame. Their faces, marked with rows of vermilion spots, seemed to wear the rubric of the edict plates of Love, [146] whose ordinances none may resist. Dusty were they with camphor and perfumes scattered in handfuls, like roads frequented by the desires[3] of youth. Like women chamberlains of a children's festival, they lashed the young folk

[1] = the world.

[2] As applied to the colts *kuṅkumapramṛiṣṭi* means 'rolling in saffron.'

[3] Lit. 'mind-chariots.'

with great wreaths of flowers. With tossing forehead marks and earrings they swayed[1] like creepers of Love's sandal tree. Like waves of passion's flood, they gleamed all resonant with the cries of anklets[2] adding music to their steps. As to what was proper to be said or not, they were as void of discrimination as the childish play of happiness. While the rapid booming of the drums[3] thrilled through their lithe frames, they cast off flower pollen, like *Ketakīs*. All day their faces were, like red lotuses, abloom; by night they slept no more than night lotuses. As if possessed, they were surrounded by throngs of princes[4]. Like endearments, they stole away the heart; like songs, they kindled the flame of desire; like the symptoms of stoutness[5], they gave rise to joy. Adding passionateness to passion itself, a glow to love, a joy to joy, a dancing motion to dancing, festivity to festival, in ogling they seemed to drink with the white (shells) of their eyes, in scolding to imprison in cages of rays from their nails, in gestures of anger to lash with curling eyebrows, in making love to pour a rain of all (sweet) feelings, in deftly moving to scatter transformations.

In other places, where under the terror of chamberlains' wands the people had made room, [147] the king's wives essayed the dance, a brilliant[6] throng with a forest of white parasols held above them, as if they were wood nymphs roaming beneath trees of paradise. Some, wrapt in loose shawls hanging from both shoulders, swayed as if mounted on play swinge. Some, with wavy robes torn by the edge of golden armlets, were like rivers lined by crossing ruddy-geese. Others, whose bright side glances were bounded by earrings entangled in tufts of white waving chowries, were like pools

1 The Bombay text has *lasantyo* 'flashing.' The words for 'forehead marks' and 'earrings' may be for the sake of the simile translated 'bunches of leaves.'

2 Or—punningly—'of *haṃsas*.'

3 Or—punningly with the *ketakīs*—'the booming of clouds.'

4 Or 'magicians.'

5 It is a great cause of congratulation when a Hindu grows *fat*,—they hold it implies a virtuous life and a good conscience.

6 The Bombay text has *vilesur* for *virejur*.

with *haṃsas* plucking at forests of blue lotuses[1]. Others, from whose tripping feet[2] trickled a dew of lac-reddened sweat that besprinkled the palace *haṃsas*, resembled moonlight nights when the twilight casts a glow upon the moon's disk. Others, with brows curved in derision at the contortions of chamberlains bending beneath golden girdles placed about their necks, seemed love-nets with outstretched arms for toils.

All womankind being thus set dancing, the earth, crimsoned by trickling lac from their feet, seemed rosy with the flush of love. Their round gleaming bosoms made the festival like a mass of auspicious pitchers[3]. Their tossing arms caused the world to seem nought but rings of lotus roots. Their sparkling playful smiles created as it were a season all of lightning flashes. The days seemed dappled by the light of dancing eyes. Brilliant ear chaplets of *Çirīṣa* flowers cast a green tint upon a daylight seemingly of parrots' tails. Dark hanging *Tamāla* sprays of braided hair shed a blackness as of collyrium on the prospect. Uplifted tendril-like hands made all creation gleam like one red lotus-bed. The radiance of rainbow-tinted gems infused a colour of jays' wings into the sunlight. Echoing with clusters of tinkling ornaments, the heavens seemed nought but clanging bells. Even old ladies shouted like maniacs. [148] Old men even lost all shame, as though bewitched. The wise forgot themselves, as if intoxicated. Even hermits' hearts were all agog for a dance. The king gave away all his fortune. Heaps of wealth, like Kuvera's treasuries, were plundered by the folk on every side.

This great festival ended, another period of time passed gradually by. Rājyavardhana was now nearing his sixth year, while his majesty Harṣa could just manage five or six paces with the support of his nurse's finger. His majesty wore upon his head a mustard amulet, like a spark of his valour's fire just peeping forth. His form was stained yellow with *gorocanā*,

[1] Their eyes are the blue lotuses, the white chowries the *haṃsas*, and the earrings their beaks.

[2] Or—punningly—'speeding rays.'

[3] A pitcher full of water is an auspicious omen.

as if his inborn warrior's prowess were coming to light. His neck was ornamented with a row of great tiger's claws linked with gold, like buds of pride bursting from his heart. He could manage a child's first indistinct cries, the prelude as it were of truth. His innocent smiles won his kinsmen's hearts, as flowers do bees. Tiny teeth, growing like buds of happy smiles and watered with the dew of his mother's cuplike breasts, were beginning to adorn his lotus mouth. The womenfolk in the harem safeguarded him like honour; the ministers of state preserved him like a state secret; the young nobles held fast to him as to virtue; his kindred cherished him like the family prestige; the swords of guards caged him in like a lion's whelp.

It was at this time that queen Yaçovatī became pregnant with Rājyaçrī, even as Nārāyaṇa's form with the earth. And when the time of her delivery was come, as the pool gives birth to the lotus bed with its long red stalks and roots[1], as the rains to the autumn sweetly vocal with wild geese[2], as the spring to woodrows with their limbs all fair with[3] flowers, [149] as the sky to the shower of wealth flashing with grains of gold, as the tide to gems with a flood of light, as the new-moon time to the crescent which delights all men's eyes, as Çacī to Jayantī a sight for a thousand eyes[4], as Menā to Gaurī wooed by all mountains[5], so Yaçovatī gave birth to a daughter, who added to the two sons formed a further ornament, like the line of a necklace above her two bosoms.

About this time Yaçovatī's brother presented his son Bhaṇḍi, a boy about eight years of age, to serve the young princes. Tufted with tossing side-locks of curly hair, the boy was like a reborn Kāma with his head encircled by the smoke line of the flame of Çiva's anger. Darkened on one side of his body by an earring of sapphire, whitened on the other by the light of a pearl in his ear-ornament, he was like

[1] Or—punningly—'with long lotus eyes.'

[2] Or 'with a voice sweet as a wild-goose's.'

[3] Or 'tender as flowers.'

[4] *Sahasrākṣa* is also a name of Indra, 'for the God of the Thousand Eyes.'

[5] Or 'kings.'

a compound Avatar of Viṣṇu and Çiva. A diamond bracelet bound about his stout forearm suggested a rejuvenated Paraçu-Rāma, betokened by the cord of his axe, which was itself all worn away in his slaughter of the Kṣatriyas. Curved bits of coral were tied to his neck string, as if he were a reincarnate Hiraṇyakaçipu wearing bits of Narasiṃha's claws broken against his adamantine breast. Though still a child, he bore himself stiffly, like a seed of the tree of valour.

To this additional son the king's regard was equally attached, as Çiva's sight to his third eye. [150] The princes also, the heart's joy of all creatures, derived a greater splendour from the company of this naturally courtly child, as do April and May when accompanied by the southern Malaya breeze. Growing in due course step by step with a fourth brother, as it were, namely the people's joy[1], they came to manhood. With stout thighs like pillars, forearms broad as propylaea, long arms like bars, wide chests like panels, stately as tall ramparts[2], they were like the gateway of a great city strong to afford refuge to a whole world.

Charming[3] were they and not to be gazed upon, like sun and moon overpowering the world by the flame of their flashing splendour and effulgence; manifested, like fire and wind, in radiance and power; adamantine in the hardness of their frames, like the immovable Himālaya and Vindhya in conjunction; fit to bear the yoke of the Kṛita age, like two great bulls; like Aruṇa and Garuḍa, borne on horses and well-proportioned[4]; like Indra and Viṣṇu, with the gait of elephants[5]; like Karṇa and Arjuna, bedecked with ring and diadem; like the eastern and western heavens, capable of procuring the uprising and setting of all great lights. In their over-

[1] For the simile cf. *Raghu-V.* x. 78.

[2] Or 'with tall Sāl trees.'

[3] Few of the puns in this paragraph can be represented in translation. The word *abhirāmadurnirīkṣyau* may also be taken with 'fire and wind.'

[4] Referring to Aruṇa and Garuḍa the compound *harivāhanavibhaktaçarīrau* will mean 'having their bodies divided in carrying, the one, the Sun, the other, Viṣṇu.'

[5] Or 'mounted on lordly *nāgas*,' sc. Indra's elephant and Viṣṇu's serpent Çeṣa.

weening pride they could scarce contain themselves in the hovel of earth straitened by the too great proximity of the shore's boundary[1]. They scorned the very shadows [151] averted from the light; they blushed that even their reflections should approach men's toe-nails; they were pained at the coward breaking even of one of their hairs; they felt shame at the second umbrella mirrored in their crest-jewels. The name of master, even as given to the Six-faced God[2], grated upon their ears; a counterpart, even as seen in their mirror, caused their eyes to smart; to clasp hands even in twilight adoration seemed to plunge a spear into their brows; the very bow borne by the clouds distressed their hearts: even painted kings that would not bow appeared to burn their feet. They honoured not even the sun's light, content with a bounded sphere; they scoffed even at the ocean, whose Glory was carried away by a mountain (Mandara)[3]; they sneered at the potent wind that wore no warlike shape[4]. It was torture to them that even Himālaya should be fanned by Yaks' tails, agony that the very seas should have their conchs, intolerable that even Varuṇa should be a rival overlord of the four oceans. The very monarchs, whose parasols they seized not, they left void of splendour[5]. Gracious though uncourted, they poured honey with their lips even upon unassuming people[6]. The stocks of evil kings, however far removed, their hot anger caused to wither. Day after day their hands, begrimed with the marks of sword play, seemed defiled by quenching the fire of all other monarchs' prowess. By the deep twang of their bows at recreation time they seemed conversing after recent dalliance with the queens of the quarters. Thus were the names Rājyavardhana and

1 Comp. Dryden, 'Cooped up he seemed in earth and seas confined.' *Māna* may mean 'size,' as well as 'pride.'

2 Kārtikeya.

3 At the churning of the ocean: otherwise 'whose glory was carried off by kings.'

4 Or 'made no war.'

5 A pun on *chāyā*, as meaning 'shadow' and 'splendour.'

6 Or—punningly—'even upon the temperate their lips, though they were not addicted to wine, rained wine.'

Harṣa proclaimed abroad over all the earth, in so much that in a very little time they attained to fame in other Continent Isles likewise.

[152] One day their father, having summoned them, retired in their company after dinner to his private apartments and affectionately addressed them :—'My dear sons, it is difficult to secure good servants, the first essential of sovereignty. In general mean persons, making themselves congenial, like atoms, in combination, compose the substance of royalty[1]. Fools, setting people to dance in the intoxication of their play, make peacocks of them[2]. Knaves[3], working their way in, reproduce as in a mirror their own image. Like dreams, impostors by false phantasies beget unsound views. By songs, dances, and jests unwatched flatterers[4], like neglected diseases of the humours, bring on madness. Like thirsty *cātakas*, low-born persons[5] cannot be held fast. Cheats, like fishermen[6], hook the purpose at its first rise in the mind, like a fish in Mānasa. Like those who depict infernos, loud singers paint unrealities on the canvas of the air[7]. Suitors[8], more keen than arrows, plant a barb in the heart. [153] For these reasons I have appointed to wait upon your highnesses the brothers Kumāragupta and Mādhavagupta, sons of the Mālwa king, inseparable as my arms from my side; they are men found by frequent trials untouched by any taint of vice, blameless, discreet, strong, and comely. To them your highnesses also will show a consideration not enjoyed by the rest of your dependants.'

[1] *Pārthiva* has double meaning, (1) royal, (2) earthen, 'the substance of earth.' Similarly *samavāya* and *dravya*.

[2] *Mayūra* beside 'peacock' means also 'rogue's jests.' *Bāliçāḥ*, (1) children, (2) triflers, alludes to the play of children making the peacocks dance.

[3] *Pallavika* has double meaning (1) knave, (2) tendril.

[4] *Vātikāḥ*=(1) knaves, (2) connected with the humours. A vitiated state of the wind is said to cause madness.

[5] *Akulīna* as applied to *cātakas* means 'not resting on the earth.' 'Thirsty' goes also with flatterers.

[6] *Jālikāḥ* has both meanings.

[7] *Ambara*=(1) ether, the vehicle of sound, (2) canvas.

[8] *Atimārgaṇāḥ*=(1) importunate persons, (2) keen arrows.

So much said, he ordered the chamberlain to summon the pair. After a brief interval the two princes, whose eyes were fixed upon the entrance, saw Kumāragupta, the elder brother, entering with the chamberlain. He was a young man neither very tall nor very short, in age about eighteen years. He planted weighty steps, as if to steady the ground, which trembled with the movements of numerous kings. A pair of rather slim shanks, issuing from not over-prominent knee joints, sallied as it were from thighs showing thick hard flesh of compact growth due to incessant practice in leaping. His hollow sides tapered at the waist, as if his middle, like that of Mandara, had been rubbed down by the serpent Vāsuki when whirled about in the fury of gods and Asuras. A chest of vast breadth offered room for unbounded feelings of respect for his master. With quiet and graceful motions his pendulous arms appeared to be carrying him across the not easily traversed ocean of manhood. Upon his stout forearm, where it was marked by the bowstring's scar, shone a spray of light from the jewelled bracelet of his left wrist, like a sprouting bud of his valour's fiery flame. From the jewel of his ear-ornament there descended upon his huge shoulder a tawny light, like an antelope skin worn in sign of dedication to the use of arms[1]. His face, whose cheeks reflected the decorated figures of armlets with upstanding points, suggested a moon with Rohiṇī set in its heart. A downcast eye with pupil fixed and still seemed to give a lesson in decorum to the lotuses, whose faces are uplifted with desire for Lakṣmī[2]. [154] For a crest he bore an *Āmlātaka* flower, like his loyalty, upon his head. He displayed a graceful flexibility such as might have been presented by a nation of bows affrighted by his merciless breaking of their rings. He derived a dignity from senses conquered even in boyhood and, like conquered foes, kept well under his control. The law of princely nobility was the trusted mistress whom he followed. Resplendent as he was, the noble nature within made his brilliance soothing as a sun with a moon inside it. From the hardness of his

[1] Cf. *Manu* ii. 41.

[2] Or 'glory.' This prince, *though* desirous of glory, had a downcast look.

frame he seemed to wear down the very mountains. His happy graciousness was as if he were selling to joy the people whom he purchased by his look.

Behind him came his younger brother Mādhavagupta, who for height and dignity[1] resembled a moving realgar mountain. In the guise of a low topknot of *Mālatī* flowers great glory seemed to be imprinting upon his head a father's[2] kiss at going forth. His meeting brows seemed to bespeak the late union of those irreconcilables, youth and decorum. With profound gravity he kept his gaze fixed, like his loyal devotion, upon his heart. Cooled by a smearing of the purest sandal paste and provided with a pillow in the shape of his necklace, his breast was like a broad slab of moonstone for glory to rest upon when wearied by her round of brief visits to numberless rival kings. He had the eye of a gazelle, the nose of a boar, the broad shoulders of a buffalo, the forearm of a tiger, the prowess of a lion, the gait of an elephant, bribes, as it were, offered by the frightened creatures after losing all else in the chase.

[155] Entering, they bowed from afar till their four limbs[3] and heads touched the ground, then assumed a suitable position indicated by a kindly glance from the king. After a momentary pause he gave them instructions from that day forth to wait upon the princes. 'As your majesty commands' they answered, and rising, saluted Rājyvardhana and Harṣa by swaying their heads again and again to the earth. They on their part saluted their father. From that hour the two were, like opening and shutting, never absent from the range of the princes' eyes,—like inspiration and exspiration, night and day before their mouths,—like a pair of arms, ever constant at their side.

Meanwhile Rājyaçrī gradually grew up in daily increasing familiarity with friends expert in song, dance &c. and with all accomplishments. In a comparatively limited period she came to maturity. On her alone fell the glances of all kings,

1 Or—punningly—'yellowness.'
2 *Guruṇā*=(1) great, (2) father.
3 Sc. their knees and hands.

like arrows on the targe, and sending envoys, monarchs sought her hand.

One day the king, standing on the roof of the seraglio, heard a man in the outer court sing an *āryā* couplet which had suggested itself to him:—

> 'At the time of the bosoms'[1] swelling, growing with the passing of each rainy season,
> 'A daughter brings low her father, like a river its bank, in a whirlpool of agitation.'

Hearing this, the king dismissed the servants, and said to the queen at his side:—'Our darling Rājyaçrī, my queen, is now grown a young woman. The thought of her, like her noble qualities, never for a moment leaves my heart. As soon as ever girls near maturity, their fathers become fuel to the flame of pain. The swelling of her bosoms[1] darkens my heart, as clouds the day. [156] It is a law of right, by whomsoever framed not with my consent, that children born of our body, dandled at our breasts, never to be abandoned, are taken from us by the unexpected arrival of someone unknown to us. Truly, these indeed are the brandmarks of this transient life. Herein has sorrow's fire more than in aught else a power to burn, that whereas both are our offspring good men grieve at a daughter's birth. Hence is it that to their daughters noble men offer water even at birth[2] in their tears. For this fear sages, neglecting marriage, dispensing with domestic life, take refuge in desolate forests. Who indeed can bear to part with a child? The more that suitors' envoys flock in, the deeper does wretched anxiety retire, as if abashed, into my heart. What can we do? In spite of all, householders must follow the ways of the world. In general too, though a bridegroom may have other merits, the wise especially incline towards good family. Now at the head of all royal houses stand the Mukharas, worshipped, like Çiva's foot-print, by all the world. Of that race's pride, Avantivarman, the eldest son, Grahavarman by name, who lacks not his father's virtues, a prince like the lord of planets

[1] Or—punningly—'clouds.'

[2] Water is offered to the dead at a funeral (*jalāñjali*): see Colebrooke's *Essays*, vol. II. p. 177.

descended upon earth, seeks our daughter. Upon him, if your majesty's thoughts are likewise favourable, I propose to bestow her.'

To these her husband's words the queen with tearful eyes and a heart alarmed by love for her daughter replied:—'Mothers, your majesty, are to their daughters no more indeed than nurses, useful only in rearing them. In their bestowal the father is the judge. Love for a daughter however far far exceeds love for a son, pity causing the difference. My lord only knows how all our lives long she is a care to us.'

His resolution taken in the matter of his daughter's bestowal, the king sent for his sons and acquainted them also with his purpose. Then on a day of good omen, in the presence of the whole royal household, he poured the betrothal water upon the hand of an envoy extraordinary, who had arrived previously with instructions from Grahavarman to sue for the princess.

[157] He having gleefully departed with his mission accomplished, the royal household, as the marriage days drew near, assumed an aspect brilliant, charming, exciting, and auspicious. All the world bedecked itself with betel, perfumes, and flowers, distributed with a lavish hand. From every country were summoned companies of skilled artists. Under the charge of royal officers came whole villages, bringing loads of serviceable gifts. Emissaries conveyed presents from many a king. The favourites busied themselves in the disposal of troops of relatives, come in answer to invitations. Leather workers, wild with intoxication—having been treated with wine—flourished in their hands drumsticks, with which they sharply struck the festal drums, till they boomed again. Mortars, pestles, stone blocks and other utensils were bedecked with pounded perfumes[1]. Successive trains of troubadours, appearing on every side, crowded the courts, where images of Indrāṇī were being set up. Carpenters, presented with white flowers, unguents,

[1] For *piṣṭapañcaṅgula* cf. *supra* p. 45, and the *Jātaka* (ed. Fausböll) II. p. 256, ll. 2–3.

and clothes, planned out the marriage altar. Workmen mounted on ladders, with brushes upheld in their hands and plaster pails on their shoulders, whitened the top of the street wall of the palace. Torrents of water from pounded saffron now being washed stained the feet of the nation. The courtyards were seas of elephants and horses, suitable for bridal gifts, which were undergoing inspection. Throngs of astrologers, set calculating, investigated the characteristics of different moments. Crocodile-mouthed conduits, conveying scented water, filled a variety of pleasure ponds. The outer terraces resounded with the din of gold-workers engaged in hammering gold. Plasterers were beplastered with showers of sand which fell over them from freshly erected walls. A group of skilled painters painted auspicious scenes. Multitudes of modellers moulded clay figures of fishes, tortoises, crocodiles, cocoanuts, plantains, and betel trees. Even kings girt up their loins, and busied themselves in carrying out decorative work set as tasks by their sovereign, being variously engaged in polishing mosaic floors of red lead, or erecting the posts for marriage platforms, which they strewed with handfuls of liquid *ātar-paṇa* pigment, reddened with cochineal disposed about them, and adorned at the top with mango and *Açoka* twigs. [158] From the furthest orient had come the queens of all the feudatories, noble, high-bred, shapely, well-clad, unwidowed dames with lines of vermilion powder glittering on their foreheads. Thronging the household, they sang sweet well-omened songs containing allusions to the bride and bridegroom's families; or with fingers steeped in divers colours dyed neck-strings; or employed their skill in leaf and plant painting to adorn polished cups and collections of unbaked clay-ware; or stained skeins of cotton thread for bamboo baskets and fabrics of wool for marriage amulets; or manufactured cosmetics, compounded of saffron paste clotted by *balāçanā* essence, and face unguents adding distinction to beauty; or made strings of cloves mingled with *Kakkola* fruit, containing also nutmegs, and large bright lumps of crystalline camphor threaded in the intervals.

The palace was arrayed in textures flashing on every side like thousands of rainbows, textures of linen, cotton, bark silk, spider's thread, muslin, and shot silk, resembling sloughs of snakes, soft as the unripe plantain's fruit, swaying at a breath, imperceptible except to the touch. Some were being made by ancient city matrons, cunning in divers ways of cutting and measuring; some, made already, were being dyed by washermen, who beamed with respect for the courtly old ladies of the harem; some, after dyeing, had been shaken by servants clinging to either end, and were drying in the shade; some, now dry, were having all the charm of sprays reproduced in their twisted shapes: in some cases the spotting with saffron paste had been begun, and in others the fragile stuffs were torn, while grasped by servitors, who lifted their arms to clutch them. Couches, whose gay coverlets cast the *haṃsa* tribes into the shade; bodices overlaid with starlike pearls; countless thousands of canvas and cloth pieces, divided up for various uses; [159] awnings bright with soft, freshly dyed bark silk; marquees, whose roofs were covered all over with garments, and posts swathed in strips of variegated silk; all these gave to the court an aspect brilliant, attractive, exciting, and auspicious.

The queen Yaçovatī, though only one person, seemed in the flurry of the marriage festival multifariously divided, her heart being with her husband, her curiosity with the bridegroom, her love with her daughter, her attentions with the invited ladies, her injunctions with the servants, her body accompanying her motions, her eyes busy in looking after things done and omitted, her joy permeating the festival. The king likewise ever and anon despatched a female camel to his gratified son-in-law, and however apt the servants, intently watching his face, might be in executing his orders, yet in the distraction of fatherly affection he did everything in person along with his two sons.

Thus the royal household became as it were the essence of freedom from widowhood; a world seemed born full of auspiciousness; the prospect seemed composed of troubadours, the sky turned into drums, the roaming domestics to be all ornament, creation looked nought but relatives, time appeared composed of bliss, the splendid festival seemed to blossom forth with all Lakṣmī's bloom. It was as if there were a treasure trove of happiness, a realisation of life's purpose, a ripening of good deeds, a youth of felicity, a new reign of delight, a fulfilment time of desires. Calculated as it were by the people's fingers, watched for by the banners on the highways, welcomed by reverberations of auspicious music, invoked by astrologers, attracted by wishes, embraced by the hearts of the bride's women friends, the marriage day arrived. [160] Instantly at dawn all strangers were expelled by the chamberlains, and the royal family was drawn apart.

Anon the groom-in-waiting, having entered, introduced a young man of fair exterior, saying, 'A betel-bearer, your majesty, by name Pārijātaka, arrived from the bridegroom's presence.' With a graciousness due to esteem for his son-in-law the king inquired of the man while still at a distance, 'Young sir, is Grahavarman well?' Hearing the king's voice, he advanced a few paces at a run, and stretching out his arms, courtier that he was, bent his head for some time to the earth; then rising said, 'He is well, as your majesty observes, and sends respectful greetings to your majesty.' Understanding him to have come with tidings of the bridegroom's arrival, the king after offering hospitality sent him back with this charge, 'At the first watch of the night see that no mishap arise owing to the passing of the marriage hour.'

When the day was ended, having transferred to the bride's face as it were the beauty of all his lotus beds, while the sun glowed like the foot of the bridal day's loveliness; when the pairs of ruddy-geese were parting in shame, as it were, that their love should be eclipsed by the bride and bridegroom's affection; when, flecked like a pigeon's throat[1], the afterglow, with its delicate texture of red silken rays,

[1] The word *kapotakaṇṭhakarbure* is best taken with the 'afterglow' and not with what follows; *karbura* may mean 'yellow' or 'golden.' For the 'yellow' cf. Psalm 68. 13 Sept.: πτέρυγες περιστερᾶς περιηργυρωμέναι καὶ τὰ μετάφρενα αὐτῆς ἐν χλωρότητι χρυσίου.

gleamed like the banner of felicity in the sky; when the dark, like the dust of the bridegroom's approaching train, was besmirching the heavenly spaces, and, as if all ready to effect the favourable conjunction, the starry array was rising; while, like an auspicious marriage bowl, the moon's disk was shooting up with ever growing[1] halo of whiteness from the Udaya hill, and, as the lovely radiance of the bride's face swallowed up the dusky gloom, the night-lotus beds with faces supine seemed to scoff at the idly-risen moon: [161] then true to his time the bridegroom drew nigh. Before him with red gold-studded chowries incessantly flashing ran footmen, like desires with the topmost shoots of passion standing out. The horizon was filled with troops of horses, which were welcomed, as it seemed, by answering neighs from the prick-eared steeds of the capital. Throngs of mighty elephants with chowries waving at their ears, arrayed in trappings all of gold, with gay housings and twanging bells, seemed to re-form the darkness dissolved by the rising moon. He came mounted on an elephant whose muzzle was bedecked with a zodiac of pearls[2], even as the lord of night rides the eastern heaven. All about him was a hubbub of dancing troubadours shrilling forth the notes of divers birds, as when the new spring comes with his groves[3]. An array of lamps, incensed with dripping perfumed oil, made yellow all the world as with a cloud of saffron toilet powder. His head, with its flowery topknot set amid a blooming jasmine wreath, seemed to laugh to scorn the moonlit evening with its halo and its moon. He had formed for himself a mock *vaikakṣaka* wrap with a wreath of flowers, like a flowery bow taken from Kāma vanquished by his beauty. Joyous with the low hum of bee tribes delirious with pride in the fragrance of the flowers, he resembled a Tree of Paradise born and descended again with Çrī upon the earth. His heart drawn on as in eagerness

[1] *Vardhamāna* also means a 'dish.'

[2] *Nakṣatramālā* = (1) 'the moon's asterisms,' (2) 'a string of 27 pearls.'

[3] Cf. Kipling, *Beast and Man in India*, p. 225: 'In Western India the bridegroom rides, covered with tinsel and gay clothing, in the midst of a moving square of artificial flowers and bushes, counterfeiting a garden, borne on long platforms on the heads of coolies.'

to behold his new bride's countenance, he appeared almost to fall forward on his face.

On his arrival at the gate the king and his sons, accompanied by their royal retinue, went forth on foot to meet him. Dismounting he bowed, and the king with outstretched arms gave him a hearty embrace, like Spring embracing Kāma. Next in order he embraced Rājyavardhana and Harṣa, and the king, taking him by the hand, led him within doors, where he honoured him with a seat equal to his own and with other attentions.

Soon Gambhīra, a wise Brāhman attached to the king, said to Grahavarman, 'My son, by obtaining you Rājyaçrī has at length united the two brilliant lines of Puṣpabhūti and Mukhara, whose worth, like that of the Sun and Moon houses, is sung by all the world to the gratification of wise men's ears[1]. Previously you were set fast by your merits[2] on the king's breast, like the Kaustubha jewel on Viṣṇu's. [162] But now you are one to be supported, like the moon by Çiva, on his head.'

Even while he spoke, the astrologers, approaching the king, said, 'Your majesty, the moment approaches: let the bridegroom proceed to the bridal house.' The king bidding him rise and go, Grahavarman entered the women's apartments, and, disregarding the thousands of glances that like opening blue lotuses fell upon him from women curious to see the bridegroom, passed on to the door of the bridal house, where he stayed his attendants and entered.

There amid a company of relatives, friends, and servants, mostly women, he espied his bride, whose face, hidden, like the morning twilight, by its roseate veil[3], dulled the gleaming lamps by its radiance. Not too tightly embraced by womanhood, which seemed alarmed by her excessive delicacy, she appeared, by the long soft sighs which her bosom, choked with

[1] Or 'of Budha, the regent of Mercury and son of the moon, and Karṇa, the son of the sun.'

[2] Or 'cords.'

[3] There is a pun in *aruṇa*, which also denotes the 'dawn.' The dawn also dims the lamps.

fright, could scarcely utter, to bemoan her departing maidenhood. Trembling she stood motionless with bashfulness, as if fearing to fall, gazing with a quiver of terror in her mind at that lotus-red hand so soon to be grasped: so might *Rohiṇī* gaze at the moon when near eclipse[1]. Her body was white with sandal, as though born of a (white) lotus bed whose amassed loveliness had been a gift from the moonlight. A fragrance of flowers breathed about her, as if she had come forth from the heart of spring. The perfume of her breath attracted the bee tribes, as if she were sprung from the Malaya breeze. Love followed in the train of one who seemed a reborn Ratī. Compounded of all gem-like natures, brilliancy, loveliness, intoxication, fragrance and sweetness, the product of the Kaustubha jewel, the moon, wine, the tree of paradise, and ambrosia, she seemed a second Çrī formed by the ocean in his rage with gods and asuras[2]. [163] The soft light of an earring produced an ear-pendant of pearly rays like clusters of white *Sindhuvāra* flowers. Her cheek's surface, a glade all green with the emerald glow of her ear-ornament, formed a pleasance, as it were, for the fawnlike[3] gleam of her eye; and thus she seemed to chide her shamefaced friends and heart, which, bewildered by the interesting spectacle of a bridegroom[4], ever and anon essayed to raise a glance.

No sooner had that thief of hearts made his entrance than he was delivered over by his bride into the clutches of love. Most deftly he performed all that in the marriage hall the bridegroom is made to do by women with faces lit by a mocking smile. Then, his bride having been arrayed in the dress proper for the ceremony, he took her by the hand, and going forth, came to an altar whitened with new plaster and surrounded by invited kings, as when the slopes of Himālaya were girt by mountains gathered to the wedding of Çiva and

1 *Rohiṇī* 'the red one' gazes at the white moon when near eclipse. The *nakṣatras* are the moon's wives.

2 The first Çrī or Lakṣmī was produced by the ocean (always spoken of as rich in jewels) at the mythical churning along with the objects mentioned in this sentence.

3 Or 'lovely.'

4 Or perhaps 'eager to see the bridegroom and the ceremony.'

Pārvatī. Gleaming around it were earthen dolls, whose hands bore auspicious fruits, and which had five-mouthed cups bristling with dew-besprent blades of barley and enemies, faces painted with soft colours[1]. Brāhman witnesses busied themselves in kindling the flame, which smoked under logs heaped up by the teachers. Close to the fire unsoiled green *Kuça* grass was set, and hard by were bundles of pounding stones, antelope skins, ghee, garlands[2], and fuel, while a sparkle of parched grain was mixed with dark *Çamī* leaves placed in new baskets. This altar the bridegroom ascended, as the moon with *his* beauty mounts the heavens. As the god of the flowery bow came with Rati to the red *Açoka*, so he drew near the fire with its tremulous sprays of red flame. The fire being fed, [164] he marched round towards the right, attended by the very flames, which as if curious to see the bride's face took a rightward twist. And as the rice oblation was let fall, the blaze, whitened by the gleam of nails, seemed to smile[3] in amazement at the bride and bridegroom's unprecedented grace of form.

Anon a tempest of tear drops, clear as great pearls, showed itself in the bride's face, which yet displayed no discomposure, and, as if to quench the fire's image in her cheeks' clear oval, she burst into weeping. With eyes brimming with tears the women of the family raised a lugubrious cry. All the bridal rites being fully completed, the husband bowed with his wife to their parents, and then entered their chamber. About its portals were figured the spirits of Love and Joy. Bees going before like friends raised a hubbub. The charmed lamps, which lighted it, swayed in the wind of the bees' wings, as if trembling in fear of a blow from their ear-lotuses. At the foot of a blossoming red *Açoka* carved on one side stood the god of love aiming his shaft, the arrow drawn to the string, and a third of his eye sideways closed. A fair well-upholstered

[1] So the Kashmir and Bombay texts and the commentator. The Calcutta text has *amatramukhaiḥ* 'goblet-mouths.'

[2] The Bombay and Kashmir texts read *-sruk-*, 'spoons,' 'ladles, which seems preferable.

[3] The nails represent the teeth shown in smiling.

bed with pillows was guarded on the one side by a golden rinsing vessel, on the other by a golden figure holding an ivory box, like Lakṣmī incarnate with an upright lotus stalk in her hand. At the bed's head stood a night bowl of silver bedecked with lotuses, like the moon come to join company with the flowery god.

There, while the bashful young bride slept with her face averted, the bridegroom spent the night in gazing at her images in the mirrors of the jewelled walls, like family goddesses come in curiosity to hear their first words and seen through jewelled loopholes. Abiding in his new father's house, by his noble nature raining ambrosia as it were upon his new mother's heart, he spent ten blissful days, ever varying with continually renewed tokens of favour; and then, leaving regret like a palace porter behind, [165] and taking all men's hearts with him like provisions named in the dowry, he managed to secure his dismissal from the king and set out with his bride to his native country.

Here ends the fourth chapter—entitled The Exposition of The Emperor's Birth—of the Harṣa-Carita composed by Çrī Bāṇa Bhaṭṭa.

CHAPTER V.

[166] As the inconstant lightning, having shown a splendour,
lets fall the thunderbolt,
Fate after ordaining happiness to men superadds heart-rending affliction.
As Ananta, moving his coils, lays the mountains in ruins, so does the one endless time by its revolutions
Lay great souls low in the dust, many together, respecting none.

Subsequently the king one day summoned Rājyavardhana, whose age now fitted him for wearing armour, and, as a lion despatches his whelp against the deer, placed him at the head of an immense force and sent him attended by ancient advisers and devoted feudatories towards the north to attack the Hūṇas[1].

For several stages my lord Harṣa followed his march with the horse. When however his brother had entered the region which blazes with Kailāsa's lustre, being at youth's adventure-loving age, he spent several days away from camp on the skirts of the Himālaya, where lions, çarabhas, tigers, and boars are plentiful, a fawn-eyed hunter with his bright form dappled by the radiant glances of love-smit[2] wood-nymphs. His bow drawn to the ear, he emitted a rain of shining shafts, which in a comparatively few days left the forests empty of wild creatures.

One day however at the fourth watch of the night[3], dawn

[1] Cf. *Viṣṇu Pur.* vol. II. pp. 133, 134.
[2] Or perhaps 'anxious (for their protégés).'
[3] This is a sign of near fulfilment.

being almost come, he saw in a vision a lion burning in an overpowering forest fire, which reddened the whole sky with a sea of flickering flame. [167] Into that same fire he saw the lioness, leaving her cubs, hurl herself with a plunge. At this the thought arose in his heart—'Stronger of a truth than steel are the bonds whose tissue is love, when even brutes are drawn on by them to acts like this.' On awakening his left[1] eye incessantly throbbed; a mysterious tremour overspread his frame; his heart started without cause from its internal moorings; for no reason at all a profound dejection came over him. What could it mean? Various conjectures wracked his mind, until losing all self-command he bowed his face in thought, so that the fixed pupils of his partridge eyes seemed to make the earth for an instant a bed of sprouting land-lotuses. A void as it were was in his heart during that day's sport, and, when the sun had ascended to mid-day, he returned home, where, lying on a bamboo couch stretched on the ground with a pillow white as moonshine and cool sandal unguent covering its frame, he remained with small hand-fans softly waving on either side, full of apprehension.

Anon he beheld afar off a certain Kuraṅgaka approaching with a billet tied in a forehead-wrap of rags of deep indigo hue[2]. Weariness and heat had combined to give him such a blackness of body, that he seemed turning into charcoal through some inner fire of grief. Disguised as the dust excited by the quick trot of his hurried approach, the very earth appeared to pursue him out of curiosity to learn news of its king. Flapped by the opposing breeze, the long hem of his robe fanned both his flanks, just as if his rapid advance had given him wings. Impelled from behind by his master's charge, drawn on from the front by prolonged emissions of weary breath, the sun's image shaped in his oozing forehead seeming to snatch at the writing in eagerness to learn its import, his body empty of every sense, as if he had dropped them in his haste, he stumbled vacantly upon an even enough road, as

[1] The right would have foretold *good* news.

[2] The dark colour symbolizes the bad news.

though overweighted by the purport committed to the letter. [168] One might compare him to a fragment of a black cloud soon to let fall a thunderbolt of ill-news, a smoke whorl of a fire of sorrow soon to blaze, a seed of a paddy of sin soon to bear its harvest; a very courier of ill-omen.

At that sight Harṣa's heart was cloven by a terror taking shape from the previous succession of evil omens. Approaching with a bow, Kuraṅgaka presented first the despondency seated in his looks and then the writing, which the prince took in his own hand and read. With its contents affliction penetrated to his soul, and, looking the picture of desolation[1], he inquired what was his father's sickness. With eyes dropping tears and lips the faltering accents Kuraṅgaka made a two-fold answer 'It is, my lord, a violent fever.' At this news Harṣa's heart was instantly splintered into a thousand pieces. Anxious for the preservation of his father's life, he rinsed his mouth and conveyed to Brāhmans the whole of his regal equipage, jewels and gold and silver to a vast amount. Then without taking food he started up and calling to a youth who stood in his presence sword to forehead, ordered him to saddle his horse. The grooms having hastily run up to bring it, he mounted and set out alone with a tremour at his heart.

Startled by the conch's sudden call to horse, the cavalry made ready in haste, and came galloping in, troop after troop, from every side, filling the abyss of heaven with the loud tramp of resonant hoofs. On the way deer, passing from right to left[2], foreshadowed the approaching end of the lion king. Facing the sun's flaming circle, a crow on a burnt-out tree uttered its dreadful cry, as if to cleave the prince's heart. Straight against him came a naked Jain, bedecked with peacock's tail-feathers[3], a fellow all lampblack as it seemed with

[1] *Avagraharūpo.* Kailāçcandra Datta's text reads *āvignarūpo* 'with confusion in his looks.' For the idea in *avagraharūpo* cf. c. VI. p. 202, ll. 9–11 (text).

[2] The opposite of the *pradakṣiṇa* or respectful order. The insolence of the deer betokens the lion's death.

[3] To sweep insects out of his path for fear of taking life.

the collected filth of many days besmirching his body. [169] This inauspicious celebration of his departure deepened the prince's apprehensions. His heart softening with filial love, surmising now this, now that; his eyes immovably fixed upon his horse's shoulder; followed in silence—for all amusing talk was at an end—by his royal escort; he in a single day accomplished a distance amounting to many days' journey. When the adorable sun, despondent as it seemed at the news of the king's sickness, bent downwards with waning splendour, he refused, despite the frequent admonitions of Bhaṇḍi and the other affectionate nobles, to take food. Footmen being sent ahead to secure a relay of villagers to show the best way, he passed the night in the saddle.

On the morrow at noon he reached the capital, but its sounds of triumph were departed, sunk the booming of its drums, checked its minstrelsy, its festivity expelled. No troubadours sang, no merchandise was exposed for sale in the shops. Here and there gleamed the smoke whorls of the Koṭihoma rite[1], which, twisted by the force of the wind, resembled crumpled horns of Yama's buffalo ploughing up the place, or death's net lines encircling it. Overhead roamed flocks of crows, which, cawing harshly in the day time, like the tinkle of iron bells adorning Yama's buffalo, announced the approach of calamity. Here loving kinsmen were keeping a fast to appease Ahibradhna[2], lying before his image. There young nobles were burning themselves with lamps to propitiate the Mothers. In one place a Dravidian was ready to solicit the Vampire[3] with the offering of a skull. In another an Āndhra man was holding up his arms like a rampart[4] to conciliate Caṇḍī. Elsewhere distressed young servants were pacifying Mahākāla by holding melting gum on their heads. In another place a group of relatives was intent on an oblation of their own flesh, which they severed with keen knives. Else-

[1] An oblation to propitiate adverse planets.

[2] Çiva. The Bombay text reads *Ahirbudhna*.

[3] *Āmardako · Vetālo, Raudradevatābheda ity anye.* Comm.

[4] Kailaççandra Datta reads *-āntra-* 'entrails of a sacrificed animal,' for *-bāhuvapra-*.

where again [170] young courtiers were openly resorting to the sale of human flesh. Thus the capital seemed polluted with the ashes of cemeteries, encircled by ill-omens, pillaged by fiends, swallowed up by the Kali age, hid beneath mounds of sin, sacked by the raids of demerit, victimized by the taunts[1] of transience, appropriated by the mockeries of fate; vacant, wrapped in slumber, robbed, abashed, deluded, fallen in a swoon.

No sooner had he entered than in the bazaar street amid a great crowd of inquisitive children he observed an Inferno-showman[2], in whose left hand was a painted canvas stretched out on a support of upright rods and showing the lord of the dead mounted on his dreadful buffalo. Wielding a reed-wand in his other hand, he was expounding the features of the next world, and could be heard to chant the following verse:—

> Mothers and fathers in thousands, in hundreds children and wives
> Age after age have passed away: whose are they, and whose art thou?

With this still further rending his heart Harṣa arrived in due course at the palace door, now shut to all the world. Dismounting, he perceived a young physician named Suṣeṇa coming out with a disquieted mien, like one reft of his senses. After receiving his salute the prince asked whether there was any improvement in his father's condition or not. 'Not at present,' was the reply, 'but there may be when he sees your

[1] The Kashmir text, however, and Kailaçc. read *adhikārāiḥ* ('rule') for *dhikkārāiḥ*.

[2] *Yamapaṭṭaka* 'one who exhibits pictures of Hades.' Cf. Kipling 'Beast and Man in India' p. 123: 'One of the most popular of the pictures sold at fairs is a composition known as *Dharmrāj*, a name of *Yama*, the Hindu Pluto, and also broadly for Justice. The Judge is enthroned and demon executioners bring the dead to receive their doom. The river of death flows on one side of the picture and those go safely across who hold a cow by the tail, while others are torn by terrible fishes. Chitragupt, the clerk or recording angel of Yama, considered to be the ancestor of the *kayasth* or clerkly caste, sits in an office with account books exactly like those of a Hindu tradesman, and according to the record of each soul, punishments or rewards are given...*Duts* or executioners torture offenders, while the blest sail upwards in air-borne chariots.'

highness.' So amid the salutations of the chamberlains he slowly entered the palace. There he found people bestowing all their goods in presents, worshipping the family gods, engaged in cooking the ambrosial posset[1], performing the Six Oblation sacrifice[2], offering tremulous *Durvā* leaves besmeared with clotted butter, chanting the Mahā-Māyūrī hymn[3], purifying the household, completing the rites for keeping out the spirits by offerings. Earnest Brāhmans were occupied in muttering Vedic texts; [171] Çiva's temple resounded with the murmur of the Hendecad[4] to Rudra; Çaivas of great holiness were bathing Virūpākṣa's image with thousands of vessels of milk[5]. Seated in the courtyard were kings, distressed in mind at failing to obtain a sight of their sovereign: bathing, eating, and sleeping had become mere names to them, and their clothes were foul from neglect of the toilet, while they passed day and night motionless as though pictured, awaiting bulletins from the king's personal attendants who came bursting in from the inner apartments. On the terrace was a woe-begone group of less intimate servants, discussing the king's sad plight in whispers: here was one imagining errors on the part of the doctors, there one reading out descriptions of incurable diseases, one recounting bad dreams, one imparting stories of demons, one publishing communications from astrologers, one droning out portents; one again reflecting upon the transiency of things, chiding this mutable world, censuring the mockeries of the Kali age, and accusing fate; another indignant with dharma and reproaching the gods of the royal household; a third commiserating the lot of the afflicted young nobles.

Scanned by his father's servants with eyes that brimmed with fast flowing tears, the prince passed on into the third

[1] Of milk, ghee, and rice offered as a life-preservative to the gods.

[2] '*Prajāpate svāhā' iti ṣaṇṇām devatānāṃ nāma grihītvā ṣaṇṇām evāhutīnām prakṣepaḥ ṣaḍāhutihoma ucyate.* Comm.

[3] *Mahāmāyūrī · Bāuddhavidyā.* Comm. Cf. Bendall, Catal. Nepal MSS. p. 49.

[4] *Rudrāikādaçī · Çivamantraḥ.* Comm.

[5] Or perhaps 'washing Çiva's thousand milk vessels.' *Virūpākṣa* = Çiva, because of his third eye.

court, where he now detected an odour of boiling oil, butter and decoctions emitting a steam scented with various herb draughts.

In the White House a deep silence reigned. Numerous lackeys thronged the vestibule; a triple veil hid the salon; the inner door was closed; the panels were forbidden to creak; closed windows kept out the draughts[1]. Anguished attendants, chamberlains furious at a tramp of footsteps on the stairs, all orders issued in noiseless signs. [172] Not quite near the king sat a man in armour; in a corner stood one bearing a gargling bowl, flurried by frequent summonses; in the Moon Chamber crouched the silent ministers of state; the screened balcony was occupied by women of the family distracted by profound grief; in the quadrangle a cluster of despondent servants. A few loving friends had been admitted. The physicians were in terror at the deep-seated ravages of the disease, the king's advisers sunk in dejection, the purohit stupefied; friends despaired, pandits were torpid[2], faithful feudatories in agony; the chowrie-bearer had lost his wits, the bodyguard was emaciated with grief. The favourites saw the accomplishment of their wishes fade away; beloved princes, having out of loyal affection abandoned sustenance, fainted with loss of strength; young nobles were prostrate on the ground from night-long watching. Grief lay heavy on a group of heirs to ancient houses; the chamberlains were shrivelled up with sorrow; the court poets had laid aside their glee; confidential servants uttered despairing sighs; from the pale lips of the king's mistresses the betel stain had fled.

The head cook was intent on the preparation of the diet ordered by perplexed physicians. Attendants were drinking streams of water from uplifted cups[3] in order to distract the pain of the king's dry mouth. Gourmands were being fed to relieve his craving. All the dealers were busy in providing a

[1] Or 'small apertures had been formed to secure ventilation,' as Kailāçcandra Datta, which seems preferable.

[2] Kailāçc. reads '*viprāṇa*' 'half-dead' for *nidrāṇa*. The Kashmir text has *vidrāṇa*, which is probably right, cf. text p. 89 l. 12 and note.

[3] But v. comm. *uccaṣakam* · *apagatapānabhājanam* '*empty* cups.'

pharmacopœia of drugs. One might infer the sick man's fearful thirst from the incessant calls to the waterman. Butter-milk was freezing in pails packed in ice; a collyrium-stick had been cooled with camphor powder placed on a moist white cloth; in a new vessel besmeared with wet clay was whey for a gargle. Water trickled from soft bundles of fibres covered with delicate (red) lotus leaves; on the ground where were cups of drinking water lay bunches of blue lotuses with their stalks. Boiled water was being cooled by passing in a stream from cup to cup; red sugar diffused a pungent odour. On a stand stood a sand jar for the sick man's eyes[1] to rest upon; fresh water-plants were coiled round a dripping globe; [173] a crystal platter gleamed with parched groats and barley-meal; a paste of flour and curds was held in a yellow emerald cup[2]; a collection of crystal, pearl, and shell vessels was sprinkled with powders and infusions of cooling herbs. Piles of myrobalans, citrons, grapes, and pomegranates were at hand. Lustral water was being scattered by fee'd Brahmans. A flat stone was stained with forehead unguents which a maidservant was pounding.

There he saw his sire preparing by a camp-lustration, as it were, of burning fever for the conquest of the next world. On a couch uneven[3] from his restless movements he tossed like venom-tortured Çeṣa on the Milky Sea. Like the drying ocean of doomsday[4], he was white with a dust of pearl powder[5]; but black death was uprooting him, as the black demon[6] up-rooted Kailāsa. As they touched him, the hands of the attendants engaged in ceaselessly smearing him with sandal were as white in the palm as if turned to ashes by contact with his burning limbs: while in the guise of the sandal

[1] For *-āntaracakṣuṣi* read *-āturacakṣuṣi* with Kailāçc. In the next compound Kailāçc. reads *-galagolayantrake* 'coiled round *the neck of* a globe' for *-galadgolayantrake*.

[2] Or, if we omit *pīta* with Kailāçc. and take *masāra* = *nīlamaṇi*, 'a sapphire cup.'

[3] Literally 'wavy.'

[4] *Kṣayakāle* = (1) at doomsday, (2) at his death.

[5] Or 'pearls, sand, and dust.'

[6] *Daçānano . vyādhiḥ Rākṣasaçca.* Comm. The demon is Rāvaṇa.

ointment his abiding[1] glory seemed to be saying farewell on his departure to another sphere. Incessantly applied petals of red, white, and blue lotuses seemed to blot his body with the falling glances of death.

On his head a thick[2] silken cloth bound round his hair told of never-ceasing shocks of pain, and, swollen with intolerable anguish, a network of dark veins stood out upon his forehead's page, a dreadful spectacle, as if death's finger were drawing lines to show the number of days ere the end. As if in horror at the sight of death's approach, the pupils of his eyes had retreated a little inwards. A stream of hot breath, rippled by waves of grey rays which issued from a line of dry teeth, suggested a river seen in a mirage. A tongue darkening, as if scorched by that burning breath, bespoke the convulsions of an appalling complication. On his breast lay gems, pearl-necklaces, sandal, and moonstones, as if he were making himself meet for the sight of death's emissaries. Tossing his arms in the contortions of his agony, he seemed seeking to cool the feverish heat with a shower bath formed of rays from the nails of his vibrating hands. Even his images, as they fell on the neighbouring liquids, jewelled floor, and concave mirrors, [174] seemed to bespeak the extremity of the heat[3]. A swoon, whose touch brought relief, he honoured like a wife in whom was all his trust. All about him, noted by the affrighted physicians, were symptoms of death, like the letters of Yama's summons. On the eve of the Great Journey, he was leaving to his kinsmen's hearts the inheritance of his pains, while, wedded as he was to soul-weariness, his bodily charm was as if in jealousy deserting him. Against him disease had concentrated its powers; emaciation let fly all her darts. Helplessness had taken him in hand: pain had made him its province, wasting its domain, lassitude its lair. Stung was he by dejection, appropriated by self-abandonment, enslaved by

1 *Sthāsnunā* 'abiding' = (1) everlasting, (2) staying behind on earth.
2 Kailāçc. reads *nibaddha-* 'bound about him' for *niviḍa-*.
3 I.e. by retreating into these cool objects.

sickness, dandled by death, the target of the south[1]; quaffed by qualms, devoured by sleeplessness, swallowed by sallowness, gulped down by spasms; a captive to calamity, a prey to pains, a city sacked by torments; fate laid hands upon him, destiny descried him, transience sniffed upon him, nothingness overbore him; mortality had taken his measure[2], affliction seized her advantage, distraction made him her dwelling; he was on the confines of doom, on the verge of the last gasp, at the outset of the Great Undertaking[3], at the portal of the Long Sleep, on the tip of death's tongue; broken in utterance, unhinged in mind, tortured in body, waning in life, babbling in speech, ceaseless in sighs; vanquished by yawning, swayed by suffering, in the bondage of wracking pains.

Seated by his side and touching him on head and breast was queen Yaçovatī, her eyes swollen with ceaseless weeping, her body grey with various medicinal powders, fanning him, though her hand grasped a chowrie, only with her sighs, and crying again and again 'My lord, are you asleep?'

At this spectacle the prince's mind, devastated by the first shock of grief, became apprehensive of destiny, and he deemed his father already a dweller in the realm of death. [175] For a moment he was as it were divorced from consciousness. Discarded by firmness, tenanted by agitation, left empty of delight, mastered by despondency, he seemed to have a heart of fire within him. Stricken as it were by deadly poison, his swooning senses left him in a darkness beyond the gloom of hell, a vacancy exceeding that of space, and he was at a loss how to act. He brought his heart into contact with fear, and his head with the earth.

As soon as the king perceived his darling son while still at some distance, swayed even in that extremity by overpowering affection, he ran forward in spirit to meet him, and putting out his arms, half rose from the couch, calling to him 'Come to me, come to me.' When the prince hastily drew

[1] The region of the god of death.

[2] Kailāçc. reads *parikalpitam* for *parikalitam*. Not so the Kāshmir text.

[3] Kailāçc. reads *pravāsasya* 'journey' for *prayāsasya*.

near with dutifully downcast looks, he raised his son's head by force, and, taking him to his bosom, seemed in his fondness to plunge into the heart of the moon's disc, to dive in a great lake of nectar, to bathe in a mighty torrent of *haricandana* sap, to be sprinkled by the waters of Himālaya[1]. Limb pressed to limb, cheek joined to cheek, closing eyes which flowed with incessant drops forming on their lashes, he held his son in a long embrace, forgetting all the torment of the fever. At length reluctantly released, the prince drew apart[2] and bowed low; then, having greeted his mother, returned and sat down near the couch, where his father gazed upon him with eyes that seemed to drink him in with their fixed unblinking look. Again and again he touched him with trembling palms, and, speaking with some difficulty—for his throat was dry through sickness,—'My boy,' he said, 'you are thin.' Whereat Bhaṇḍi explained that it was three days since the prince had taken food.

At this the king, after a long sigh, found strength to say in tear-choked accents:—'I know, my boy, your filial love and exceeding tender heart. At times like this[3] overmastering, all-afflicting family affection distracts even a sober man's mind. For this reason you must not give yourself over to sorrow. Consumed as I am by the fever's fierce heat, I am still more so by your distress. Your leanness cuts me like a sharp knife. Upon you my happiness, my sovereignty, my succession, and my life are set, and as mine, so those of all my people. The sorrows of such as you are a sorrow [176] to all people on earth; for no families of small worth are adorned by your like. You are the fruit[4] of stainless deeds stored up in many another life. You bear marks declaring the sovereignty of the four oceans, one and all, to be almost in your grasp. By your mere birth my end is attained, I am free from the wish to live. Only deference to the physicians makes me drink their medicines. Furthermore, to such as

[1] All these images suggest 'coolness' or relief from the heat of the fever.

[2] Read *apasṛitya* with Kailāçc.

[3] Kailāçc. reads '*īdṛiçeṣu vidhureṣu*' 'in such afflictions as this.'

[4] Kailāçc. reads *phalam asyāneka*,—explaining *asya* as = *mama*.

you, who through the merits of a whole people are born for the protection of all the earth, fathers are a mere expedient to bring you into being. In their people, not in their kin, are kings rich in relatives. Rise therefore, and once more attend to all the needs of life. Not till you have eaten will I myself[1] take my diet.'

At these words the flame of sorrow blazed up still more fiercely in the prince's heart, as if to consume it. One short moment he paused, and then being again[2] charged by his father to take food, he descended from the White House with these thoughts in his mind:—'This great crash[3] has come without warning, like a bolt from a cloudless sky. Even a common grief is a breathing death, a disease without antidote, a plunge into fire without being reduced to ashes, a living abode in hell, a shower of coals without light, a sawing in twain without cleavage, a lancet's stroke that leaves no scar. What then of deeper afflictions? What shall I do now?'

Escorted by one of the king's officers, he proceeded to his own apartments, where he partook of a few mouthfuls, mouthfuls which, as if of smoke, evoked tears, as if of fire awoke a burning in his heart, as if of poison brought on swoons, as if of mortal sin aroused disgust, as if of alkali inflicted pain. While rinsing his mouth, he ordered his chowrie-bearer to fetch tidings of his father's state. Having gone and returned, the man reported that the king still remained as before: whereat the prince in distress of mind rejected the betel, and when the sun inclined to setting, summoned all the physicians in private, and with a despairing heart inquired what steps under such circumstances should be taken. [177] 'Your highness,' they answered, 'reassure yourself: in a very few days your father will be reported restored to his proper self and pristine condition[4].'

Among their number, however, was a young doctor of

[1] Kailāçc. reads for *svayaṃ sukham* 'with an easy mind.'

[2] Kailāçc. reads *punaḥ punar* 'again and again.'

[3] *Mahāpralayo* om. Kailāçc.

[4] *Prakṛiti*, as the comm. observes, is an ominous word, implying 'ante-natal state.'

Punarvasu's race named Rasāyana, a youth of about eighteen years of age, holding an hereditary position in the royal household, in which he had been cherished like a son by the king. He had mastered the Āyur Veda in all its eight divisions, and, being naturally of an acute intellect, was perfectly familiar with the diagnosis of diseases. He now stood silent and tearful with downcast looks. Being appealed to by the prince, 'Friend Rasāyana, tell me the truth, if you see anything at all unpromising,' he replied 'To-morrow at dawn, your highness, I will state the facts of the case[1].'

At that very instant the keeper of the palace lotus pools, comforting a ruddy-goose, chanted aloud an Aparavaktrā couplet:—

> 'Fortify, O bird, thy heart; freely abandon grief; pursue the path of discretion:
> 'With the beauty of the red-lotus pools the sun hies himself to Sumeru's peak.'

Versed in the omens of words, the prince on overhearing this relaxed his hopes for his father's longer life. The physicians gone, he lost all fortitude, and at nightfall went up again to his father's presence, where in anguish of heart he spent a sleepless night prolonged by grief, listening without cessation to his father's cries such as, 'The heat is terrible, bring pearl necklaces, Hariṇī!—place jewelled mirrors on my body, Vaidehī!—anoint my brows, Līlāvatī!, with bits of ice—give me camphor powder, Dhavalākṣī!—apply a moonstone to my eye, Kāntamatī!—set a blue lotus on my cheek, Kalāvatī!—give me a rubbing with sandal, Cārumatā!—[178] make a brisk[2] breeze with a cloth, Pāṭalikā!—assuage the heat with lotuses, Indumatī!—refresh me with wet clothes, Madirāvatī!—bring lotus fibres, Mālatī!—wave a palm leaf, Āvantikā!—bind tight my whirling head[3], Bandhumatī!—support my neck, Dhāraṇikā!—place an ice-cooled hand upon my bosom, Kuraṅgavatī!—shampoo my arms, Valāhikā!—

[1] *Yathāvasthitam* may however be masculine = 'the king's real condition': so Kailāçc. trans.; in the comm. he gives *prakṛitam*.

[2] *Pāṭaya* (Kailāçc. *paṭaya*). *paṭuṃ kuru* 'make brisk.' Comm.

[3] Lit. 'imprison my runaway head.' Kailāçc. notes a var. lec. *bādhamānam*.

squeeze my feet, Padmāvatī!—clasp tight my body, Anaṅgasenā!—what hour? Vilāsavatī!—sleep will not come, tell stories, Kumudvatī!'

At dawn the prince descended, and, though a horse was held in readiness by a groom advancing to the palace door, went on foot to his own quarters. There in hot haste he despatched express couriers and swift camel riders one after another to procure his brother's coming. After washing his (tear-soiled) face he rejected the toilet appurtenances brought by the servants. Hearing from distracted young princes standing before him an indistinct murmur 'Rasāyana, Rasāyana,' he asked 'Well, friends, what of Rasāyana?,' whereat they all at once became silent. Being further pressed, however, they with sorrowful reluctance explained 'Your highness, he has entered fire.' The prince became (ashy) pale, as if scorched by an inner fire, and his grief-blinded heart, torn up by the roots, refused to be steadied. 'A noble man,' he thought, 'would rather not be than like an ordinary person utter unwelcome and distressing words. His generous nature, maintained in trying circumstances, has like unadulterated gold acquired a greater brilliance by entering fire.' Again he thought 'Rather was this to be expected of his love. Was not my father his father, my mother his mother, we his brothers? [179] Even when other masters are taken away, a life retained is a cause of shame in the world: how much more in the case of my auspiciously-named father, who was to his dependants ambrosia itself, a veritable kinsman, unfailing in favours! In burning himself he has acted as the time demanded. Nay, what does fire destroy of him who abides in glory steadfast to the world's end? He has but fallen in the flames; 'tis we who are burnt. Blessed indeed is he, a chief among the fortunate: but hapless this royal house, deprived of such a noble youth. As for me, what exacting task, what relic of duty, what preoccupation prevents this unfeeling life from even now going its way[1]? What hindrance

[1] The Kāshmir text reads *prasthāniṣṭhurāḥ*, perhaps to be taken as one word, 'bent on departing': Kailāçc. has *prasthāḥ* for *prāṇāḥ*. The Comm. (*prasthā . agragāminaḥ*) evidently read *prasthāḥ*.

is there that my heart bursts not in a thousand parts?' Thus sorrow-stricken, he went not to the royal lodging, but disregarding every duty, threw himself upon a couch and remained wrapped in his shawl from head to foot.

Such being the prince's state and the king's condition remaining the same, the hands of the people seemed rivetted to their cheeks, streams of tears modelled upon their eyes, their looks fastened on the ends of the noses, sounds of wailing graven in their ears, lamentations a natural growth upon their tongues, sighs budding on their mouths, syllables of woe painted upon their lips, sorrows stored up in their hearts. Frighted, as it were, by the fire ot scalding tears, sleep dwelt not in the hollows of their eyes: smiles vanished, as if dissipated by the wind of sighs: speech, as if consumed to nothingness by hot pain, went not forward. Even in tales no jests were heard: none knew whither musical parties had gone. Dances were as much forgotten as if they belonged to the past of previous births; even in dreams no finery was used. There was not even a rumour of pleasure: the very name of food was unspoken. Groups in taverns were like flowers in the sky[1]: troubadours' voices seemed conveyed to another world: [180] recreation appeared to belong to a different cycle of existence. Again, it seemed, was Kāma scorched by a fire, that of sorrow: even by day none left their couches. In slow successiou too there appeared in the world portents many and great together on every side, betokening the fall of a lofty spirit and filling all creatures with apprehension of the king's death.

Thus:—first the earth, heaving in all her circle of great hills[2], moved as though she would go with her lord. Next the oceans, as though remembering Dhanvantari[3], rolled

[1] I.e. were non-existent.

[2] The *Kulācala's* are seven in number, viz. *Mahendra* (the Northern parts of the Ghāts), *Malaya* (the Western Ghāts), *Sahya* (Northern parts of Western Ghāts), *Çuktimat* (doubtful), *Ṛikṣaparvata* (Mts. of Gondwāna), *Vindhya*, *Pāriyātra* (Central or Western Vindhya).

[3] Or 'seeking (another) Dhanvantari' to heal the king. Read *Dhănvantarer* with Kailāçc., who also has *āture tasmin* for *antare tasmin.* Dhanvantari was produced at the churning of the Ocean.

with waves noisily plashing upon each other. High in the heavenly spaces, apprehensive of the king's removal, appeared comets like braided locks with awful curls of far-extended flame[1]. Beneath a sky thus lowering with comets the world seemed grey, as with the smoke of a Long Life sacrifice commenced by the sky regents. In the sun's circle, now shorn of its radiance and lurid as a bowl of heated iron, some power, studious of the king's life, had presented a human offering in the guise of a horrid headless trunk. The lord of white effulgence, gleaming 'mid the round rim of his flaming halo, seemed to have raised a rampart of fire in alarm at Rāhu's greedily opening jaws. The quarters, won by the king's valour, glowed red as though they had in anticipation entered fire[2]. All crimsoned with flowing showers of bloody dew, the earth, his spouse, appeared to have shrouded herself in a gown of red cloth to die with him. The portals of the heavens were blocked with untimely masses of dark cloud, as though the regents, fearing the tumult of the monarch's death, had closed their iron door-panels. Loud grew the awful, heart-riving bursts of thunder-storms, crashing like the patter of drums that are beaten at the out-goings of the king of the dead. The sun's brilliance was dimmed by dust-showers brown as camel-hair, which started up, as it were, beneath the hoofs of Yama's approaching buffalo. Rows of jackals lifted high their muzzles in a discordant howl, like firebrands catching fire from flames that fell from the sky[3]. In the royal mansion the images of the family goddesses, [181] whose braided hair at its parting lines gave forth smoke in token of their distress[4], seemed to be mani-

[1] The quarters of the heavens are compared to wives fearing for their husband's death. Widows wear braided hair. *Vitataçikhikalāpa-vikaṭakuṭilāḥ* may punningly mean 'curly and long as a peacock's outspread tail.'

[2] There are puns in *-prasādhitāḥ* (also 'decked in the king's splendour') and *anuraktāḥ* ('red' and 'devoted').

[3] Cf. the name *ulkāmukha*='jackal.' Kailāçc. reads *jvālābhiḥ* for *jvālāḥ*.

[4] Cf. Vergil *Georg.* I. 480 '*Et maestum illacrimat templis ebur aeraque sudant.*'

festing their grief by dishevelled locks[1]. A swarm of bees, ranging feverishly about the Lion Throne, produced the illusion of Kālarātri's[2] tossing plaits of curling hair. Never for an instant ceased the croak of crows hovering above the women's quarter. From the centre of the white umbrella's circle an old vulture, screaming on high, tore with nimble beak a bit of a gem —the kingdom's life as it were—red as a piece of juicy meat.

Distressed by these mighty signs, the prince could scarce live through that night. On the morrow a woman approached from the palace with such a tinkle of ornaments breaking in her hurried advance that she seemed a proclamation of the victory of dismay. The clash of her anklets, as they moved on her hurrying feet, set the craning *haṃsas* of the palace cackling, as if from a (respectful) distance they were asking 'What? What?'; while in a blindness of tears she seemed to learn the way from tame cranes screeching in answer to the girdle, which as she stumbled rang upon her broad hips. Her forehead having been cut in collisions with unnoticed doors, a mass of blood like a red shawl's fringe covered her weeping face. Her cane, which she was casting away, looked like a stream from her golden bracelet, melted apparently by the heat of grief. Her fluttering shawl, waving in the wind of her breath, suggested a snake trailing its slough behind. Hanging over her sloping shoulders, tossed by the wind, and black as strips of *Tamāla* bark, her hair covered her bosom in a dangling unbraided mass in keeping with her grief. As she incessantly waved her hand, which through the pain of beating her breasts was swollen and dark almost like copper in the palm, one might have thought it scorched through wiping away her hot tears. The people near her, imaged in her cheek, she seemed to bathe in her eyes' broken cascade, as if they were soon to enter the fire of sorrow. Under the quivering rays that issued from her restless eyes the very

[1] In times of misfortune the hair of the family goddesses is supposed sometimes to smoke; the smoke is the dishevelled hair.

[2] A form of Durgā: the name (*Kālarātri*='Night of Doom') is used here by reason of its appropriateness. The black strings of bees represent the plaited hair.

day grew black, as if burnt by her grief. It was Velā, Yaçovatī's head attendant, inquiring of everyone[1] where the prince was. [182] Welcomed by the people's despairing looks, she drew near, and letting both hands fall upon the mosaic, so that as she bent her head the rays from her teeth seemed to besprinkle her pallid lips in a falling shower, 'Help, help, my lord,' she cried; 'though her husband lives, the queen has taken a certain resolution.'

At the news of this further grief the prince, as if his strength of mind had given way, as if melted by sorrow, drained by thought, carried off his feet[2] by pain, clasped by alarm to her bosom, lost all power of action. With returning consciousness, 'Callous that I am,' he thought, 'the assault of grief, oft as it falls upon my heart, yet like a hammer's stroke upon hard flint, evokes fire indeed, but reduces not my frame to ashes.' Rising, he went in haste to the women's apartments, where while still at a distance he heard cries like these from queens resolved to die:—'Beloved Mango, take thought to yourself, your mother is seeking another home—I am going, darling jasmine cluster, bid me farewell—Without me, sister pomegranate by the house, you are now to be defenceless—Forgive, red *Açoka*, my kicks[3] and sins in plucking your sprays for ear-ornaments—I see you, seraglio *Vakula*, wayward child as you are become through those mouthfuls of wine—Clasp me tight, dear *Priyaṅgu* creeper; I am passing beyond your reach—Friend Mango at the porch, you must render me the funeral libation of water[4], since you are my child—See you forget me not, brother parrot in your cage! What say you? I am taken away from you—May we meet again, *çārikā*, in dreams—Mother, to whom shall I entrust the tame peacock who clings in my path?—Nurse, you must fondle this pair of *haṃsas* like children—Ah hapless me! not to have enjoyed the marriage festivities of this couple of ruddy-geese—Go back,

[1] Read *pratipuruṣam* with Kailāçc.

[2] *Tulita* is supported by the alliteration: Kailāçc. has *ākulita* 'dumbfounded.'

[3] '*Sanūpuraraveṇa strīcaraṇenābhitāḍanaṃ dohadaṃ yad açokasya tataḥ puṣpodgamo bhaved*' ap. Kailāçc. Cf. *Mālavikāgn.* III.

[4] I.e. the *jalāñjali* offered at a funeral.

fawn deer, mother's darling—Chamberlain, fetch my favourite lute, I must embrace it—Take a good look at me, Candrasenā—Vindumatī, this is my last greeting—[183] Let go my feet, girl—Venerable old widow friend, why do you weep? I am in the hand of fate—Chamberlain, old friend, why pass respectfully round an unlucky woman like me?—Control yourself, foster sister, why do you fall at my feet?—Clasp me by the neck, sister, for the last time—Cruel, I have not seen my dear friend Malayavatī—This humble greeting, Kuraṅgavatī, is for goodbye—Sānumatī, this is my last obeisance—This, Kuvalayavatī, is our final embrace—Pardon, friends, our lovers' quarrels.'

Entering with these sounds burning in his ears, he saw his mother just issuing forth, after giving away all her wealth and assuming the vestments of death, with the purpose of entering the fire, like Sītā, before[1] her lord. Still wet from her recent bath, she resembled the holy Çrī just risen from the ocean. Like the sky with its double twilight tints, she wore two saffron-brown robes. Enveloping her form, like a silken shawl; she wore the tokens of her unwidowed death, reddened by a tissue of light from lips stained with the deep dye of betel[2]. Hanging between her breasts was a red neck-cord, suggesting a stream of blood pouring from a broken heart. Her necklace, the thread of which was drawn aside by the hooked point of a cross-bent earring, seemed a halter of white silk compressing her throat. Her limbs being all aglow with moist saffron paste, she appeared to be swallowed in the pyre's devouring flames, while she filled the bosom of her robe with white tears like flower offerings to its blaze. At every step she scattered in dropping bracelets a kind of farewell present to the family goddesses. From her neck down to her instep hung wreaths of strung flowers, as if she were mounted on a death-swing with garlands for cords.

An ear-lotus resonant with bees humming within seemed to be saluting her lotus eyes. The domestic *haṃsas*, lovers

1 With reference to Sītā 'before' = 'in presence of.'

2 Satīs are burnt in all their ornaments. Kailāçc. reads *avidhavā* separately 'though no widow,' and *-paṭalam pāṭalam.*

of her jewelled anklets, moved in a circle round her, as if to make the ceremonial circuit[1]. Her hand carried a picture representing her husband, which she held as steadfast as her heart, where he dwelt, was fixed on death. Lovingly, like a pennon of wifely love, she clasped her lord's spear-haft, reverently tied with waving strings of white flowers. Before the king's umbrella, spotless as her life, she shed tears as to a kinsman.

She was giving instructions to her husband's ministers, who grasped them with difficulty, their eyes being stopped by torrents of tears that welled up as they fell at her feet. [184] Her ears caught the sound of wailing in the house, where a group of old kinsmen, grieving at their courteous dismissal, were adding to the clamour. The roars of the caged lions took her heart captive, resembling, as they did, her husband's utterance. Her nurse and her conjugal love had combined to beautify her: an old woman and swooning, familiar both, supported her: a friend and agony, comrades in adversity, embraced her: servants and pain were about her, clasping every limb: great princes and sighs attended her[2]: behind came aged chamberlains and heavy griefs. Even upon her husband's favourite hounds she cast a tearful eye: she fell at the feet even of rival queens: to even the painted figures she offered greeting: before even the domestic birds she clasped her hands: to the very brutes she said farewell: she embraced the very trees about the palace.

'Mother,' cried the prince while still afar, his eyes filling with tears, 'do you also abandon hapless me? Be merciful and turn back,' and so in the act of speaking fell at her feet till his crest was almost lovingly kissed by the light of her jewelled anklets. As he lay there with his head touching her feet, her youngest and dearest son in such distraction of mind, the queen Yaçovatī, propped up[3] by a great frenzy of grief like a mountain, carried away into the Tartarean darkness of a swoon, overborne by the full tide of love

[1] Read *pradakṣiṇīkriyamāṇām* with Kailāçc.

[2] Read *kulaputrair ucchvasitaiçca* with Kailāçc.

[3] Cf. Persius Sat. I. 78, '*Antiopa aerumnis cor luctificabile* fulta.'

rising in might like an outburst of accumulated tears long pent up, could not in spite of all her efforts check the torrent of her weeping. Her bosom heaved convulsively, betraying the resistless will of grief: her throat was choked distressfully with sobs: her lip quivered with exceeding agony, and her tightened nostrils repeated the tremor: closing her eyes, she deluged her clear cheeks with flowing rills of tears: then raising her face a little, she covered it with the hem of her shawl, wherein her shining nails showed forth in a row, like a spring of lucid tears welling up through the thin interstices. [185] Loud[1] and long she wept like some mean woman, while with anguished heart and dripping breasts she recalled to mind from the day of his birth all the childish years when he lay in her bosom. Then[2], as her thought recurred to home and kin, full oft she moaned, calling aloud upon her parents, 'Mother! father! look not upon me as a sinner that in my sore affliction I have set out for the other world': crying to her dear elder son far away, 'Alas darling! that I, all ill-fated, see you not': lamenting her daughter, now settled in her father-in-law's house, 'Defenceless are you now': reproaching fate, 'Merciless power, how have I offended?': inveighing in various ways against herself, 'No woman has had such an evil portion as I': suddenly reviling death, 'Remorseless one, thou hast stolen me away!'

When this outburst of grief had died away, she lovingly raised her son, and with her hand wiped his streaming eyes, which, as if melting, seemed to flow only the more[3] when the rays from her nails clustered in masses on his lashes. Her own eyes also she wiped, as, again and again refilling, they were distressed by a trickling succession of tiny drops, while their whiteness, swallowed up by a deep red, departed, their corners were swoln with scalding tears, and their lashes bestarred with pearls[4] of lucid dew. Then she set behind her ear a curl, which, loosened by her distress, clave

[1] *Muktakaṇṭham* 'uncontrollably.'

[2] Insert *ca* with Kailāçc.

[3] Or simply 'in torrents.' The rays are the white tears.

[4] *-tāra-* is omitted by Kailāçc.

to her tear-moistened cheek: pushed aside a mass of tresses entangled with a disordered and fallen ear-ornament: drew back with her hand a shawl which, being wet and filled with a torrent of tears, had somewhat slipped: bathed her lotus face, whose beauty, marked with thin red lines impressed by the shawl's hem, wore a rippled appearance, with water poured from a silver flamingo-mouthed vessel tilted by a hunchbacked girl[1]: wiped her hands on a white cloth held by mutes[2]: stood for some time with her eyes fixed immoveably upon her son's face, and then after many long sighs spoke.

'It is not, dear, that you are unloved, without noble qualities, or deserving to be abandoned. With my very bosom's milk you drank up my heart. If at this hour my regard is not towards you, 'tis that my lord's great condescension comes between us[3]. Furthermore, dear son, [186] I am not, like glory[4] or the earth, incompassionate, a requisite of sovereignty, ever craving for the sight of another lord. I am the lady of a great house, born of a stainless ancestry, one whose virtue is her dower. Have you forgotten that I am the lioness mate of a great spirit, who like a lion had his delight in a hundred battles? Daughter, spouse, mother of heroes, how otherwise could such a woman as I, whose price was valour, act? This hand has been clasped by even such a hero, thy father, a chief among princes, peer of Bharata, Bhagīratha, and Nābhāga. Upon this head have the subservient wives of countless feudatories poured coronation water from golden ewers. This forehead, in winning the honourable fillet of chief-queen, has enjoyed a thing scarce accessible to desire. These breasts have worn robes swayed by the wind of chowries waved by captive wives of foes; they have been sucked by sons like you. Upon

[1] In this clause read with Kailāçc. *taraṅgitam iva ca*, *lāvaṇyaṃ*, and *kubjikā-* for *kuñjikā-*: the two last readings are in the Kashmir text. By a series of puns the queen's face is compared to a lotus, *taraṅgitam* in this connection meaning 'wave-tossed.'

[2] Kailāçc. has *kalamūkakara-* not *loka-*. He also inserts *dhāutadhavale* before *vāsaḥçakale* and reads *pāṇiṃ* for *pāṇī*.

[3] For '*antaritā*' Kailāçc. reads '*antaritam*.' The sense is the same.

[4] Cf. '*çūrasamāgamāikavyasaninyā lakṣmyā*' Kādambarī.

the heads of rival wives have these feet been set; they have been adored with diamond-wreaths of diadems by the bending matrons of a whole capital. Thus every limb has fulfilled its mission: I have spent my store of good works, what more should I look to? I would die while still unwidowed. I cannot endure, like the widowed Rati[1] to make unavailing lamentations for a burnt husband. Going before, like the dust of your father's feet, to announce his coming to the heavens, I shall be high esteemed of the hero-loving spouses of the gods. Nay, what will the smoke-bannered one[2] burn of me, who am already on fire with the recent sight of his heart-rending pains? Not to die, but to live at such a time would be unfeeling. Compared with the flame of wifely sorrow, whose fuel is imperishable love, fire itself is chilly cold. How suits it to be parsimonious of a life light as a bit of rotten straw, when that life's lord, majestic as Kailāsa, is passing away? Even should I live, yet after the mortal sin of slighting the king's death the joys, my son, of my son's rule will touch me not. In those that are consumed by grief felicity[3] is ominous, accursed, and unavailing. Not in the body, dear son, but in the glory of loyal widows[4] would I abide on earth. [187] Therefore dishonour me no more, I beseech you, beloved son, with opposition to my heart's desire.'

So saying she fell at his feet. But the prince hastily drew them away, and bending down, held her in both his arms, and raised her prostrate form. Pondering the inevitableness of grief, deeming that act to be the better part befitting a lady of rank, recognizing her fixed resolution, he stood in silence with downcast looks.

[1] *Çambhunā tu hate kāme tatpatnī ratisañjñitā*
Mumoha purato dṛiṣṭvā patim bhasmāvaçeṣitam ||
Jātasañjñā muhūrttena vilalāpa ha citradhā
Yadvilāpād vane vāpi samaduḥkham abhūt tadā ||.
Kailāçc. from Skanda Purāṇa.

[2] I.e. fire.

[3] There is a pun in *bhūtiḥ*, which may also denote 'ashes.'

[4] *Viçvastānāṃ · vidhavānām* Comm. cf. A.K.

True is it that, even when made timorous by affection, a noble nature resigns itself to what accords with place and time. Having embraced her son and kissed his head, the queen went forth on foot from the women's quarter, and, though the heavens, filled with the citizens' lamentations, seemed to block her path, proceeded to the Sarasvatī's banks. Then, having worshipped the fire with the blooming red lotus posies of a woman's timorous glances, she plunged into it, as the moon's form enters the adorable sun. The other, distracted at his mother's death, departed 'mid a throng of kinsmen to his father's side, and found him with his vital forces nearly spent, revolving his eyeballs as the declining lord of stars (the Moon) revolves his stars. Overcome with excess of intolerable grief, robbed by affection of all self-control, he clasped those lotus feet which had been fondled by the assembled crests of all proud kings; and uttering a cry, burst like a common man into a long fit of weeping, raining from clouded eyes a most pellucid stream of tears. It seemed as if an inner fire were melting his moonlike face, the light-texture of his teeth turning to water, the loveliness of his eyes oozing out, the ambrosia of his countenance trickling away.

The king, whose eyes were closing[1], recovering consciousness as the sound of the prince's ceaseless weeping fell upon his ear, uttered in faint tones these words:—"You should not be so, my son. Men of your mould are not infirm of heart. Strength of soul is the people's mainstay, and second to it is royal blood. With you, the vanguard of the stout-hearted, the abode of all preëminence, what has weakness to do? [188] To say you are the lamp of our line were almost depreciation of one whose brilliance compares with the god of day. To call you a lion among heroes is like a reproach to one whose prowess is seconded by penetrating insight[2]. To

[1] But the commentator explains *uparudhyamānadṛiṣṭir* as 'having his consciousness impeded.' Kailāçc. reads *uparirudhyamana-* 'eyes turned up.'

[2] If we keep *çaurya* (which Kailāçc. omits), it will be 'heroism and penetrating insight.'

declare this earth yours is almost a vain repetition, when your bodily marks proclaim an universal emperor's dignity. To bid you take to yourself glory is almost contradictory, when glory has herself adopted you. 'Succeed to this world' is a command too mean for an intending conqueror of both worlds. 'Appropriate my treasury' is a grant of little service to one whose sole craving is for the accumulation of fame spotless as moonlight. 'Make prize of the feudatory kings' is almost meaningless, when your virtues have made prize of all beings. 'Support the burden of royalty' is an injunction misbecoming one accustomed to support the burden of the three worlds. 'Protect the people' is but reiteration, when the sky has your long arm for its bar. 'Guard well your dependants' is an incidental duty to a peer of the world's Guardians. 'Practise yourself in arms,' to one whose forearm is blackened by the bow-string's callous brand how can this advice be given? 'Check levity' is an utterance without excuse towards one whose senses even in tender years were held in check. 'Annihilate your foes' is a suggestion of your own inborn valour." With these words on his lips the lion king closed his eyes never to open them more.

In that hour the sun too was reft of the brilliance which was *his* life. Ashamed as it were of his own sinfulness involved in the taking of the king's life, he now bent low his face. As if scorched within by a fire of sorrow for the monarch's decease, he assumed a coppery hue. Slowly, slowly he descended from the heavens, as if in compliance with earthly usage to pay a visit of condolence. As though to present an oblation of water to the king, he drew nigh to the western ocean. As soon as the water was presented, his thousand hands became red as if burnt in sorrow's flame. [189]

With radiance thus subdued, as if the mighty emperor's death had brought on a deep distaste for life and colour, the light-coroneted god entered the hollows of the mountain caves[1]. Cool grew his heat, as though moistened by the

[1] Like an ascetic.

gathering storm of the people's tears. The world assumed a lurid tinge, as if from the colour of all humanity's tear-flushed eyes. The day grew black, as if scorched by the heat of countless people's burning sighs. From the day-lotuses their glory departed, as though it had started to follow the king. As the shadows passed on, the earth became dark as with grief for her lord[1]. Like the heirs of noble houses, anguished *cakravākas,* abandoning their wives, resorted with piteous cries to the outskirts of the water[2]. Alarmed as it were at their widowhood, the lotuses hid their treasure chambers[3]. The red glow oozed away, like a bloody flow from the sky-queens' bursting hearts. In due course the lord of splendour had gone to the other world, leaving only the afterglow behind[4]. Like a banner of the dead, the twilight came all ruddy with a lurid expanse spreading far and wide over the heavens. Dusky streaks, like the lines of black chowrie ornaments upon a bier, were seen obstructing the view[5]. A night black in all its quarters was mysteriously built up, like a pyre with black beams of aloe wood[6]. With smiling faces the beauteous night lotuses adorned themselves in ivory-petalled buds and formed for themselves white garlands of wreathed filaments, like wives in readiness to follow their lord to death[7]. Like the tinkling

[1] The puns here turn on the various meanings of *chāyā*=(1) brightness, (2) shadow, and *çyāmā*=(1) black, (2) lady. The puns require the reading *parivṛitṭa-* for *parivṛita-*: the shadows have retraced their course eastwards.

[2] Or 'vicinity of the woods': cf. Comm. *vanaṃ · toyaṃ vipinaṃ ca.* The nobles seek the woods, the birds the water.

[3] The lotuses are compared to queens, who, alarmed by the breaking of the royal umbrella (implying the king's death), hide their treasures (*koça*=(1) buds, (2) treasures). *Chattrabhaṅga* also refers to the umbrella-like leaves fading.

[4] As the king himself had gone, leaving only affection behind.

[5] *Darçanapratikūlāsu* taken with the chowries will mean 'ominous to view.'

[6] Or—with the night—'black in its quarters as aloe wood.'

[7] 'Beauteous night lotuses' may also punningly mean 'night lotuses like Satīs': 'ivory-petalled buds' (='buds with petals white as ivory') also means 'earrings of ivory.'

bells of the gods' descending chariot were heard the voices of birds settling in their nests in the tree tops. In the eastern quarter the moon appeared in sight, like the umbrella of Indra come forth to welcome the king on his journey along the heavens.

At that hour the feudatories and townsmen headed by the family priest, taking upon proffered shoulders [190] the bier of this Çivi-like[1] king, bore him to the river Sarasvatī, and there upon a pyre befitting an emperor solemnly consumed all but his glory in the flames. As for my lord Harṣa, through all that night, terrible as Bhīmarathī[2], he sat with the princes sleepless on the uncushioned ground, surrounded by all the connections of the royal household in a dumb sorrowing company like an universal assemblage of living beings; while his tears rained down like an outpouring of the flood of affection which, heated by sorrow's fire, flowed only within. In his heart he thought:—'Now that my father is taken away, the world of the living has reached its goal: a chasm sunders the progress of mankind; the eldorados of desire are laid desolate, veiled are the portals of joy. Truthfulness is lulled to sleep, the people's livelihood is made a spoil, vanished is the love of heroism, sweet speech annihilated. Banished are all kinds of manly sports, ended is delight in battle, pleasure in the virtue of others is laid low, men of trust are an exhausted stock. No place is there for great feats, no profit in the Çāstras, no prop for the spirit of heroism, discernment is passed into a legend. Let men offer water[3] to might, let the protection of the people go a begging, let chivalry bind her widow's braid, let sovereign glory flee to a hermitage[4], let

[1] Çivi gave up a part of his own flesh to save a pigeon from a hawk.

[2] *Bhīmarathī* = 'the night of doomsday,' or 'that night in a man's life which follows upon 77 years, months, and days,' or, according to the commentator, 'a river in hell.'

[3] Sc. as at a funeral.

[4] The words *samāçrayatu rājyaçrīr āçramapadam* are, as Kailāçc. observes, ominous of *Rājyaçrī's* fortunes, since they may also mean 'let R. flee to a hermitage.'

the earth array herself in two white robes[1], let merriment wear a pair of bark dresses, let valour mortify herself in forest seclusions, let heroism put on rags. Whither now must gratitude go to seek him? Where again will the creator get such atoms for the construction of great spirits? The ten regions now find themselves empty of virtue, the world has become a darkness unlighted by duty, fruitless now is the birth of those who live by the sword. Without my father whence are to come those gatherings of heroes when throughout the day the cheeks of warriors bristle as stories go round full of the delight of famous fights? Would that even in a dream I might once more see his lotus face with its long red eyes[2]! [191] Even in another birth might I but clasp again those arms more massive than pillars of steel! Even in another world might I but hear his voice, deep as the roar of the churned Milk Ocean, calling me "son" in accents like a torrent of ambrosia.'

While the prince was engaged in these and other meditations, the night drew drearily enough to a close. Anon the cocks began to clamour wildly, as if in grief. The courtyard peacocks precipitated themselves from the tops of the trees on the garden mounts[3]. The birds, forsaking their homes, started forth for the forest. The gloom suddenly grew thin and swooned away. The lamps, as their oil[4] failed, inclined towards extinction. Robed in the bright red bark dress of the dawn, the sky seemed to have betaken itself to a mendicant's life. Like the fragments of the king's bones, the stars, all grey as a swallow's neck, were being gathered up by the appearance of morning[5]. Droves of wild elephants, their humps covered with mountain minerals[6], had set out towards divers pools, rivers, and fords. Like a

[1] Sc. like a widow.

[2] Or—of the lotus—'buds.'

[3] Or—for the sake of the implied simile—'houses, hills and trees.'

[4] Or—punningly—'self-love.'

[5] Read *samuccīyamanāsu* with Kailāçc. *Prabhātasamayena* may also be translated 'by the morning ceremony of gathering the bones' (*asthicayana*).

[6] Or—punningly—'having pots filled with the king's ashes.'

funeral *piṇḍa* ball of pure white rice[1], the moon dropped upon the verge of the western ocean's sand isle. Gradually his light paled, as if through the smoke which spread from the king's flaming pyre; in his heart appeared a blackness as of a dark scar due to his burning sorrow for the king: chastened in mien as it were by the agony depicted in the moon-like[2] faces of the departed monarch's whole harem, and distracted with yearning for his already vanished Rohiṇī, he drew nigh to his setting. Like my lord the king[3], the sun had mounted the heavens, and like the sovereignty, the course of night had changed.

Roused by the appeals of groups of wise kings, like the lotus beds by awaking flamingos, my lord Harṣa started up, and passed with eyes aflame out of the palace. In the women's apartments only a few sorrow-stricken chamberlains were left, and the domestic *haṃsas* were dumb and inert now that the tinkle of anklets had ceased. In the court[4] stood his father's servants, like a herd of wild elephants whose leader is fallen. Near his post the king's sorrowing elephant lay motionless and dull with his rider weeping on his back. [192] The royal steed occupied the stable yard, as might be known[5] from the lamentations of the marshal. In the empty audience chamber the clamorous cry of 'Victory' was still. Thus the prince passed on to the Sarasvatī's bank, and having bathed in the river, offered water to his father. After the funeral bath, he stayed not to wring his hair, but having put on a pair of white silk robes, proceeded home full of sighs, umbrella-less, with none to clear his path, and, though a horse was led up, on foot: while his eyes, flushed like a red lotus and rivetted to the end of his nose, seemed vomiting forth his sorrow's flame for fear of burning his father, who now

[1] Or—with the moon—'pale as a ball of pure white wax.' Kailāçc. inserts *çarvaryām* 'at night.'

[2] *Vidrāṇa*, as before, ='stupefied.' *Proṣita* may perhaps go with *purandhri*, if on pp. 149 sqq. all the queens enter fire.

[3] Read *rājanīva* (for *rājatīva*) with Kailāçc.

[4] *Kakṣyā* may also denote the elephant's girth cord: so Kailāçc.

[5] *-kathite*. Kailāçc. reads *-kvathite* 'anguished' and mentions *-vyathite* 'distressed' as an alternative.

survived only in his heart, and his lower lip, though unstained by betel and now for a long time washed clean, yet, being naturally red as a spray of the tree of Paradise, appeared by its colour, as the hot sighs came forth, to emit lumps of flesh and blood from a cloven heart.

On the same day the king's favourite servants, friends, and ministers, whose hearts were held tight by the bonds of his many virtues, went forth, and in spite of the remonstrances of tearful friends, abandoned their loved wives and children. Some consigned themselves[1] to precipices: some stationed themselves at holy fords in the neighbourhood. Some in agony of heart spread couches of grass, and quieted their great sorrow by abstinence from food: some, beside themselves with passionate grief, plunged like moths into the flame. Some, in whose hearts burnt a fire of fierce pain, took vows of silence and sought refuge on the mount of snows: some to cool their heat lay on couches of twigs along the Vindhya slopes, where wild elephants bedewed their bodies with a shower bath from their trunks. Some, indisposed for a courtier's life, abandoned the gratifications within their reach, and lived on a limited diet[2] in vacant forest openings: some by feeding on air became emaciated[3] hermits, rich only in virtue. Some assumed red robes and studied the system of Kapila in the mountains: some, tearing off their crest jewels, bound the ascetic's knot upon their heads, and made Çiva their refuge: others [193] by enveloping themselves in trailing pale-red rags displayed the bright afterglow of their love. Others again reached old age in sylvan hermitages, where the deer licked their forms with the ends of their tongues[4]: others finally took vows, and roamed as shaven monks, bearing water in pots and in the

[1] For *babandhuḥ* Kailāçc. has *babhañjuḥ*. For the custom cf. Daçak. *Pūrvapīṭhikā ucchvās.* 4 *sub init.*

[2] Or as the commentator (*piṇḍakāiḥ · çarīrāih*) suggests 'with emaciated frames.'

[3] Lit. 'with prominent veins.'

[4] Kailāçc. has *jihvātala* 'surface of their tongues.'

hollows of their eyes, both equally red in colour and rubbed by their hands.

My lord Harṣa's condition underwent no change. Wild with grief for his father, he turned away from all the avocations of life, regarding glory as a curse, the earth a mortal sin[1], royalty a disease, pleasures serpents, home a hell, family ties a bondage, life an infamy, the body an infliction, health a blot, vigour a result of sin, food a poison, poison ambrosia, sandal a flame, love a saw, heartbreak a felicity. He was closely attended by young nobles of ancient houses, which had enjoyed the favour of the court for generations, venerable trusted advisers wearing an inherited dignity, old Brāhmans versed in Çruti, Smṛiti and Itihāsa[2], anointed counsellors of royal rank endowed with learning, birth and character, approved ascetics well trained in the doctrine of the Self, sages[3] indifferent to pain and pleasure, Vedāntists skilled in expounding the nothingness of the fleeting world, mythologists expert in allaying sorrow. Under their influence the prince was never allowed even in thought to follow[4] the dictates of grief, and through their solicitations he gradually lost his distaste for food and the other dues of life. His thoughts recurring to his brother, thus he mused:—"Pray heaven my brother, when he learns of our father's death, a type of the world's dissolution, may not after a bath of tears assume two robes of bark! or seek [194] a hermitage as a royal sage! or, man-lion as he is, enter a mountain cave! Though his lotus eyes brim with a flood of tears, may he yet look upon the lordless

1 Whence the contagion of governing it would excite disgust.

2 Kailāçc. here inserts *adhigatanikhilajinavacanaviditaviparītabhavasthitayo dharmadeçanāpaṭīyāṃsaḥ pārāçariṇaḥ* 'mendicants skilled in inculcating Dharma and acquainted by knowledge of Buddha's teaching in full with the contradictions in men's notions of life.'

3 Here Kailāçc. has in place of *munayaḥ* '*samāçritāḥ sanābhayaḥ cittajñāçca pradhānasacivāḥ niṣkāraṇabāndhavāçca munayaḥ*' 'sympathising dependent kinsmen, great ministers expert in reading people's thoughts, and sages who acted as disinterested kinsmen.' This agrees with the Comm.'s *sanābhayaḥ · sagotrāḥ*, which has no reference to the Calc. or Kashm. text.

4 Kailāçc. reads *çokānupravaṇam anucaritum* 'to act in pursuance of headlong grief.' This also was read by the Comm.

earth[1]! Tormented by the poisonous pangs of a first loss, may the best of men yet remember himself[2]! Never may indifference due to the transitoriness of things lead him to slight the advances of sovereign glory! All aflame with the fire of direful pain, may he have recourse to the coronation bath! Once arrived here may he not, when pressed by the kings, display a contrary mind! True, my noble brother was deeply devoted to his sire. He was for ever singing to me our father's praises[3], 'Think you, Harṣa, that any man ever did or will possess such a stately frame, tall as a golden palm[4], such a great lotus of a face with its upturned looks abloom all day with ove for the sun's rays[5], such stave-like arms, bright as diamond pillars, such smiles mocking the grace of the lazy sot Haladhara? What other is high-minded, valiant, and generous?'" Amid these and other thoughts he could scarce pass the time, waiting with longing heart for his brother's advent.

Here ends the fifth chapter—entitled The Death of The Great King —of the Harṣa-Carita composed by Çrī Bāṇa Bhaṭṭa.

[1] Kailāçc. with the Comm. understands a negative here and translates 'may he not consider the earth helpless': but?

[2] 'Remember me' Kailāçc. (trans.).

[3] For '*-çlāghayā mām*' Kailāçc. reads *-çlāghāyām*. The Kashmir text has the unintelligible *-çlāghayā mām*.

[4] Kailāçc. reads *punaḥ* (sic) *vapuḥ kāñcanatālataruprāṃçupramāṇam* for *punaḥ kāñcanatālataruprāṃçu kāyapramāṇam*. The Kashmir text agrees with Kailāçc. except that it omits *vapuḥ*.

[5] An allusion to his devotion to the sun, cf. c. IV. For '*divasam unmukhavikasitam mukhamahākamalam*' Kailāçc. has *divasamunmukhaṃ vikasitam mukhakamalam*. The Kashmir text agrees with those of Calcutta and Bombay.

CHAPTER VI.

195] Even as a conqueror, Death gathers his troop of heroes,
Assembling them from this place and that on the earth, sending forth his own secret emissaries to bring them in.
The sin of smiting the confiding rouses the anger of the mighty to the destruction of the cruel one,
As the twang of the sapling which an elephant breaks robs the lion of his sleep.

The Brāhman who consumes the departed spirit's first oblation had now partaken of his meal. The horror of the days of impurity had passed. The various appurtenances of the royal bier[1], beds, chairs, chowries, umbrellas, vessels, carriages, swords and the like, now become an eyesore, were in course of distribution to Brāhmans. The bones, in shape like sorrow's spearheads[2], had been carried with the people's hearts to sacred fords. A monument in brick had been set up on the sepulchral pile. The royal elephant, victor in mighty battles, had been abandoned to the woods. Gradually the lamentations subsided, the outcries became rarer, the tears ceased to flow; the sighs were less vehement, the exclamations of despair sank to a murmur, the couches of despondency began to disappear. Ears were now capable of listening to reason, hearts in a mood to be heedful of kind attentions, the king's virtues could now be computed. Grief

[1] Read *nṛipatikaṭa-* with the Kashmir text for *nṛipanikaṭa-*.

[2] Read *kalpitaçokaçalyeṣu* with the Kashmir text. The fragments of bone are spearheads in the people's hearts.

was becoming a moral theme[1], the poet's pathos[2] had had its day. Only in dreams was the king present to the eye, only in hearts did he reside, only pictures retained his outline [196], only poetry preserved his name.

At this season my lord Harṣa, having on a certain occasion laid aside his occupations, saw himself unexpectedly surrounded by a great company of silent downcast nobles headed by the whole assemblage of his aged kinsmen. At this spectacle he reflected, 'What else can it be? This sorrow-stricken throng of people announces my dear lord's arrival,' and so with a tremour at his heart questioned one of them, a man of distinguished bearing, as he entered, 'Come, speak; is my noble brother arrived?' 'As your majesty says,' he slowly answered, 'he is at the door': whereat the prince, whose mind was softened with supreme sorrow added to[3] brotherly affection, all but poured out his life along with a gushing torrent of tears.

Anon, heralded by lamentations, which, uttered[4] by the chamberlain, entered like servants in advance, the elder brother came in sight amid a throng of servants pale and worn with many days' neglect of bathing, eating and sleeping, and reduced in numbers by their long and rapid march. Only one or two, chiefly domestics, could be distinguished. The umbrella-bearer was wanting, the superintendent of the wardrobe lagged behind, the pitcher-carrier had collapsed, the spittoon-bearer was prostrate, the betel-bearer panted, and the sword-bearer limped. The prince's form was grey all over with the dust of the roads, as though his helpless heritage[5], the earth, had made him her refuge. Long white bandages, bound about arrow-wounds received in battle while conquering the Hūṇas, dotted his form like side-glances from his approaching royal glory. Limbs emaciated, as though for

[1] *Pradeçavṛittitām āçrayati* '*declamatio fiebat.*'

[2] *Kavirudites̤u = duhkhoddīpanakāleṣu* 'occasions for kindling grief afresh.'

[3] *Nihita* lit. 'placed in': there is probably a pun, the fire of sorrow (*manyu*) being placed in the oil of affection.

[4] Or—punningly with reference to the servants—'admitted.'

[5] *Kramāgatayā* contains a pun 'gathered on his way.'

the preservation of the king's life he had offered their flesh in sorrow's fire, told of the heaviness[1] of his grief. Upon his crestless head, with its hair miry and disordered and its jewel gone, he seemed to bear grief visibly enthroned. His forehead, lined by sweat oozing under the heat, appeared to weep with yearning to fall at his father's feet. With a broad river of tears he ceaselessly bedewed the earth, as though it had swooned on the death of its honoured lord. His grief-worn cheeks seemed channelled[2] by the fall of that incessant stream of tears. [197] From his round lips the betel stain had faded away, as if they were melted through coming in the way of his burning breath[3]. Darkened by the rays of his sapphire ornament, of which only the amulet was left, the region of his ear seemed burnt by a great flame of sorrow at the recent news of his father's death. Though his beard showed but a faint growth, yet his face, being fringed with a tassel of rays from the dark pupils of his fixed downcast eyes, looked black with the long growth of mourning. He was as a lion distressed and left without a refuge by the fall of a great hill[4], like the day turned into darkness and faded in splendour by the setting of the lord of light, like Nandana robbed of its shade by the crash of its tree of Paradise[5], like a quarter of the heavens vacant through the exile of its sky elephant, like a mountain quivering and rent by a crushing thunderbolt[6]. Purchased by leanness, made a bondsman to misery, a domestic to despair, a disciple to the demands of grief, appropriated by affliction, dumb with taciturnity, pressed down by depression, all a sweat through hot pain,

[1] There is an oxymoron in the antithesis between the emaciation of the limbs and the heaviness of the grief.

[2] 'And many a furrow on my grief-worn cheek
Has been a channel for a flood of tears.' Moss.

[3] The commentator, who explains *adharavimbenāpi* as instrumental of circumstance, must have read this in place of *adharavimbenopalakṣitam*.

[4] Or 'king.'

[5] *Kalpapādapo* may also mean 'king,' and *vichāyam* 'reft of splendour.'

[6] Or 'by the fall of a thunderbolt upon his sire.'

culled by melancholy, looted by lamentation, adopted[1] by apathy, renounced by presence of mind, disowned by discernment, repudiated by resolution, he was absorbed in a sorrow beyond the appeals of the counsels of age, the cure of good men's eloquence, the scope of sages' voices, the power of holy writ, the course of wisdom's efforts, the range of friendly offices, the sphere of sense delights, the province of gradual repair[2].

Uplifted, as it were, on an agitated sea of stormy surging love[3], Harṣa rose excitedly to meet him. But his majesty Rājyavardhana, on seeing him at a distance, felt inclined to let loose his long-stemmed torrent of tears. Extending his long stout arms, as if he would make an armful of all his sorrows, he clasped his brother's neck in abandonment of grief and drawing him now to his own worn unshawled bosom, [198] now to his neck, now to his shoulder, now to his cheek, sobbed with such violence that their hearts were almost uprooted with their moorings. The king's favourite also, as his sovereign was recalled to his mind, responded like an echo with vehement sobs. It was long before the elder brother's tears ceased to flow, and, like the rain-god in autumn, he very gradually calmed himself. Then he sat down, and, water being brought by a servant, bathed his eyes, which seemed to derive the foam line of a great torrent from the massed light of the man's nails, and, often as they were wiped, were robbed of vision by drops of tears, which, forming at the end of their lashes, impeded their opening. Then with a piece of moonlight in the shape of a towel[4] presented by the betel-bearer he wiped his face, which the hot tears had scorched. Having spent some time in utter silence, he rose and proceeded to the bath house. After a stay there he roughly wrung his unadorned locks of dishevelled and disordered hair; and with a lip which, as the remnant of its quivering emotion struggled as it were for existence, seemed to wish to

[1] Read *vṛitam* 'chosen' for the sake of the alliteration.
[2] Perhaps we should read *kālakramāpacayānām* 'gradual decrease.'
[3] For the pun on *utkalikā* 'agitation' and 'wave' cf. text p. 42 l. 9.
[4] Its whiteness and coolness are compared to moonlight.

kiss even itself now glorified by the bath, with bathed eyes whose whiteness seemed to adore the sky regents with a dropping flower offering of white[1] lotus petals opening to the autumn moon, he threw himself upon a couch placed on the courtyard terrace and having a cushion disposed beneath a low awning. There he remained without uttering a word.

My lord Harṣa also bathed and reclined in silence by his side, stretched on a blanket laid upon the ground. Glancing ever and anon upon his afflicted elder brother, he felt his heart almost split into a thousand parts. For the sight of a brother is a rejuvenescence of sorrow. To the people that day was terrible even beyond the day of their king's death. Throughout the city none cooked, none bathed, none took their pleasure; in every quarter there was no man but wept. Not otherwise did the day pass by[2]. [199] At length, hued like flesh moistened by a great flow of blood—as if he had just been shaped by Twaṣṭṛi's axe[3]—the sun sank, red as madder, in the waters of the western sea. On the (red) lotus ponds the bee tribes buzzed in distress at the closing of the calixes. Anguished by the grief of their spouses at their approaching separation, a horizon of ruddy-geese fixed a tearful gaze upon their dear friend, the sun's orb[4], now hued like a blooming *Bandhūka.* Musical with bees, graced by *kalahaṃsa* beauties, the (night) lotus pools gave forth a sound like the plaited bells upon the jewelled girdle of the roaming Çrī. In the firmament the rising clear-flecked moon shone like the pointed hump of Çiva's tame bull, when blotted with mud scattered by his broad horns.

At that hour, being solicited by the chief feudatories, who approached with inoffensive[5] admonitions, Rājyavar-

[1] Read *viçada* for *viṣada.*

[2] Owing doubtless to the recurrence of *divasaḥ* this passage from 'Throughout' to 'pass by' is omitted by the Kashmir text.

[3] Twaṣṭṛi was the artist of the gods. For the story cf. Wilson's Hindu Drama, vol. I. p. 363.

[4] The pairs of ruddy-geese spend the night on different sides of the river wailing to each other.

[5] Or perhaps 'not to be resisted.'

dhana reluctantly consented to take food. Dawn having appeared and all the kings being admitted, he addressed himself to Harṣa, who was standing near, as follows:—"My dear brother, your situation invites instruction from your elders. Even as a boy you held fast to our father's habits of thought, as to the oriflamme of the virtuous[1]. Wherefore to one so tractable my heart, softened to compliance with the decrees of fate, has something to suggest. Do not revert to the gaucherie so easy to the nature of the young and so much at variance with affection. Do not like a dullard make opposition to my wish. You are surely not unacquainted with the universal practice. What did Purukutsa when Māndhātṛi, the three worlds' protector, died? What Raghu on the death of Dilīpa, whose brow governed the eighteen continents? What Rāma on the death of Daçaratha, who in the great Asura battle mounted the chariot of the gods? What Bharata on the death of Duṣyanta, to whom the confines of the four oceans were but a cow's puddle[2]? Enough of these: [200] did not our father himself undertake the government on the decease of his auspiciously named sire, who by the pervading smoke of more than a hundred sacrifices turned the prime of Indra grey[3]? Moreover the man whom grief subdues the learned term coward: for women are the province of sorrows. Still what am I to do? It is some native cowardice or womanishness which has rendered me subject to the flame of filial grief. My mountain[4] being laid low, my tears are all set flowing like torrents. The great splendour sunk, the lamp of wisdom is vanished from my darkened prospect. My heart is on fire, and discernment, as if apprehensive of being itself scorched, visits it never even in sleep. All my manhood is melted like a thing of lac by a mighty flame of pain. At every word[5] my mind faints like

[1] Or punningly 'a pennon with a cord.'

[2] For *goṣpada* cf. Hesiod 'Works and Days,' 489.

τῆμος Ζεὺς ὕοι τρίτῳ ἤματι, μηδ' ἀπολήγοι,
μήτ' ἄρ' ὑπερβάλλων βοὸς ὁπλὴν μήτ' ἀπολείπων.

[3] A reference to the myth that Indra feared to be displaced by any one who should perform a hundred horse-sacrifices.

[4] Or 'king.' [5] Or 'step.'

a deer smit with a poisoned shaft. Like a misanthrope, my memory roves in devious wanderings. My firmness has, like our mother, departed with our sire. Daily my sorrows increase, like moneys employed by an usurer. My body, as if laden with a cloud born of the smoke of sorrow's flame, rains down a pouring drizzle of tears. 'At death every man[1] is dissolved into the five elements' is no true saying of the childish folk. Our father is become fire only, since he burns me so. The o'ermastering rebel, grief, having penned this recreant heart of mine, burns it as the submarine fire the ocean, rends it as the thunderbolt the hill, attenuates it as waning the moon, and devours it as Rāhu devours the sun. My heart [201] cannot with mere tears dismiss the fall of so noble a spirit, stately as Sumeru. At sovereignty my eye grows disordered, like the partridge's at poison[2]. My mind seeks to avoid a glory, which, as if belonging to outcasts, is of no noble sort, banner-borne, crimson of hue[3], turbaned with many shrouds of the dead. Like the house sparrow, I cannot endure to abide even a moment in a home which has become a hell[4]. I desire therefore in a hermitage to purge with the pure waters of pellucid streams that run from mountain tops this fond defilement which clings to my mind as to a garment. Therefore do you receive from my hands the cares of sovereignty, a gift not high esteemed indeed and reft of the joy of youth, like old age, which Pūru welcomed at his father's will[5]. Dismissing all the sports of youth, deliver your bosom like Viṣṇu to the embraces of Glory[6]. I have abandoned the sword." So speaking, he took

[1] *Pañcajana* 'people of the five races,' cf. the *pañca janāḥ* of the Ṛig-V.

[2] The partridge's eye is said to 'grow red' (*viraktam* also 'disgusted') on seeing poison. See Kullūka, Manu, vii. 217.

[3] The Sanskrit words may here mean 'of no Aryan lineage, outcast from pure birth, polluting assemblies'; or perhaps 'destined to be borne on the poles of outcasts.'

[4] Or 'a burnt habitation.'

[5] Yayāti, being afflicted by Indra with the curse of old age, prevailed upon his son Pūru to take the affliction upon himself.

[6] The allusion is to the youthful sports of Kṛiṣṇa with the shepherdesses before Lakṣmī became his wife.

his scimitar from the hand of his sword-bearer and flung it on the earth.

At this speech Harṣa's heart was cloven as with the stroke of a sharp-pointed spear, and he reflected: "Can my lord have been angered when away from me by a hint received from some envious wretch? Or is he seeking in this way to try me? Or is this a mental aberration born of grief? Is this perchance not my dear brother, or has he possibly said one thing and my sorrow-vacant sense apprehended another? Did he intend one thing while another escaped his lips? Is this a stratagem of fate for the downfall and ruin of our whole house, [202] an intimation of the failure of all the garnered merit of my deeds, or a freak of a whole horizon of disastrous stars? Or is it a pleasantry of the Kali age, heedless of my sire's death, that this man has, like the vilest of mankind, instigated me, as one ready for any deed, to this atrocious act, as if I were no child of Puṣpabhūti's line, no son of our sire, no younger brother of his own, void of affection and detected in fault? 'Tis like bidding a divine drink wine, a faithful servant outrage his master, a good man have dealings with the low, a chaste wife forget her honour. Thus much indeed is seemly, that on the death of so noble a sire,—a Mandara for churning like an ocean the whole ring of feudatories drunk with the intoxication of valorous frenzy,—a man should seek a hermitage, don the bark dress, and practise austerities. But as for this charge of sovereignty, it is like a rain of cinders on a drought-parched wilderness, scorching one already scorched. This is unworthy of my lord. Again, although in this world a prince without pride, a Brāhman without greed, a saint without anger, an ape without tricks, a poet without envy, a trader without knavery, a fond husband without jealousy, a good man free from poverty, a rich man without harshness, a poor man not an eyesore, a hunter without cruelty, a mendicant with a Brāhman's learning[1], a contented servant, a grateful dicer, a wandering ascetic without gluttony, a

[1] Or perhaps 'an orthodox Brāhman.'

misanthrope with a soft tongue[1], a truthful minister, and a king's son without vice are all equally hard to find, yet my lord himself has been my instructor. Who, I wonder, with such a father, a very scent-elephant among kings, fallen, with such a royal elder brother going in his young manhood to a hermitage, abandoning his throne, and rendering sterile his great pillar-like thighs and arms, could desire the clod called earth, defiled by the tears of all men's eyes, or, even were he an outcast, could court that bawd of the deeds of warrior families entitled Glory, whose low character is betrayed by the tokens of the distorted features of all the vile parasites who hang about the drunken game of wealth? How did such a deeply degrading thought enter my lord's imagination? [203] What is this blemish observed in me? Has Sumitrā's son[2] faded from his mind? Have Vṛikodara and others been forgotten? Not thus heedless of those who love him, thus singly fixed upon achieving his own ends, used my lord's high preëminence to be. Again, my lord being gone to a hermitage, who indeed could so long for life as even to entertain a thought of the earth? The lion has a countenance all glorious with a handsome mane clotted with the ichor from the heads of mad elephants which his paw, terribly arrayed with claws sharp as the points of a thunderbolt, has felled: but when he has gone forth to take his pleasure in the forest, who is left to guard his dwelling in the mountain cave? for a hero's ally is his prowess. Why is my lord thus considerate to the jilt glory as not to lead her disguised as old age, like a woodland fawn, to that same hermitage, with rags to hide her bosom, and laden with bundles of *Kuça* grass, flowers, fuel, and leaves[3]? But what avail these vain and manifold reasonings? in silence

[1] The Comm. *gopyo-dāsaḥ* points to the reading of the Kashmir text, which omits *parivrāḍ abubhukṣuḥ* and has *gopyaḥ* in place of *nṛiçaṃsaḥ*.

[2] Alluding to the far-famed younger brothers of the Rāmāyaṇa and Mahābhārata, Lakṣmaṇa and Bhīma.

[3] I.e. 'Why not wait till you are old?' It was not unusual for Hindu kings to retire in old age to hermitages.

will I follow in his train. And the sin involved in transgressing my elder's commands austerity in fine shall dispel in a hermitage." So reflecting, he stood silent and downcast, in spirit gone first to the hermitage.

By this the weeping Keeper of the Robes had provided bark dresses, as previously ordered. The women of the royal household were screaming, as if their hearts[1] had left them in alarm at the heavy strokes which their hands dealt (upon their breasts). Brāhmans with uplifted arms were wailing aloud in horror[2]. With doleful cries a group of citizens were engaged in bending before the princes' feet. Ancient courtiers ran away with tumult in their hearts. Aged kinsmen leaning on servants entered with trembling forms, disordered apparel, grief-choked voices, streaming eyes, and hearts bent on remonstrance. Despondent feudatories sighed, as prostrate they marked the jewelled mosaic with their nails. All the people had started with their children and aged to forest seclusions.

Suddenly a distinguished servant of Rājyaçrī, [204] Saṃvādaka by name, entered with flowing tears in a bewilderment of grief. Uttering a cry, he precipitated himself into the audience. Thunderstruck at this, Rājyavardhana and his brother questioned him with their own lips: "Speak, friend! speak; what stroke more unmanning than the present is fate, triumphant at the king's death, bringing upon us, in pursuance of her resolve to increase her efforts for our ruin?" "My lord," the man with an effort replied, "it is the way of the vile, like fiends, to strike where they find an opening. So, on the very day on which the king's death was rumoured, his majesty Grahavarman was by the wicked lord of Mālwa cut off from the living along with his noble deeds. Rājyaçrī also, the princess, has been confined like a brigand's wife with a pair of iron fetters kissing her feet, and cast into prison at Kānyakubja. There is moreover a report that the villain, deeming the army leaderless, purposes to invade and seize this country as well. Such are my tidings: the matter is now in the king's hands."

[1] I.e. senses. [2] *Abrahmaṇyam.*

Instantly at the news of such a fresh, sudden, unexpected, unimagined disaster the overwhelming passion of sorrow, rooted as it was, vanished from a heart previously unacquainted even by hearsay with humiliation, naturally impatient of checks from outside, filled with the pride of early manhood, claiming a birth from a heroic line, and devoted to a sister now suddenly an object of compassion. An awful paroxysm of wrath leapt fiercely into the recesses of Rājyavardhana's heart, like a lion into his cavernous abode. On his broad brow a deadly frown broke forth, darkening like Yama's sister[1] and like her wavy with wrinkled lines that writhed like Kāliya's brood in their fright at Keçin's destroyer[2]. His left hand, proudly stroking his right shoulder[3], huge as a sky-elephant's frontal hump, rained down upon it a torrent of rays from its own nails, as if to consecrate it for the enterprize of battle toils. [205] His right, whose palm filled with oozing sweat—just as though he had seized the Mālwa's hair to tear him up by the roots—and which trembled as if with yearning to grasp wanton glory's tresses, glided once more toward his terrible sword. On his cheeks appeared an angry flush, as if Sovereignty, delighted by his taking up arms, were celebrating an ovation by scattered vermilion powder[4]. His upturned right foot climbed his left thigh, as if, all kings being in his presence, it were filled with the pride of trampling upon their array of diadems. Imprinted on the jewelled mosaic, his left foot through the desperate twitching of his toes spat out a smoke, as though he would spout a flame to leave the earth widowed of men. His fresh wounds, bursting in his fierceness, spurted a bloody dew, as if to awake his valour sent by the poison of sorrow to sleep. Thus he addressed his younger brother: "This task, my noble brother, is my royal house, this my kin, my court, my land, my

1 The river Yamunā.

2 I.e. Kriṣṇa, see Viṣṇu Pur. v. 16.

3 The Comm. takes *koça* as an oath at an ordeal; but it seems here used as an expletive, cf. *bāhudaṇḍa*.

4 The people sprinkle red powder on one another at the Holi festival and at other rejoicings, cf. Kathās. 18. 122.

people guarded by their king's club-like arm: this day I go to lay the royal house of Mālwa low in ruin. The repression of this beyond measure unmannerly foe—this and no other is my assumption of the bark dress, my austerities, my stratagem for dispelling sorrow. Mālwas to maltreat the race of Puṣpabhūti!—this is the hind clutching the lion's mane, the frog slapping the cobra, the calf taking the tiger captive, the water-serpent grasping Garuḍa by the throat, the log bidding burn the fire, the darkness hiding the sun! My pain has vanished before a more vehement passion. Let all the kings and elephants stay with you. Only Bhaṇḍi here must follow me with some ten thousand horse." So speaking, he ordered the marching drum instantly to sound.

Hearing this command, my lord Harṣa, inflamed as he was with a fit of anger at the tidings of his sister's and brother-in-law's fate, felt his loving agony grow, as it were, to a greater height at the order to remain behind. [206] Speaking out, "What harm," he asked, "does my lord see in my attending him? If I am regarded as a boy, then I should all the more not be abandoned: if as needing protection, the cage of your arms is an asylum; if incompetent, where have I been tried? if in want of fostering care, separation makes thin; if unequal to hardships, I am classed as a woman; if you would have me happy, happiness marches in your train; if you think the toil of the journey great, absence is harder to support; if you would have me watch over my wife, Glory resides in your steel; if you wish me to guard your rear, valour is your rear-guard; if you argue that the feudatories are uncontrolled, they are secured by the bonds of your virtues; if you say a great man must not carry a companion with him, then you count me as distinct from yourself; if you say you are marching with a very light train, what excessive weight is there in the dust of your feet[1]? if you think it inopportune that two should go, gratify me with the commission; if you say brotherly affection is timid, the fault is mutual. Whence this your arm's excessive greedi-

[1] Sc. such as I.

ness that you desire alone to quaff the ambrosia of fame as white as a mass of the Milk Ocean's foam? Never before have I been stinted in your favours. Therefore let my lord be gracious and take me also."

So speaking, he sank his head to the ground and fell at his brother's feet. But the elder upraised him and said:—"Why thus, dear brother, by putting forth too great an effort add importance to a foe too slight for our power? A concourse of lions in the matter of a deer is too degrading. How many flames gird on their armour against a sheaf of grass? Moreover for the province of your prowess you have already the earth with her amulet wreath of eighteen continents. The winds that carry off ranges of great hills arm not against a trembling cotton yield. The sky elephants, audaciously familiar with Sumeru's flanks, butt not upon a tiny ant-hill. For a world-wide conquest you, like Māndhātri, shall grasp, in the shape of your bow with its curving frame adorned with bright gold leaf, a comet portending the world's end of all earthly kings. [207] Only, in the unbearable hunger which has been aroused in me for our enemies' death, forgive this one unshared morsel of wrath. Be pleased to stay." Such was his answer, and on the same day he set out to seek the foe.

My lord Harṣa's brother being thus occupied, his father laid to rest, his brother-in-law banished from life, his mother dead and his sister a prisoner, he could scarcely make the time pass, alone as he was like a wild elephant strayed from the herd. Many days having elapsed, on one occasion as with the night two-thirds spent he lay awake, being still despondent at his brother's departure, he heard the watchman chanting an Āryā couplet:—

'Though his virtues[1] be sung by continents, though rich be his worth like a treasure of jewels[2],
'As a squall a ship, so does fate overwhelm a hero without warning.'

[1] Or—of the ship—'cables.'

[2] Or—of the ship—'though it have amassed the prime of the ocean's treasures.'

At this his heart was still further grieved by thoughts of the instability of things; but when the night was well-nigh ended, he obtained a moment's sleep, and in a vision saw a heaven-kissing pillar of iron broken in pieces. With a throbbing heart he awoke again, and reflected:—"Why do these evil dreams thus incessantly pursue me? Day and night my eye—and not the right one—throbs expert in prophecies of evil. Dire portents again never for a moment weary of announcing the death of no mean king. Day after day Rāhu, hard by the sun's disc which shows a headless trunk, is seen to wear a bodily form no longer curtailed[1]. The Seven Sages vomit eruptions of smoke, swallowed perhaps in their time of austerity, and cover all the planets with grey. Every day dire flames are seen in the heavens, and the star groups fall from the firmament like motes of ash from the burning. The dimmed moon seems to sorrow for the downfall of the stars. Each night, as the meteors flash hither and thither, the heavens with tremulous starry eyes gaze as it were upon a mighty conflict of planets in the abysm. [208] Whistling with bits of gravel and permeated by huge flying dust clouds, the wind seems transporting the earth somewhither to signify the transmission of sovereignty. I see no fair auspice in the hour. Who shall waylay this fatality in our stock, which wastes its tender growth as an elephant a bamboo? Be it well, in any case, with my lord." After such thoughts as these he found a difficulty in encouraging his heart, which seemed in coward flight[2] from an outburst of brotherly affection in its midst. Then rising, he went through the usual round of duties.

When in the audience chamber, he saw Kuntala, a chief officer of cavalry and a great noble high in Rājyavardhana's

[1] The trunk seen in the sun seems to provide Rāhu, an eclipse demon who is all head, with a body. Varāhamihira (iii.) says, 'if a staff is seen in the sun, the sovereign will die; if something in the shape of a headless trunk, there will be danger from sickness.'

[2] '*Dravad*' may be taken in the sense of melting, 'his heart moist with an oil of brotherly affection bursting forth within.' The Kashmir text reads *antarbhinnam*.

favour, hastily enter with a dejected company entering in his train. His form was wrapped in a shawl as miry as if unbearable grief had reddened[1] its texture with a smoke of hot sighs. His looks were downcast, as if through shame at the preservation of his life, his glance fixed on the end of his nose, and his face, hairy with the long growth of mourning, mutely with uninterrupted tears bespoke his master's fall. This sight aroused the prince's alarm, but when the time came to hear the dreadful calamity, he seemed seized in every limb by all the world powers at once, water in his eyes, sighs in his moon-like mouth, fire in his heart, earth upon his breast. From the man he learnt that his brother, though he had routed the Mālwa army with ridiculous ease, had been allured to confidence by false civilities on the part of the King of Gauḍa, and then weaponless, confiding, and alone, despatched in his own quarters.

Instantly on hearing this his fiery spirit blazed forth in a storm of sorrow augmented by flaming flashes of furious wrath. His aspect became terrific in the extreme. As he fiercely shook his head, the loosened jewels from his crest looked like live coals of the angry fire which he vomited forth. Quivering without cessation, his wrathful curling lip seemed to drink the lives of all kings. [209] His reddening eyes with their rolling gleam put forth as it were conflagrations in the heavenly spaces. Even the fire of anger, as though itself burned by the scorching power of his inborn valour's unbearable heat, spread over him[2] a rainy shower of sweat. His very limbs trembled as if in affright at such unexampled fury. Like Çiva, he put on a Shape of Terror: like Viṣṇu, he displayed a Man-lion's aspect: like the sun-crystal hill, he fired at the sight of another's fierce brilliance[3]: like doomsday, his form overpowered the eye by the brilliance of twelve suns uprisen: like a world-alarming hurricane, he brought a tremour upon all monarchs[4]: like the Vindhya,

[1] Mud is often described as 'red.'

[2] Sc. the fire, as if in fear of a hotter fire, scatters water around.

[3] Or 'a second source of light.'

[4] Or 'mountains.'

he grew in sublimity of form[1]: like a great serpent, he was wroth at the insult of a vile king[2]: like Janamejaya, intent upon burning all sovereigns[3]: like Vṛikodara, athirst for his enemy's blood: like the gods' elephant, in full career to repel his foes[4]. He represented the first revelation of valour, the frenzy of insolence, the delirium of pride, the youthful avatar of fury, the supreme effort of hauteur, the new age of manhood's fire, the regal consecration of warlike passion, the camp-lustration day of resentment.

"Except the Gauḍa king," he cried "what man would by such a murder, abhorred of all the world, lay such a great soul low, as Agni's progeny did Droṇa[5], in the very moment when, having by his arm's undissembling valour subdued all princes, he had laid the sword aside? [210] Apart from that ignoble wretch, in whose minds would my lord's heroic qualities, alighting like flamingoes upon the lakes, find no favour, spotless both as a mass of Ganges foam, and recalling the memory of Paraçu-Rāma's prowess[6]? How could he, furious as the summer sun, which dries the water of the lotus pools, put forth his hands, regardless of friendly advances[7], to take my lord's life? What shall be his doom? Into what creature's womb shall he pass? Into what hell shall he fall? What outcast even would wreak this deed? My tongue seems soiled with a smirch of sin as I take the miscreant's very name upon my lips. With what design did

[1] Mbh. III. 8781 (104). The mountain swelled in order to stop the path of the Sun and Moon.

[2] Or 'conjurer.'

[3] Or 'snakes.'

[4] Or 'against a rival elephant.'

[5] Dhṛiṣṭadyumna killed Droṇa unfairly, when the latter heard the news that his son was dead. Dhṛiṣṭadyumna is called the progeny of fire because he and his sister Draupadī were produced out of the sacrificial fire. The word may also punningly mean 'the author of evil courses.'

[6] The word *pakṣapātam* may punningly mean either 'favour' or 'flight by wings': for the story of Rāma's forming a path over Kailāsa for the wild-geese cf. *Mahāvīracarita* p. 26 (Trithen) and the name *Krāuñcā*.

[7] Or—punningly—'rays, regardless of their (the lotuses') beauty.'

this mean remorseless[1] being bring my lord to his death, working his way like a worm into a sandal pillar capable of delighting a whole world? Truly now the fool, when in greed for the taste of sweet savours he laid hands upon my lord's life as honey, saw not the coming onset of a swarm of arrows[2]. By lighting up this evil path[3] this vilest of Gauḍas has collected only foul shame, like lampblack, to the soiling of his own house. Though the sun, crest jewel of the world, may be sunk in the west, is there not the moon, lion lord of the one deer that roams[4] the planet thickets, ready at once by the creator's appointment to quell the darkling foe of the road of right? Even when the goad, discipline's lawgiver, is broken, there exists for a wicked elephant's admonition the lion's still sharper claw, skilled to cleave the thick-boned heads of all mad elephants. Who is not bound to punish such vile jewellers, as it were, who deface the most brilliant gems? What now will be the wretch's fate?"

[211] Even as he thus spoke, the senāpati, Siṃhanāda, a friend of his father also, was seated in his presence, a man foremost in every fight, in person yellow as a hill of orpiment, stately as a great full-grown Sāl tree's stem[5], and tall as if ripened by valour's exceeding heat. He was far advanced in years: and, although he had oft risen from repose upon a couch of arrows, yet in point of vigorous age he seemed to scoff at Bhīṣma. So stubborn was his frame, that even old age laid but a trembling hand, timidly as it were, upon his stiff hair. He seemed while still alive to have been born anew into a lion's nature, compounded of guileless valour and having for a mane his straight locks white as a bunch of moonlight. His eyes were veiled by brows whose

[1] With reference to the worm *vigataghṛiṇena* will mean 'relieved from the heat.'

[2] Or 'bees.'

[3] Or punningly 'lamp at a loophole.'

[4] Or by paronomasia 'dims': v. *viçeṣeṇa haraṇam vihāro vichāyīkaraṇaṃ gamanaṃ ca* Comm. The moon is compared to a lion, and the deer is the Hindu counterpart of the 'man in the moon.'

[5] The Comm. has *kāṇḍaṃ skandhaḥ*, which may point to a reading *-kāṇḍa-* for *prakāṇḍa-*.

wrinkled skin hung loose, as if he shrank from the mortal sin of beholding a new master's face. His terrible visage, brightened by a thick white moustache which hid his cheeks, seemed to pour forth an untimely war time[1] in the shape of a commencing autumn white with blooming *Kāça* groves. A beard hanging down to his navel played the part of a white chowrie, fanning his master, who though dead survived in his heart. In spite of age his broad chest was rough with great gashes of wounds opening their lips as if athirst to drink the water of whetted steel's edge: and all across it ran in lines the writings of many great scars graven by the axe edge of sharp swords, as though he were making a calculation of the hour of victory in every battle; whence he might be likened to an eastern range of hills in motion[2]. In the charm of divers martial exploits he seemed to outstrip the very Mahā-Bhārata; in an unbroken career of slaughtering foes to give a lesson to Paraçu-Rāma himself: in ranging oceans[3] and in energy devoted to winning glory perforce to throw even Mandara into the shade: [212] in adapting himself to the limitations of his position[4] to surpass the very sea: in steadfastness, rigidity and elevation to shame even the hills: in circumambient effulgence of fierce native brilliance to set the sun himself at nought: in the wearing toil[5] of supporting his lord's weighty concerns to laugh even Çiva's bull to scorn. Of fury's fire he

[1] There is perhaps a pun here, as the Sanskrit might mean 'an untimely Vikrama-era' commencing with autumn instead of the spring-month Caitra.

[2] He is compared to an eastern hill because of the long line of ridges across his breast and also because of the astronomical reference to the use of this hill in calculating ascensions. The Sanskrit helps the comparison by means of a pun in *parvata*.

[3] We have here a punning reference to the ocean-churning, as the words may also mean 'in revolving in the ocean and attracting Lakṣmī &c.'

[4] *Vāhinīnāyaka* = (1) leader of armies, (2) lord of rivers = ocean. 'In not overpassing his bounds,' and 'observing the principles of generalship.'

[5] *Ghṛiṣṭapṛiṣṭha* literally = 'having an abraded back,' an idiomatic turn for 'worn out by many labours,' v. Comm. *kāryeṣu kṣuṇṇo lokeṣu ghṛiṣṭapṛiṣṭha ucyate*. *Īçvarabhāra* will punningly mean 'the weight of Çiva.'

was the rubbing stick, of valour the lordliness, of arrogance the arrogant quality, of pride the erysipelas, of violence the heart, of martial ardour the life, of enterprise the panting gasp: to the infuriate a hook, to noxious kings an elephant's goad[1], the colophon of chivalry, the family priest of martial companies, the scale-beam of the brave, the boundary overseer of the village of swords, the performer of proud speeches, the sustainer of the routed, the executor of pledges, the authority on openings in great wars, the reveille drum of battle's devotees. His very voice, deep as the booming of a drum, inspired the warriors with lust for battle, as he said:

'My lord, knaves in themselves most foul mark not how they are themselves deluded by the foul unresting vixen fortune, as crows by the koïl. The aberrations of success, like those of the lotus, include the closing of the eyes in error[2]. Hiding the sun with umbrella shades, the sluggard souls become unaware of the fierce heat of others. What indeed is a wretch to do whose looks, for ever turned away through excess of timidity, have never even beheld the faces of angered heroes[3] when the fire of rage puts forth its bristles upon cheeks tawny with the swelling of unparalleled excesses of passion? [213] Little suspects this miserable man how great souls dishonoured, like spells wrought by Brāhmans[4], in a moment consummate the ruin of whole houses. Even against the low the mighty blaze out at a blow[5]. Well does this deed, so capable of hurling irredeemably to hell, befit such an outcast from all martial gatherings. To right-thinking men, who bear in the bow a treasure precious above all else in battle, and whose is the sword, that lotus thicket for the sport of glory's *haṃsas*, even ocean-churnings and the

[1] Or 'to noxious serpents a Garuḍa.'

[2] Or—punningly—'the closing of buds at eve.'

[3] The words for 'timidity' and 'heroes' may also mean 'delicacy' and 'suns.'

[4] There is a pun in *viprakṛitāḥ*, which means (1) 'dishonoured,' (2) 'wrought by Brāhmans.'

[5] Or 'even in water electric flashes blaze out.'

like appear but mean expedients to bring fame[1] to view: what then of such expedients as his? Those for whom, as if themselves incompetent for the task, the very hills appointed by the creator to support the earth vomit forth iron to assist the stroke of clublike arms hard as the thunderbolt,—how can such stout-armed myrmidons of spotless fame even in thought dream aught impossible? Before warriors' hands, glorious in power to quell all opposition[2], the sun's rays (hands) are in respect of occupying the realms of space maimed. Only by vulgar report is Yama's dwelling in the southern quarter, essentially it is in the frown of warriors, where are terrible spaces curving with wavy lines like the Great Buffalo's horns[3]. Strange that heroes roaring like lions in battle[4] do not suddenly grow manes along with the thorny hair that bristles under the joy of conflict! The mass of wealth[5] born from the four oceans has two dreadful crucibles whereby foes are burnt, the subaqueous fire and the heart of a great hero[6]. How can the fire's natural heat rest before it has embraced all oceans[7]? Idly has the lord of serpents expanded his vast ponderous hood, when by his coils[8] he supports merely a clod of earth. Only the arms of warriors, adorned with forearms heavy as a sky elephant's trunk, know how sweet a taste does the earth provide in the enjoyment of a supremacy whose edicts are never set at nought. Like the sun, a king passes his days at his ease with radiance unimpaired, while with upturned face the goddess of lotuses[9] clasps

[1] = Lakṣmī.

[2] Or 'in overpowering all planets.'

[3] This compound goes with both *dakṣiṇāçā* and *bhaṭabhrukuṭir:* in the former case we must translate 'lines of the Great Buffalo's horns,' the Great Buffalo being that of Yama.

[4] There is here apparently a pun on the speaker's own name: the translation would be 'letting loose Siṃhanāda.'

[5] Or—punningly—'cinders.'

[6] The Kashmir text reads *mahāpuruṣāṇāṃ hṛdayaṃ dhāma.*

[7] Read *payorāçīn sahajasya* (for *payorāçisahajasya*) with the Kashmir text.

[8] Or—punningly—'by his government.' *Bhogin* 'serpent' may also mean 'king.'

[9] *Padmākara* = (1) the hands of Padmā = Çrī, (2) lotus beds.

his feet. [214] But the coward is, like the moon, deer-hearted and pallid of hue[1]: how can his glory abide steady for even a pair of nights? Expansive is the heroic spirit, raining a spray of boundless glory. The paths of prowess are levelled by the pioneer valour. The portals of pride by their very creak dispel its foes. The open realms of space to valour are lighted by the sheen of swords. Glory, like the earth, derives a loving flush from a dewy shower of the enemies' blood. Like a row of toe-nails, Royalty also glitters more brightly through rubbing against the grindstone edge of many a king's diadem jewels. Enemies' looks as well as a man's palms are darkened by ceaseless practice in arms. Hundreds of bandages bound about manifold wounds make fame as well as the body white. Hard strokes of swords, falling upon the cuirassed panels of enemies' breasts, spit forth not only sparks but also glory. Whoso, when his people have been slain by the foe, announces his heart's grief like a wise man by the breast beating of his enemies' wives, whose sighs are the wind caused by the descent of hard scimitars, whose tears are those which drip and fall on the body of a lifeless foe, who offers water by the eyes of his enemies' mistresses[2], he and none other deserves fame. No notion of kindred do the enlightened attach to bodies evanescent like a vision come and gone in sleep: with heroes, the conception of body belongs to imperishable fame. As foul lampblack does not so much as touch the diamond mirror, naturally brilliant with a radiance of ever glittering splendour, so sorrow touches not the illustrious. Once more, you are the vanguard of the stout-hearted, the captain of the wise, the foremost of the mighty, the champion of the noble, the forerunner of the illustrious, the prime of the dauntless. Here also you have cool retreats for the abode of fortitude, concealed by the shadow of a forest of strong arms, with the delight of sword-edge water within reach, and the fire of anger ever smoking in the vicinity: stout are those walls whose panels are soldiers' breasts.

[1] Literally 'pale of back': *pāṇḍurapṛiṣṭhasya · deçabhāṣayā nirlajjasya* 'shameless,' Comm.

[2] Water is offered to the dead.

Think not therefore of the Gauḍa king alone: so deal that for the future no other follow his example. [215] Wave the chowries of these mock conquerors, these would-be[1] lovers of the whole earth, by the sighs of the matrons in their harems. Excise their vicious cravings for the umbrella's shade by awnings of flocking kites blinded by the scent of carnage. Dispel with exudations of tepid blood the unhealthy flush of eyes diseased by the side glances of the harlot, ill-got fame. Assuage by the lancing of sharp arrows the tumours of preposterous hardihood[2]. By panaceas of scars from encircling bunches of iron fetters uproot the stinging pains of feet that wanton with yearning for footstools. By the letters of stern command in caustic showers allay the itching of ears alert for the cry of 'Victory.' Remove the unhealthy rigidity of stiff unbending heads by forehead applications of a sandal salve consisting of the gleam of toe-nails. With levies of tribute for nippers extract the splinters of unmannerly forwardness inflamed by the arrogance of wealth. With the radiance of gemmed footstools for lamps pierce the darkness of soldiers frowns produced by windy swelling. Overcome the complications of vain pride with a cure removing heaviness of head by the lightness of kicks. Soften the hardness of the bow-string's callosities by the warmth of clasped hands folded in a perpetual obeisance. Forsake not the path along which your sire, grandsire, and great grandsire have marched amid the envy of the three worlds. Relinquishing the grief proper to cowards, appropriate, as the lion a fawn, the royal glory which is your heritage. Now that the king has assumed his godhead and Rājyavardhana has lost his life by the sting of the vile Gauḍa serpent, you are, in the cataclysm which has come to pass, the only Çeṣa[3] left to support the earth. Comfort your unprotected people.

[1] *Çraddhākāmuka* occurs in this sense in c. III. p. 94. We might however translate 'these seekers after the reverence of the whole earth.'

[2] The Kashmir text has *vīrakāryā* 'of valorous feats.'

[3] A pun in *çeṣa* ((1) left, (2) the serpent *Çeṣa*) refers to the earth-supporting serpent.

Like the autumn sun, set your forehead-burning footsteps upon the heads of kings[1]. Let your enemies with nail-scorching clouds of smoke from sighs all hot with the vexation of consecration to new subservience and with dawning light from a horizon of trembling crest gems give your feet a dappled hue. Even Paraçu-Rāma, though reared as a solitary ascetic among the deer, though soft-hearted with the tenderness of his Brāhmanical nature, did yet, when his father was slain, frame his resolve and one and twenty times cut down and eradicated the united power of the Kṣatriya stock, which with the fierce echoing twang of its forest of bows' notched ends [216] could rob the sky elephants of their madness, and could inflame the world with fever by its array of humming bow-strings: what then of my lord, the prince of the magnanimous, whose spirit wields in the native hardness of his frame a thunderbolt? Therefore do you this very day register a resolve, and for the wreck of this meanest of Gauḍas' life take up the bow, that pennon of the sudden expedition of fate busy in gathering lives. My lord's body, baked in the flame of humiliation, cannot without the cool application of the crimson sandal-unguent of foes be relieved of this dire fever of pain. Failing the means of allaying the pain of insult, Bhīmasena did yet without the device of any Mandara[2] quaff the ambrosia of foemen's blood, as though it had been sweetened by Hiḍimbā's kisses. And Jamadagni's son bathed in pools of Kṣatriya gore, whose coolness was grateful to the touch by assuaging the fever of anger's fiery flames.'

So much said he ended, and my lord Harṣa replied:—'The advice of your eminence deserves to be acted upon. As it is, my envious arm looks with a claimant's eye upon even the king of serpents who upholds the earth. When the very planet groups rise, my brow longs to set itself in motion for their repression. My hand yearns to

[1] The words for 'footsteps' and 'kings' may denote 'rays' and 'mountains.'

[2] I.e. to churn it from the ocean. Bhīma had vowed to drink Duḥçāsana's blood to avenge the insult offered to Draupadī. Hiḍimbā is the wife of Bhīma.

clutch the tresses of the very hills that will not bow. My heart would force chowries upon even the sun's presumptuously bright hands[1]. Enraged at the title of king, my foot itches to make footstools of even the kings of beasts. My lip quivers to command the escheatment of the very quarters of heaven so wilfully occupied by their headstrong regents. How much more therefore now that such a woeful issue[2] has come to pass! My mind, brimming with passion, has no room for complying with the observances of mourning. Nay, so long as this vile outcast of a Gauḍa king, this world-contemned miscreant, who deserves to be pounded, survives, like a cruel thorn in my heart, I am ashamed [217] to cry out helplessly with dry lips like a hermaphrodite[3]. Until I evoke a storm of rain from the tremulous eyes of the wives of hostile hosts, how can my hands present the oblation of water? But small store of tears have these eyes till they have seen the smoke cloud from this vilest of Gauḍas' pyre. Listen to my vow: 'By the dust of my honoured lord's feet I swear that, unless in a limited number of days I clear this earth of Gauḍas, and make it resound with fetters on the feet of all kings who are excited to insolence by the elasticity of their bows, then will I hurl my sinful self, like a moth, into an oil-fed flame.' So saying he gave instructions to Avanti, the supreme minister of war and peace, who was standing near: 'Let a proclamation be engraved': "As far as the orient hill, whose summit the Gandharva pairs abandon when alarmed by the hurtle of the sun's chariot wheels,—as far as Suvela[4], where the calamity of Rāma's devastation of Ceylon was graven by axes hewing down the capital Trikūṭa,—as far as the western mount, the hollows of whose caves resound with the tinkling anklets of Varuṇa's intoxicated and tripping mistresses,—as far as Gandhamādana, whose cave-dwellings are perfumed with fragrant sulphur used as scent by the Yakṣa matrons; let all kings prepare their hands to give tribute or grasp swords, to seize the realms of space or

[1] Or 'rays.' [2] *Durjāte vyasane.* Comm.

[3] The Sanskrit here contains an untranslateable pun.

[4] A mountain in Laṅkā, Ceylon.

chowries, let them bend their heads or their bows, grace their ears with either my commands or their bowstrings, crown their heads with the dust of my feet or with helmets, join suppliant hands or troops of elephants, let go their lands or arrows, grasp mace-staves or lance-staves, take a good view of themselves in the nails of my feet or the mirrors of their swords. I am gone abroad. Like a cripple, how can I rest, so long as my feet are not besmeared with an ointment found in every continent, consisting of the light of precious stones in the diadems of all kings?"

Thus resolved, he dismissed the assembly, and having sent away the feudatories, left the hall once more desirous of the bath. Having risen, he performed all his daily duties like one restored to himself. And from the face of the three worlds, which had heard the vow, the day with heat allayed faded, like the spirit of self-assertion, away. [218] Later on when even the adorable sun, reft of his radiance, had disappeared, as if afraid of the loss of his own sovereignty; when even the red-lotus beds, apparently through fear, were closing and hiding the buzzing of their bees[1]; when the birds, motionless and checking as if in fright the agitation of their wings[2], were becoming invisible; when in honour of the afterglow, which, like the king's vow, embraced the whole world, all the people with bowed heads joined a forest of adoring hands; when, as if the sky regents, apprehensive of falling from their station, were erecting a circle of sky-kissing iron bulwarks, the heavens were being hidden by an array of thick mists; Harṣa did not stay long at the evening levee. The very lamps around, whose flames shook in the wind from the swaying shawls of bending kings, seemed to salute him, as he dismissed the company, and, interdicting the servants from entering, passed into the bed-chamber. There he lay prostrate and stretched upon the bed his languid limbs. As soon as he was left alone with his lamp, fraternal affection, finding its opportunity like a brigand, held him in its grasp. Closing his eyes, he beheld his senior living as it were in his heart. Without a pause his sighs issued forth, as

[1] Or 'arrows.' [2] Or 'partisans.'

if in quest of his brother's life. Covering his face with a flood of tears in place of a white shawl's hem, he wept long and silently; and these thoughts were in his heart: 'How could such a form as his possibly deserve an end like this? Our sire had a hard-knit frame like a broad mass of rock: but, like the iron-stone from the hills, my brother was harder still. How after losing him does it become me, heartless that I am, even to draw one breath? This is my love, devotion, attachment! What child even could approve of my surviving his death? Whither so suddenly has that noble unity gone? Accursed fate has parted me from him without even an effort. Unfeeling that I am, my grief has been all this time obscured by rage—fie upon it!—and I have not even abandoned myself to tears. Frail beyond question are the loves of mortals, fragile as a spider's web. Kinship can be only a conventional tie, if even I sit here apparently self-contained like a stranger when my lord has gone to heaven. What profit has dastard destiny reaped by parting a pair of happy brothers with hearts blessed in the union of mutual love? [219] My lord's virtues, once grateful to all creatures as if made of moonlight, do now that he has passed to another world verily burn, as if they had caught fire from his pyre.' These and the like mournful meditations were in his mind. When day dawned, he gave early instructions to the chamberlain that he desired to see Skandagupta, the commandant of the whole elephant troop.

Summoned by a succession of numerous people running all together, Skandagupta, not waiting for his elephant, hastened on foot from his quarters with bustling lictors forcing the people aside. At every step he questioned the chief elephant doctors, who bowed on every hand, as to the night's news concerning the favourite elephants. All around him was a bustle of groups of people belonging to the camp. In front ran throngs of unemployed persons[1], come for the purpose of bursting the animals' fastenings

[1] The comm. however explains *anāyattā · hastipārçvarakṣiṇaḥ* 'elephant attendants.'

and looking like Vindhya forests as they filled the expanse of heaven with thickets of bamboo clumps bedecked with uplifted peacocks' tails. With them were riders displaying handfuls of emerald green fodder, soliciting fresh-caught elephants, or bowing from a distance in delight at getting prime wild ones, or reporting the approach of rut in one under their charge, or ordering the drums to be mounted. First of all came some who, having been deprived of their elephants for careless offences, wore their beards long in mourning, while ragged new comers ran up in hope of the happiness of securing one. Troops of superintendents of decoys, finding at last an opportunity, were busy with hands uplifted enumerating the serviceable females. Rows of foresters with tossing badges of twigs strove by upraising forests of tall goads to announce the number of fresh captured elephants which they had secured. Crowds of mahouts displayed leathern figures for practising manœuvres[1]. [220] Emissaries from the rangers of elephant forests, sent to convey tidings of the movements of fresh herds and momentarily expecting supplies of fodder, reported the commissariat stores at villages, towns, and marts.

Beneath an aspect of indifference the bearing of a great minister, upheld by his master's favour, and a natural unbending rigidity gave to Skandagupta an air of command. He seemed to enjoin the very seas to provide a limitless supply of shells for elephants' ears, to pillage the very hills for store of red-chalk unguents to paint their heads, to deprive Indra of his Airāvata's charge over the sky elephants. His tread, heavy as when Kailāsa bent[2] beneath the weight of Çiva's step, sought, as it were, to quell the earth's pride in her power to support great weights. His swinging arms, which reached his knees and dangled as he moved, appeared to plant on either side an avenue of stone pillars for elephant posts. A somewhat full and pendulous lip, sweet as ambrosia and soft as young sprays, suggested a bait to allure the

[1] These were figures of elephants used in training the animals for battle.

[2] Or *nāmita* 'was bent' (Kashmir).

elephant of Çrī. His nose was as long as his sovereign's pedigree. A pair of long eyes, exceedingly soft, sweet, white, and large, as if they had drunk the Milk Ocean, gulped down the expanse of heaven. His forehead was full and wide beyond even Meru's flank. His hair, very long, naturally curling and rejoicing in a soft dark colour as if from growing in a perpetual umbrella shade, appeared, as its tresses tossed and quivered like young tendrils, to cut the sun's rays and despoil them of their light. Though, owing to the fall of all hostile alliances, he had abandoned the use of the bow, yet all the ends of heaven heard the echo of his great qualities[1]. With a whole army of raging elephants at his disposal, he was yet untouched by presumption[2]. Great in station, he was yet full of sweetness[3]: royal yet full of virtues[4]: chief of the generous[5] as of elephants: wearing his dependence with the enviable undaunted dignity of sovereignty: raised to a position in the king's favour, unapproachable, like a noble wife, by others and fast fixed by love to one lord: disinterested kinsman of the wise, unsalaried servant of the great, unbought slave of the prudent.

[221] Entering the palace, he saluted from a distance, leaning his lotus hands upon the earth and touching it with his head. When he had seated himself in not too great proximity, Harṣa addressed him: 'You have received a full account of my brother's destruction and my own intentions. You must therefore hastily call in the elephant herds out at pasture. The hot pain of my brother's defeat forbids even the briefest delay in marching.' Thus addressed Skandagupta replied with an obeisance: 'Let my master consider his orders executed. Loyal devotion, however, requires of me a few words. Therefore let your majesty hear.

[1] Or 'bowstrings.' [2] Or 'rut.'

[3] Or 'though made of ashes, yet full of sap.'

[4] Or 'made of earth, yet consisting of threads.' Cf. Comm. *guṇās tantavo 'pi, na hi ghaṭaḥ paṭo bhavatīti virodhaḥ* in allusion to the favourite illustration in Hindu logic: 'a crock is not a cloth.'

[5] The pun on *dānam* (=(1) a gift, (2) rut) has occurred before in Chapter II.

All that your majesty has undertaken is worthy of the nobility[1] fostered in Puṣpabhūti's line, of your own inborn valour, of your arms long as a sky-elephant's trunk, and of your peerless affection for your brother. When even the wretched worms named snakes brook no insult, how should such mines of valour as yourself? Yet the story of his majesty Rājyavardhana has given you some inkling into the despicable characters of vile men. Thus do national types vary, like the dress, features, food, and pursuits of countries, village by village, town by town, district by district, continent by continent, and clime by clime. Dismiss therefore this universal confidingness, so agreeable to the habits of your own land and springing from innate frankness of spirit. Of disasters due to mistaken carelessness frequent reports come daily to your majesty's hearing[2]. In Padmāvatī there was the fall of Nāgasena[3], heir to the Nāga house, whose policy was published by a *çārikā* bird. In Çrāvastī faded the glory of Çrutavarman, whose secret a parrot heard. In Mṛittikāvatī a disclosure of counsel in sleep was the death of Suvarṇacūḍa. [222] The fate of a Yavana king was encompassed by the holder of his golden chowrie, who read the letters of a document reflected in his crest jewel. By slashes of drawn swords Vidūratha's army minced the avaricious Māthura king Bṛihadratha while he was digging treasure at dead of night. Vatsapati, who was wont to take his pleasure in elephant forests, was imprisoned by Mahāsena's soldiers issuing from the belly of a sham elephant[4]. Sumitra, son of Agnimitra, being over fond of the drama, was attacked by Mitradeva in the midst of actors, and with a scimitar shorn, like a lotus stalk, of his head. Çarabha, the Açmaka king, being attached to string music, his enemy's emissaries, disguised as

[1] Read *abhijanasya* or *ābhijātyasya* for *ajātyasya:* the Kāshmir text has *abhijanasya ābhijatyasya.*

[2] This speech refers to a curious mass of unknown legendary history.

[3] Cf. *Viṣṇu P.* Wilson's tr. (Hall's ed. vol. iv. p. 217) Manu, vii. 149. 150.

[4] Cf. *Kathāsarit. S.* ch. 12.

students of music, cut off his head with sharp knives hidden in the space between the *vīṇā* and its gourd. A base-born general, Puṣpamitra, pounded his foolish Maurya master Bṛihadratha, having displayed his whole army on the pretext of manifesting his power. Kākavarṇa, being curious of marvels, [223] was carried away no one knows whither on an artificial aerial car made by a Yavana condemned to death[1]. The son of Çiçunāga had a dagger thrust into his throat in the vicinity of his city. In a frenzy of passion the over-libidinous Çuṅga[2] was at the instance of his minister Vasudeva reft of his life by a daughter of Devabhūti's slave woman disguised as his queen. By means of a mine in Mount Godhana, joyous with the tinkle of numerous women's jewelled anklets, the Māgadha king, who had a penchant for treasure caves[3], was carried away by the king of Mekala's ministers to their own country. Kumārasena, the Pauṇika prince, younger brother to Pradyota, having an infatuation for stories about selling human flesh, was slain at the feast of Mahākāla by the vampire Tālajaṅgha. By drugs whose virtues had been celebrated through many different individuals some professed physicians brought an atrophy upon Gaṇapati, son of the king of Videha, who was mad for the elixir of life. Confiding in women, the Kāliṅga Bhadrasena met his death at the hands of his brother Vīrasena, who secretly found access to the wall of the chief queen's apartments. Lying on a mattress in his mother's bed, a son of Dadhra, lord of the Karūṣas, encompassed the death of his father, who purposed to anoint another son[4]. Candraketu, lord of the Cakoras, being attached to his chamberlain, was with his minister deprived of life by an emissary of Çūdraka. The life of the

[1] Cf. the story of the Enchanted Horse in the Arabian Nights.

[2] *Viṣṇu Pur.* IV. ch. 24.

[3] *Asuravivaravyasaninam* 'a lover of snake palaces' or 'treasure caverns': cf. the Comm.'s *ahivivaram*. This king's councillors on this occasion disguised themselves as *vātikāḥ*, which is perhaps for *vātigāḥ* 'workers in mines or metals.' *Asuravivara* occurs *supra* text p. 108 l. 5 and p. 143 l. 9. In the former passage *vātikāḥ* appears and is explained by the Comm. as *asuravivaravyasanina ācāryāh*.

[4] Kāmandaki, *Nītisāra*, vii. 51.

chase-loving Puṣkara, king of Cāmuṇḍī, was sipped, while he was extirpating rhinoceroses, by the lord of Campā's soldiers ensconced in a grove of tall-stemmed reeds. Carried away by fondness for troubadours, the Maukhari fool Kṣatravarman was cut down by bards, his enemy's emissaries, with the cry of 'Victory' echoing on their lips. In his enemy's city the king of the Çakas, while courting another's wife, was butchered by Candragupta concealed in his mistress' dress. [224] The blunders of heedless men arising from women have been brought sufficiently to my lord's hearing. Thus, to secure her son's succession, Suprabhā with poisoned groats killed Mahāsena, the sweet-toothed king of Kāçi[1]. Ratnavatī, pretending a frenzy of love, slew the victorious Jārūtha of Ayodhyā with a mirror having a razor edge[2]. Devakī, being in love with a younger brother, employed against the Sauhmya Devasena an ear lotus whose juice was touched with poisoned powder. A jealous queen killed Rantideva of Viranti with a jewelled anklet emitting an infection of magic powder[3]: Vindumatī the Vṛiṣṇi Vidūratha with a dagger hidden in her braided hair[4]: Haṃsavatī the Sauvīra king Vīrasena[5] with a girdle ornament having a drug-poisoned centre: Pauravī the Paurava lord Somaka by making him drink a mouthful of poisoned wine, her own mouth being smeared with an invisible antidote.'

So much said, he ended and went forth to execute his master's orders. His majesty Harṣa complied with all the forms of royalty. But while he, according to his vow, was commanding his march for a world-wide conquest, in the abodes of the doomed neighbouring kings manifold evil portents spread abroad. Thus:—herds of black spotted antelopes roamed restlessly hither and thither, like imminent glances of death's emissaries[6]. In the courts resounded the

[1] Kāmandaki, *Nītis.* vii. 52. [2] *Ibid.* 53.
[3] *Bṛihatsaṃhitā* lxxviii. 1, Kāmandaki vii. 53. Read *visara.*
[4] Cf. Varāhāmihira, *Bṛihat-Saṃhitā* lxxviii. 1, Kāmandaki vii. 54.
[5] Kāmandaki vii. 53.
[6] The India Office MS. has *aviprakṛiṣṭakāladṛiṣṭayaḥ.*

hum of swarms of honey bees, types of the clatter of deserting glory's anklets. With streams of flame issuing from cavities of hideous open mouths, ill-omened jackals dismally even in the day time howled long and with no fair presage. Down swooped vultures, red as young monkeys' faces in the roots of their wings, as if full well acquainted with dead men's flesh. All at once the trees in the parks put forth untimely flowers, as though to say farewell. Vehemently wept the statues in the halls, beating their breasts with strokes of agitated palms. The warriors, as though their heads had vanished in fear of the near clutching of their hair, beheld themselves headless in their mirrors. [225] Upon the crest gems of the queens appeared footprints marked with wheels, conchs and lotuses[1]. The chowries of the slave women slipped suddenly from their hands. Even in lovers' quarrels the soldiers, averted from their mistresses, turned their backs for a long while away. On the elephants' cheeks were parted the honey-symposia of the bees. As if sniffing the scent of Yama's buffalo, the panting steeds refused to eat the green young grass, ripe[2] though it might be. In the courtyards the sluggish peacocks would not dance, though coaxed by girls clapping music accompanied by the sound of tossing bracelets. Near the gateways night after night troops of dogs howled shrilly without cause, upturning their faces as if their eyes were fixed upon the moon's deer. Shaking her forefinger as if to count the dead, a naked woman wandered all day long in the parks. Upon the inlaid pavements uprose lines of grass swaying like the curved hairs upon a deer's hoofs. With braided locks and eyes not from collyrium[3] lustrous, appeared in the wine of their goblets the reflections of the lotus faces of warriors' wives. The lands shook as if affrighted at their approaching seizure. Upon the

[1] Natural marks on an emperor's feet; cf. Varāhamihira, *Bṛihat S.* lxix. 17.

[2] Literally 'clustering': *stambakarim* · *baddhastambaṃ pakvaṃ vā* Comm.

[3] Widows braid their hair and omit the use of collyrium. Read with the MS. *nirañjanalocana-*.

bodies of the soldiers a crimson rain might be seen to have fallen, in hue ruddy as blooming *Bandhūka* flowers, and suggesting the clots of red sandal juice wherewith doomed criminals are decked[1]. As if to lustrate a doomed glory[2], blazing meteors ceased not to fall in showers, setting the star-clusters afire with eruptions of incessantly flashing sparks. At the very first a furious hurricane swept along, from every house bearing away, like a chamberlain, chowries, umbrellas and fans[3].

Here ends the sixth Chapter—entitled The King's Vow—of the Harṣa-Carita composed by Çrī Bāṇa Bhaṭṭa.

1 Cārudatta in the Mṛiochakaṭikā, Act x., describes himself, when led to execution, as 'dragged like a beast to sacrifice, decked with the marks of red sandal on his limbs and besprinkled with meal and pounded incense.'

2 The meteors act the part of the torch which was carried round the sacrificial animal, see *Ait. Brāhm.* ii. 5.

3 We may here note a few small variations of reading by the Kashmir text in the above paragraph :—(1) for *aviprakriṣṭāḥ* 'at no great distance' *praviṣṭa*—'having entered' with 'emissaries,' (2) for *ajire* 'in the courts' *ciram* 'for a long time,' (3) for *ciram açivārtham* 'long and with no fair presage' *upaçiviraṃ çavārtham* 'near the camp for corpses,' (4) 'in the halls' omitted. There are also unimportant misreadings *prarūḍhaprasarāḥ* for *-praṇayāḥ* 'full well acquainted,' *pāṇipallavāḥ* for *-pallavāt*, *caṣaṇa-* for *caṣaka-* 'goblets,' *ātmāpa*(*hāra*) 'seizure,' *tarantī* for *apaharantī* 'bearing away.' The MS. has no. (3), though without *çavārtham*, and also the following :—text p. 225 l. 4 *aghaṭanta* for *vyaghaṭanta*, l. 10 *kaṭakeṣu* for *vāṭakeṣu*, l. 11 *nirañjanalocanaruci* (? *ruñci*), l. 12 *ceṭījanānām* for *bhaṭīnām*.

CHAPTER VII.

[226] **To the vowed hero the earth is a courtyard pediment, the ocean a dyke,**
Hell is dry land, and mount Sumeru an ant-hill!
Strange is it that the mountains bow not when the stout-armed wields the bow!
Of what account at all are the wretched crows termed enemies?

Some days having passed, on a day with care calculated and approved by a troop of astronomers numbering hundreds, was fixed an hour of marching suitable for the subjugation of all the four quarters. The king had bathed in golden and silvern vessels, like autumn clouds which were skilled[1] in pouring water; had with deep devotion offered worship to the adorable Nīlalohita[2]; fed the up-flaming fire, whose masses of blaze formed a rightward whorl; bestowed upon Brāhmans sesamum vessels of precious stones, silver, and gold in thousands, myriads also of cows having hoofs and horn tips adorned with creepers of gold-work[3]; sat upon a throne with a coverlet of tiger skin; duly anointed first his bow and then his body down to the feet with sandal bright as his own fame; put on two seemly robes of bark silk marked with pairs of flamingos; formed about his head a chaplet of white flowers to be, like the moon's digit, a sign of the supreme[4]; [227] drawn to the

[1] Or 'white,' the rainless autumn clouds being so.

[2] = Rudra-Çiva.

[3] This clause is much curtailed in the Kashmir text, which omits all mention of gifts to Brāhmans, and by a zeugma makes the king *sacrifice* the cows.

[4] *Parameçvara* = (1) king, (2) Çiva.

region of his ear a fresh *gorocanā*-spotted *Dūrvā* spray like a sprout of light from the emerald in his ear-ornament; and wound upon his forearm together with the seal-bracelet an amulet to prosper his going. After being sprinkled on the head with a spray of lustral water scattered by the hand of the highly honoured and delighted Purohit, he had sent away valuable equipages, and divided among the kings ornaments anointing the heavens with a copious light of jewels, had loosed the prisoners, and bestowed suitable gifts of favour upon distressed pilgrims and nobles; and had installed his right arm, which by a reminding throb at the moment brought itself as it were to notice, in the office of subduing the eighteen continents. Finally with all good omens pressing forward officiously, like devoted servants, in the van, amid a clamourous cry of 'Victory!' from the delighted people, he issued forth from his house, like the Golden Foetus from Brahmā's egg, to set on foot an age of gold.

The starting place was fixed at a large temple built of reeds not far from the city and close to the Sarasvatī. It displayed a lofty pillared gateway, an altar supporting a golden cup adorned with sprays, affixed chaplets of wild flowers, wreaths of white banners, strolling white-robed people, and muttering Brāhmans. During the king's stay there the village notary appeared with his whole retinue of clerks[1], and saying, 'Let his majesty, whose edicts are never void, even now bestow upon us his commands for the day,' so presented a new-made golden seal with a bull for its emblem. The king took it. As soon however as a ball of earth was produced, the seal slipped from the king's hand and fell face downwards upon the ground, and the lines of the letters were distinctly marked upon the nearly dry mud and soft earth of the Sarasvatī's bank. Apprehensive of an evil omen, the courtiers were depressed, but the king thought in his heart: 'The minds of the dull are indeed blind to reality. The omen signifies that the earth shall be stamped with the single seal of my sole command: [228] but the rustics

[1] *Karaṇi*, cf. the Hindi *Kirāṇī*, 'a clerk.' The Comm. suggests an alternative rendering 'requisites for writing.'

interpret otherwise.' Having thus mentally welcomed the omen, he bestowed upon the Brāhmans a hundred villages delimited by a thousand ploughs. That day he spent in the same place, and when night arrived, complimented all the kings and retired to rest.

At the close of the third watch, when all creatures slept and all was still, the marching drum was beaten with a boom deep as the gaping roar of the sky elephants. Then, after first a moment's pause, eight sharp strokes were distinctly given anew upon the drum, making up the number of the leagues in the day's march.

Straightway the drums rattled, the *nāndīs*[1] rang out joyously, the trumpets brayed, the *kāhalas* hummed, the horns blared; the noise of the camp gradually increased. Officers occupied themselves in arousing the courtiers. The heavens were confounded by a confused noise of drumsticks added to a rapid tapping of mallets[2]. Commanders mustered crowds of barrack superintendents[3]. Thousands of torches lighted by the people made inroads upon the darkness of night with their glare. Loving pairs were roused from sleep by the tramp of the women of the watch[4]. Shrill words of command from the marshals dispelled the slumbers of blinking riders. Awakened elephant herds vacated their sleeping stalls. There was a shaking of manes from troops of horses risen from sleep. The noisy camp resounded with mattocks uprooting ground fastenings. Elephant hobbles rattled as their pins were extracted. Rearing horses curved their hoofs at the clear low noise of chain-keys brought towards them. [229] A clanking sound of halter fetters filled the ten regions to overflowing, as the foragers loosed the rutting elephants. Leathern bags, bursting with fullness, were extended upon the dusty backs of elephants, which had been

[1] A drum which is beaten for a good omen. *Guñjā* or *kuñjā* here translated 'trumpet' is explained by the Comm. as a horn with rings of lac *çaṅkhabhedo yatpṛiṣṭhe jatu parikalitaṃ bhavati.*

[2] For this characteristic of breaking camp in India cf. Twining 'Travels in India,' pp. 92 and 484.

[3] The Comm. notes a var. lect. *pāṭhīpati* with uncertain meaning.

[4] Cf. *yāmakinyaḥ* c. IV. p. 137 l. 5 (text).

rubbed down by strokes from wisps of hay. Servants of house-builders[1] rolled up awnings and cloth screens belonging to tents and marquees. Leathern sacks were filled to roundness with bundles of pegs. Store-room stewards collected stores of platters. Many elephant attendants[2] were pressed to convey the stores. The houses of the neighbourhood were blocked with clusters of cups and vessels, which were lifted upon numerous elephants, while the riders kept the animals steady. Wicked elephants were loaded with a cargo of utensils hurriedly tossed upon them by travel-practised domestics. Amid the laughter of the crowd helpless corpulent bawds lagged as they were with difficulty dragged along with hands and legs sprawling sideways[3]. Many huge and savage elephants trumpeted as the free play of their limbs was checked by the tightening of the girth-bands of their gaudy housings. A jangling of bells taking place in the elephant troop inflamed all ears with fever. Camels, as sacks were set on their backs, bellowed at the outrage. The carriages of the high-born nobles' wives were thronged with roguish emissaries sent by princes of rank. Elephant riders, deceived as to the time of starting, searched for new servants. Highly honoured footmen led the fine[4] horses of the king's favourites. An array of gay gallants employed thick unguents to draw circular lines of camphor on their persons[5]. To the saddles of marshals were fastened martingales with wooden figures of deer[6], bells, and reeds attached. [230] Apes were placed among troops of horses whose grooms were entangled in a network of coiled

[1] *Gṛihacintaka* = ? 'house-artists.'

[2] *Nālīvāhikaḥ. kariṇām vāsa(ghāsa ?)grahaṇaniyukto hastipako meṭhākhyaḥ.* Comm.

[3] Or 'dragged by the hands of sideways-bowing servants'?

[4] But the Kashmir and Bombay texts read *vāravājini* 'show horses' in place of *varavājini.* We might translate 'the king's favourite show horses.'

[5] The Comm. explains *nāsīra* as either (1) camphor, as in the text, or (2) vanguard, which will require the rendering 'thick unguents fit for the adornment of the vanguard.'

[6] Cf. Comm. *lavaṇakālāyī* (sic) *mṛigākṛitir açvānām dārumayī kriyate.*

reins[1]. Stablemen dragged along half-eaten shoots[2] to be eaten at the morning manoeuvres. Loud grew the uproar of foragers shouting to one another. Much crashing of stables resounded as the young rearing horses swerved in the confusion of starting. Women, hastening at the call of riders whose elephants were in readiness, presented unguents for the animals' heads. The low people of the neighbourhood, running up as the elephants and horses started, looted heaps of abandoned grain. Donkeys ridden by throngs of boys[3] accompanied the march. Crowds of carts with creaking wheels occupied the trampled roads. Oxen were laden with utensils momentarily put upon them. Stout steers, driven on in advance, lagged out of greed for fodder lying near them[4]. In front were carried the kitchen appliances of the great feudatories. First ran banner-bearers. Hundreds of friends were spectators of the men's exits from the interior of their somewhat contracted huts. Elephant keepers, assaulted with clods by people starting from hovels which had been crushed by the animals' feet, called the bystanders to witness the assaults. Wretched families fled from grass cabins ruined by collisions. Despairing[5] merchants saw the oxen bearing their wealth flee before the onset of the tumult. A troop of seraglio elephants advanced where the press of people gave way before the glare of their runners' torches. Horsemen shouted to dogs tied behind them. [231] Old people sang the praises of tall Tangaṇa horses which by the steady motion of their quick footfalls provided a comfortable seat. Deckhan riders[6] disconsolately contended with fallen mules. The whole world was swallowed up in dust.

1 *Avarakṣiṇy · açvabandhanarajjuḥ* Comm.

2 The Comm.'s *prāuḍhiko · yogyāçanārthaṃ prasevako yo bukkaṇa iti prasiddhaḥ* seems to point to a reading *prāuḍhike* 'bags' for *prārohake* 'shoots.'

3 Or, taking *celam* as = *vastram*, 'loaded with bundles of clothes.'

4 The Comm. however says *lambamāno · gardabhadāso banijāṃ karmakaro vā*, which would require the translation 'greedy for &c. were driven on by *donkey boys*.' Cf. *lambanā · gardabhadāsāḥ* p. 236, l. 9 (text).

5 *Vidrāṇāḥ · saçokāḥ* Comm. Cf. *supra* p. 68 note.

6 'There are no mules in the Deckan,' Comm.

At the hour of marching the front of the king's residence became full of chieftains arriving from every side, mounted on female elephants, with riders holding up bows striped with gold leaf, swords grasped by confidential servants occupying the inner seats, chowries waved by betel bearers, sheafs of javelins in cases under the charge of those who sat at the back, and saddles curving with scimitars and bristling with golden arrows[1]. Girths, confining on either side the ends of the saddle, kept their cloth cushions motionless and gave a firm seat. The clash of their swaying foot-rests augmented the sound from the precious stones in their anklets[2]. Their shanks were covered with their proper covering[3] of delicate tinted silk. Their copper-coloured legs were chequered with mud-stained wraps, and a heightened white was produced by contrast with trousers soft and dark as bees[4]. They wore tunics darkened by black diamonds glistening on bright forms[5]; chinese cuirasses thrown over them[6], coats and doublets showing clusters of bright pearls, bodices speckled with a mixture of various colours, and shawls of the shade of parrots' tails. Fine waistbands[7] were wound about flanks made thin by exercise. Servants ran up to loose dangling earrings which had become entangled with pearl necklaces, tossed by their movements. [232] Their ear-ornaments clashed as they struck against earrings budding with gold filagree work. The stalks of their ear-lotuses were fixed in their turbans. Their heads were wrapt in shawls of a soft saffron

[1] *-nalaka-* ?

[2] Read *pādabandha-* (·*pādakaṭaka*, 'anklet') with Comm.

[3] The Kashmir text and the Comm. read *-svasthānasthagita-* for *svasthaganasthagita-*.

[4] The sense here is far from clear. The Comm. writes *piṅgā · jaṅghikā, anye jaṅghālety āhuḥ | satulā · ardhajaṅghikā ity, anye ardhajaṅghālety āhuḥ*. The Kashmir text reads *sitāṅgaiḥ* for *piçaṅgapiṅgaiḥ*.

[5] Read *mecakakañcukaiç*.

[6] The Kāshmir text and the Comm. read *apacita · parihitam pūjitaṃ vā*.

[7] *Çastam · paṭṭikūṭhoraḥ kaṭisūtram ity arthaḥ*, Comm.: but the Calcutta and Bombay texts read *çastram* 'fine scimitars fastened to &c.'

hue. They had linen turbans[1] inlaid with bits of crest gems. Clouds of bees formed as it were peacocks' feathers in their topknots. Their elephants' housings were bedabbled from long travel. The recesses of the world were filled with proud restless warriors who bounded along, gay with round Kārdaraṅga shields of various colours and chowries tossing in front of them. The abysses of the heavens resounded with the noise of the tinkling golden ornaments upon hundreds of prancing Kāmboja horses. The sharp tapping of hundreds of fiercely beaten *lambā* drums deafened the cavities of men's ears. Their names were proclaimed aloud. And craning footmen awaited their commands.

When the adorable sun arose, the signal conch rang out repeatedly, announcing the moment of the king's arraying the army. After a brief interval he came forth, riding upon a female elephant, which by the play of its flapping ears, swaying as it moved, seemed on this the king's first expedition to be producing an assemblage of earth-supporting elephants[2] for a conquest of the different quarters. An auspicious umbrella, distinguished by a turquoise rod and, by reason of the bits of ruby inlaid at its top, glowing as in anger at the sight of the sunrise—this, and a tunic of new silk, which clung about him, softer than the plantain fruit, as if he were a second king of snakes, recalled the day of the ambrosia churning when clouds of the Milk Ocean's foam whitened the skies[3]. Raised while still young, like the tree of paradise, to the station of an Indra, he veneered the heavens with a powder for placing the whole world at his disposal in the shape of the pollen from the bunches of flowers in his ear-wreath, which was tossed abroad by the wind of the flapping chowries. [233] His splendour seemed to drink up

[1] The Kāshmir text and the Comm. read for *-colaiḥ -kholaiḥ*: *kholaḥ · çirastram*, 'helmets' or 'turbans.'

[2] I.e. by reason of the reverberations of the sound.

[3] Or punningly 'wearing robes white as the Milk Ocean's foam.' By a complicated series of puns the king is compared to the day of the Ocean churning. The white umbrella is the white-clouded sky and he with his white robes is the serpent Çesa whirled in the Milky Ocean. Read *lohitāyat(ay)ā* with MS. A.

the very rising sun, whose golden image appeared in his fronting crest-gem. His lip, smeared deep with betel and vermilion, was like a seal assigning away the various island continents in fief to loyal affection[1]: while in the guise of a horizon of light from pearl necklaces, he forced chowries upon the very heavens. With his brows capriciously raised a third part in reviewing the royal company, he seemed to enjoin tribute upon even the three worlds. The long rampart of his arms appeared to embrace the seven great ocean fosses with protecting love. Tightly embraced by Glory, having with her all the sweetness of the milky ocean, he was, as if made of ambrosia, drunk in by thousands of eyes upraised in curiosity by the people of the camp. The weight of his great qualities seemed to sink him deep in royal hearts all moist with affection; the flood of his magnificence to anoint the very marrow[2] of the beholders. Like the Lord of the Immortals, he appeared busy in wiping away the stain of his elder brother's[3] slaughter: like Pṛithu, sweeping away all the gathered kings[4] with intent to cleanse the earth: like the sun, preceded by thousands of ushers, like rays, heralding his appearance[5] and clearing the way, nimbly moving in deft performance of their duty, stern in enforcing order, effecting as it were the seizure of the very regions of space, which were hidden by the press of frightened fleeing people, teaching the very wind decorum by swallowing up his goings in a mass of waving pennons, expelling the very sun's rays, which were repelled by a cloud of dust upraised by hurrying feet, keeping aloof the very day, which was hurled aside by the light from a foliage of golden maces.

Then as the company of kings bowed, with bodies dutifully bent down, hearts thrilling with fear, heads all agleam with the light of golden diadems whose gems were loosened

1 *Anurāga* may punningly mean 'redness.'

2 *Majjanniva*, *majjāmapi*, MS.

3 Indra killed Viçvarūpa, the three-headed son of Tvaṣṭṛi, who was *agraja* in the sense of being a Brāhman.

4 Or 'hills,' cf. Visnu-P. i. 13. 82.

5 Lit. 'causing light,' or 'crying Ho! people.' The other adjectives have a punning application to the sun.

by their motions, and crests emitting dust from tossing flowers, [234] the rays of their blazing crest jewels, waving downwards, aslant, and upwards, seemed like flocks of jays engaged in producing fair omens[1]. As they soared like courtyard peacocks to the sky, now dense with cloud-masses of dust, it was as if the sky-regents were fixing at their doors festoons of soft sprays from the tree of paradise[2]. Thus welcomed with bows, the hero of heroes, purchasing as it were the kings' souls in the shape of adoration, distributed among them tokens of his favour, such as quarter glances, side-glances, full glances, raised eyebrows, half-smiles, jests, plays upon words, inquiries after their health, return greetings, careless movements of the brow, and instructions, according to their several deserts.

The king having started, the echo of musical instruments spread loudly hither and thither about the four quarters of heaven, like the snorting of sky elephants affrighted at the tumult. As, angered against their brethren in the sky, the elephants emitted their triple flow, the tracks of the ichor torrent, all black with bees, appeared to pour thousands of Kālindī's rills[3]. The sun's radiance being crimsoned with masses of vermilion powder, the birds[4] feared that the sunset was come. The booming of the drums was lost in the noise of elephants' ear-flapping, strengthened by the uproar of bees. A host of waving chowries swallowed up the whole totality of things moving and motionless. The sky became an unbroken white with clots of foam, pure as *Sindhuvāra* chaplets, tossed by the breath of the cavalcade. Forests of umbrellas, with upright golden stocks and white as massed

[1] Cf. Mālatī Mādhava, Wilson's trans. 'Hindu Theatre,' II. p. 66—

'As the countless jewels shoot
Their blaze into the sky, the heavens reflect
The countless hues, as if the peacock's plumage,
Or the mixed colours of the painted jay,
Played through the air &c.'

[2] The clouds represent the doors, the colours of the gems the leaves of the tree of paradise. Read *vandanamālā*.

[3] The waters of the Kālindī or Yamunā being dark-blue in colour.

[4] I.e., as the Comm. explains, 'the ruddy-geese.'

bunches of *Tagaras,* drank up the day, and the eight regions were lost behind their close array. Blinded by a night of dust, the day blossomed out in a morning light from lines of coronet gems. The heavens were deafened by the din which the horses made with their clanging golden and silvern rows of chariot ornaments. As if to quench utterly the fire of foemen's valour, [235] the elephants bedewed the circle of the quarters with a hot drizzle of ichor. The light of crest gems, flickering like lightning, stole from all eyes the power to open. The king himself was surprised at his forces, and casting his eyes in every direction beheld an army starting out of its encampment, in appearance like the animate world tumbling at an aeon's commencement from Viṣṇu's belly, the ocean overflooding the world in a stream from Agastya's mouth, the Narmadā's flood rolling a thousand rills after being dammed and let loose again by Arjuna's thousand arms. Meanwhile a multitudinous babble was going on as follows:—'March on, my son!' 'Good sir, why do you lag? Here is a galloping horse.' 'Friend, you hobble like a lame man, while the vanguard here is coming furiously upon us.' 'Why are you hurrying the camel? Don't you see, you pitiless brute[1], the child lying there?' 'Rāmila, darling, take care not to get lost in the dust!' 'Don't you see the barley-meal sack leaks? What's the hurry, Go-ahead?' 'Ox, you are leaving the track and running among the horses.' 'Are you coming, fishwife?' 'You female elephant, you want to go among the males.' 'Hullo, the peasack is awry and dribbling: you don't heed my bawling.' 'You're going astray down a precipice: quietly, you self-willed brute.' 'Porridge man, your jar is broken.' 'Laggard, you can suck the sugar cane on the way.' 'Quiet[2] your bull.' 'How long, slave, are you to gather jujube fruit?' 'We have a long way to go; why do you linger, Droṇaka, now? this long expedition is at a

[1] *Niḥçūka* here and in c. VIII. p. 263 l. 10 and 276 last line (Bomb. Ed.) = 'pitiless.' *Çūka* in the sense of compassion is quoted by lexicographers, cf. B. and R. s.v.

[2] The Kashmir reading *prasāraya* is perhaps preferable; '*drive on* your bull' with the preceding sentence.

standstill for one rascal[1].' 'The road in front is all ups and downs: old fellow, see you don't break the sugar kettle.' 'The load of grain is too heavy, Gaṇḍaka: the bullock can't carry it.' 'Quick, slave, with a knife cut a mouthful of fodder from this bean field: [236] who can tell the fate of his crop when we are gone[2]?' 'Keep away your oxen, fellow! this field is guarded by watchmen.' 'The wagon is stuck fast: harness a strong pulling steer to the yoke.' 'Madman[3], you are crushing women: are your eyes burst?' 'You confounded elephant driver, you are playing with my elephant's trunk.' 'Trample him, you savage brute.' 'Brother, you are tripping in the mire.' 'O friend of the distressed, raise this ox from the mud.' 'This way, boy! in the thick of the dense elephant squad there is no getting out.'

Here groups of elephant men, bachelors, knaves, donkey boys, camp followers, thieves, serving men, rogues, and grooms, sated with an easily acquired meal of plentiful readily pounded remnants of grain, expressed their approval of the camp in bold[4] boisterous jubilation[5]. There poor[6] unattended nobles, over-whelmed[7] with the toil and worry of conveying their provisions upon fainting oxen provided by wretched village householders and obtained with difficulty, themselves grasped their domestic appurtenances, grumbling as follows:—'Only let this one expedition be gone and done with.' 'Let it go to the bottom of hell.' 'An end to this world of thirst.' 'Good luck to this servitude of ours.' 'Goodbye to this camp, the pinnacle of all unpleasantness.' Here swiftly running in a line, as if tied together—as it were

[1] Read with MS. A *niṣṭheyam*.

[2] Or 'when people are away.'

[3] *Yakṣapālita* may, however, be a proper name.

[4] *Āṇḍīrāḥ · pragalbhāḥ*, 'bold,' Comm. who also suggests *rāṇḍīrāḥ* 'harlots' sons.'

[5] Read *kelikalāiḥ* (not *kekikalāiḥ*) with the Kāshmir text and the Comm.

[6] The Kāshmir text and the Comm. here insert *-vṛiddha-*, 'old.'

[7] *Gatasaṃyogair · utpannacittakṣobhair*, 'distracted,' Comm. Read *-āyāsāvegāgatasaṃyogair*.

on board a ship gliding down a very rapid current—[237] were the king's hired porters, carrying black hard clubs as heavy as trunks of trees, bearing golden footstools, waterpots[1], cups, spittoons, and baths, pushing every one aside in irrepressible pride at being in charge of their sovereign's property with himself at hand: also bearers of kitchen appurtenances with goats attached to thongs of pig-skin, a tangle of hanging sparrows and forequarters of venison, a collection of young rabbits, potherbs, and bamboo shoots, buttermilk pots protected by wet seals on one part of their mouths which were covered with white cloths, baskets containing a chaos of fire-trays, ovens, simmering pans, spits, copper saucepans, and frying-pans[2]. Here, with cries of 'The labour is ours, but when paytime comes some other rascals will appear,' village servants, set to scare on[3] the feeble oxen tripping at every step, were indiscriminately badgering the whole body of nobles. There the whole country side had come in eager haste from both directions out of curiosity to see the king, and fools of grant-holders, issuing from the villages on the route and headed by aged elders with uplifted waterpots, pressed furiously near in crowds with presents of curds, molasses, candied sugar, and flowers in baskets, demanding the protection of the crops[4]: flying before their terror of irate and savage chamberlains, they yet in spite of distance, tripping, and falling, kept their eyes fixed upon the king, bringing to light imaginary wrongs of former governors, lauding hundreds of past officials, [238] reporting ancient misdeeds of knaves. Others, contented with the appointed overseers, were bawling their eulogies:—'The king is Dharma incarnate'; others, de-

[1] The Kāshmir text reads *paryaṅka* 'palanquins', and the Comm. *karakas ·tāmbūlādhārah*, 'betel-box.'

[2] The sense of the Sanskrit words is here in several cases doubtful.

[3] For *kheṭane* the Kāshmir text and the Comm. read *skhalane · preraṇe*, which we translate. For *kheṭacetakaiḥ* the Kashmir text has *khalaceṭakaiḥ* 'rascally servants.'

[4] The printed texts here insert some words which recur below; v. note on next page and Appendix.

spondent at the plunder of their ripe grain, had come forth wives and all to bemoan their estates, and to the imminent risk of their lives, grief dismissing fear, had begun to censure their sovereign, crying 'Where's the king?' 'What right has he to be king?' 'What a king!' Hares[1] ran about hither and thither, pursued by furiously running crowds armed with clubs, and struck at every pace like polo balls[2]: others were caught by throngs coming upon them all at once and torn in pieces, while others[3] by skill in plunging between the legs of divers animals and eluding many riders' dogs by dodging, managed in spite of showers of clods, clubs, sticks, axes, stakes, spades, hoes, knives, and poles to effect their escape, screaming the while with all the energy left them. Elsewhere a cloud of dust was raised by bands of running foragers with loins a mass of fodder bundles and grey with chaff, sickles swinging from one part of their ancient saddles, loose dirty blankets made of bits of old wool, and, dangling in tatters, torn jerkins presented by their masters. In one place riders were intently occupied in rehearsing the approaching Gauḍa war[4]. Here all the people, busy with orders to fill up muddy places, were cutting bundles of grass. There shrieking quarrelsome Brāhmans, mounted on the tops of trees, were being expelled by the rods of chamberlains standing on the ground. There village dogs, entrapped by bits of food[5], were being tied in leashes. Elsewhere again horses, driven by princes emulous for victory, enlivened the scene by their collisions.

Thus the camp, exciting interest by manifold incidents, [239] was like the doom's-day ocean gone abroad to swallow the world at a gulp, hell formed to embower great serpents[6], Kailāsa created for the dwelling of the supreme. Like the

[1] Cf. Hdt. iv. 134.

[2] *Girigudakaiḥ*: cf. B. and R. *giriguḍa* 'play-ball' and reff. The Comm. gives the meaning 'clod.'

[3] Insert *anyair* with MS. A.

[4] The Sanskrit compound here is almost identical with that omitted above: v. note on previous page.

[5] Read *grāsākṛiṣṭa* for *grāmākṛiṣṭa* with the Kashmir text.

[6] Or 'kings.'

storehouse whence the Prajāpatis brought forth the four ages, it showed a succession of all creatures: like austerities, it was replete with toil, yet like them bringing the noble onwards in their way.

With such a spectacle before his eyes Harṣa arrived at the encampment. Reaching his quarters, he heard the stout-armed princes around expressing their zeal in such talk as this:—'It was the famous[1] Māndhātṛi who opened the way to world-conquest. With the irresistible onset of his chariot Raghu in a brief time set the world at peace. Seconded by his bow, Pāṇḍu imposed tribute on the array of kings haughty in the pride of inherited prowess, nobility, and wealth. Having crossed the realm of China, the Pāṇḍava Arjuna, in order to complete the Rājasūya sacrifice, subdued Mount Hemakūṭa, whose caves resounded with the twang of the bow-ends of the angry Gandharvas. No obstacle save resolution do the conquests of heroes know. Though shielded by Himālaya with all its snows, the impotent Druma[2], fearing a trial of strength, bore like a servant the exactions of the Kuru king. Not too ambitious, surely, of conquest were the ancients, seeing that in a small part of the earth there were numerous monarchs such as Bhagadatta, Dantavakra, Krātha, Karṇa, Kaurava, Çiçupāla, Sālva, Jarāsandha, and Sindhurāja. King Yudhiṣṭhira was easily content since he endured quite near at hand the kingdom of the Kimpurushas, when the conquests of Dhanañjaya had made the earth to shake. A fainéant was Caṇḍakoça[3], who, having subdued the earth, penetrated not into the Amazonian realm. How insignificant is the distance between the Snowy Range and Gandhamādana! The land of the Turuṣkas is to the brave but a cubit[4]. Persia is only a span. The Çaka realm but a rabbit's track. In the Pāriyātra country, incapable of

[1] Read *tatrabhavatā* (not *-ām*) with the Kāshmir text and the Comm.

[2] Druma was the king of the Kinnaras.

[3] There is an oxymoron in the expression *alasaç Caṇḍakoçaḥ*, since *caṇḍa* means 'violent.'

[4] Read *kiṣkus* for *kiṣku*—with the Kashmir text.

returning a blow, a gentle march alone is needed. [240] The Deckhan is easily won at the price of valour. Mount Malaya is hard by the Dardura rock, whose cave temples are pleasant with the fragrance of sandal branches tossed by the wind from the southern ocean's waves; and Mahendra joins Malaya.'

At the door of his lodgings Harṣa graciously dismissed the chiefs on either side by motions of his brows; then entering, he dismounted and retired to a seat in the outer audience tent, where, after dismissing the assembly, he remained for a short time. Anon the chamberlain, resting both his hands on the earth, announced that Haṃsavega, a confidential messenger sent by the heir apparent of Assam[1], waited at the gate. 'Admit him at once' the king graciously commanded. Inspired by courtesy and respect for the king, the chamberlain went forth in person; and soon Haṃsavega, whose very exterior, delighting the eye with graceful flexions, belied the weight of his qualities, entered the palace in courtly style, followed by a long train of men carrying munificent presents. While still at some distance he embraced the courtyard with his five limbs[2] in homage. At the king's gracious summons to draw near he approached at a run and buried his forehead in the footstool: the king having laid a hand on his back, he approached again[3] and once more bowed. Finally he assumed a position not far away, indicated by a kindly glance from the king, who, turning his body a little aside, sent away the chowrie-bearer standing between, and face to face inquired familiarly, 'Haṃsavega, is the noble prince well?' 'At this moment,' was the reply, 'he is well, since your majesty so respectfully inquires with a voice bathed in affection and moist with a flow of friendship.' After a momentary pause he went on in courtly terms: [241] 'Excepting only a heart replete with respect, a present worthy of your majesty, who is a vessel for the grandeur of

[1] Prāgjyotiṣa. [2] I.e. hands, feet, and head.

[3] For the construction *nyastahastaḥ priṣthe pārthivena* cf. Raghu. V. vi. 20 *nṛipāṇāṃ çrutavṛittavaṃçā* for *çrutanṛipavṛittavaṃçā*.

governing the four oceans, is with difficulty attainable in the world. Nevertheless my master, in his endeavour to add substance to his message, has fulfilled the destiny of this umbrella derived from Varuṇa, a family heirloom—Ābhoga its name—by consigning it to a worthy charge. It manifests many wonder-moving miracles. Every day, to give coolness to its shade, the moon's rays, from their stored-up thousands, penetrate it one by one. This having entered, pure sweet showers of moon-bright water, skilled to teach the lore of chattering teeth, drip at will and as long as desired from its jewelled ribs. Whoso, like Varuṇa, is or is to be sovereign of the four oceans, him and no other does it honour with its shade. Fire does not burn it, nor wind bear it away, nor water wet it, nor dust defile it, nor age corrode it. Let your majesty honour it with a glance. My commission you shall hear[1] in confidence.' So speaking, he turned round and commanded one of his own men to rise and display it.

The words were scarcely spoken when the man rose, raised it aloft, and drew it from its wrapper of white bark-silk. Even as it was drawn forth in its exceedingly white splendour, it seemed as if Çiva had burst into a wild laugh, the circle of Çeṣa's flattened hoods had leapt gleaming up from hell, the Milk Ocean had stood fixed in circular shape in the sky, an autumn array of clouds had joined company in the firmament, Pitāmaha's swan equipage had rested with poised wings in the ether, the day of the moon's birth from Atri's eye had appeared to the people with all the charm of its disc of white effulgence, the instant of the lotus' uprising from Nārāyaṇa's navel had been revealed, the delight of gazing to satiety upon the moonlit twilight had been granted to the eye, a vast round sand-isle of the heavenly Ganges had emerged in the bosom of the sky, and the day been exchanged for the full-moon night. [242] Distressed[2] by apprehension of a moonrise, the pairs of ruddy-geese in the

[1] Read *çroṣyasi* (for *çroṣyati*) with the Kashmir text. So the MS.

[2] Read *dūyamāna* (for *hūyamāna*) with the Kashmir text.

neighbouring lotus pools slowly and softly parted, dropping the ends of lotus fibres from their busy beaks. Closing their voiceless lips in fear of a gathering of autumn clouds, the groups of domestic peacocks turned away in despondency. In a mad joy at the moon, opening their petals with a broad gleaming smile, the white lotus beds awoke.

With wonderment in their minds the king and chiefs, as their glance mounted up in the line of the handle, gazed with awe upon that great world-marvel of an umbrella, which might be compared to the triple world's forehead mark, the White Island's babyhood, the autumn moon's partial incarnation, Dharma's heart, the moon-world's palace, Empire's mouth with its white circle of teeth, the sky's circular hair-parting showing a white line of pearls in array[1], the moon's halo with its white centre of great effulgence, Airāvata's round ears at rest in all the loveliness of their white smiling shells, the world-adored track of Viṣṇu all pale with Ganges' white eddies[2]. Tied around its rim was a circle of small chowries, made of lotus fibre from Mānasa and resembling the flames of light from Varuṇa's diadem. To its point was attached for an emblem a *haṃsa* with pinions poised as if waiting anxiously to hear the tinkle of imperial glory's anklets. Its charming stock was a smooth miraculously stiffened lotus root from Mandākinī, like a Vāsuki with closed hoods, converted to a rod. Its whiteness seemed to cleanse the Zodiac, its outgoing flood of radiance to veil the day, its height to depress the heavens. It was like an ascent of all fair omens, a white bower for Glory, a cluster of flowers on the tree-trunk of Brahmā[3], the moonlight's round navel, the white smile of Fame, the gathered foam of the water of all swords' edges, the nucleus of heroism's splendour.

[243] This having been first inspected by the king, the servants in due order displayed the remaining presents. Among them were famous ornaments inherited from Bhaga-

[1] The reference is to the galaxy.
[2] The Ganges is said to issue forth from Viṣṇu's foot.
[3] Sc. the world.

datta and other renowned kings, ornaments which crimsoned the heavenly spaces with the light of the finest gems: the prime of sheeny crest jewels: pearl necklaces which seemed the source of the Milk Ocean's whiteness: silken towels, pure as the autumn moon's light, rolled up in baskets of variously coloured reeds: quantities of pearl, shell, sapphire, and other drinking vessels, embossed by skilful artists: loads of Kārdaraṅga leather bucklers with charming borders, bright gold-leaf work winding about them, and cases to preserve their colour: soft loin-cloths smooth as birch bark: pillows of *samūruka* leather[1], and other kinds of smooth figured textures: cane stools with the bark yellow as the ear of millet: volumes of fine writing with leaves made from aloe bark and of the hue of the ripe pink cucumber: luscious milky betel nut fruit, hanging from its sprays and green as young *hārīta* doves; thick bamboo tubes containing mango sap and black aloes oil, and fenced round with sheaths of *Kāpotikā* leaves, tawny as an angry ape's cheeks: bundles contained in sacks of woven silk and consisting of black aloe dark as pounded collyrium, *Goçīrṣa* sandal stealing the fiercest inflammation away, camphor cool, pure, and white as bits of ice, scent bags of musk oxen, *Kakkola* sprays, clove flower bunches, and nutmeg clusters, all bristling with masses of ripe fruit: cups of *ullaka*[2], diffusing a fragrance of sweetest wine: [244] heaps of black and white chowries: carved boxes of panels for painting, with brushes and gourds[3] attached: curious pairs of *Kinnaras*[4], ourang-outangs, *jīvañjīvaka* birds, and mermen, with necks bound in golden fetters: musk deer scenting the space all round them with their perfume: female *camara* deer, used to running about the house: parrots, *çārikās*, and

[1] *Samūruka* is a kind of deer.

[2] The Comm. doubts whether this is the juice of a kind of fragrant fruit or a kind of decoction.

[3] Sc. to hold the paints.

[4] The *Kinnaras* are described as mythical beings in the shape of men with horses' heads, perhaps originally a kind of ape. Some species of ape may be meant here.

other birds enclosed in gold-painted bamboo cages and chattering copious wit: partridges in cages of coral: and rings of hippopotamus ivory, encrusted with rows of huge pearls from the brows of elephants[1].

Delighted at the sight of the umbrella, the king mentally welcomed it as a fair omen on his first march, and addressed himself in friendly terms to Haṃsavega, saying:—'I marvel not, fair sir, to obtain from the prince, rich in every precious gift, as the moon was got from the ocean, this great umbrella, fit to be held above the head of the Supreme. The first lessons of the great are in conferring favours.' The collection of presents having next been removed, after a moment's pause, 'You require rest, Haṃsavega,' he said, and dismissed him to the chamberlain's house. Rising himself, he bathed, and then, seeking fair auspices, entered eastward the shade of Ābhoga.

The very moment he entered, such a coolness arose from the shade that the moon seemed to have become his crest jewel, dew-dropping moon-stones seemed to kiss his forehead, camphor dust to melt upon his eyes, a frost from drops of dissolving snow to form pearl necklaces, a rain of *Haricandana* juice to fall without a pause upon his breast, his heart became cool as if made of night-lotuses, an invisible melting ice seemed to anoint his limbs. Astonished he thought, [245] 'What but an undying alliance could be a fit return for this present?' At the hour of dining he sent to Haṃsavega the remains of his toilet sandal enclosed in a polished cocoanut wrapped in a white cloth, a pair of robes touched by his person, a waistband called Pariveça whereof one part[2] showed clusters of clear pearls like autumn stars, an ear-ornament called Taraṅgaka, reddening the day with the light of a precious ruby, and a plentiful repast. In this and other proceedings the day was spent.

Anon the light-wreathed sun, his form dimmed by the great masses of dust from the encamped array,

[1] These pearls are often alluded to in Sanskrit poetry, e.g. Kumāra-S. i. 6.

[2] Or perhaps 'with the name 'Pariveça' formed by groups of &c.'

dipped in the western ocean, as if to cleanse his polluted frame. As though to announce to the god the presentation of the umbrella Ābhoga, he departed to Varuṇa's quarter. By the closing of all the day-lotus beds the earth with all her isles seemed prematurely to clasp hands in obeisance before her lord. Like a glow of affection for the king, the twilight flush, akin to the proffered homage of the whole animate creation, took the world in its embrace. The eastern heaven grew dark, as if alarmed at the Gauḍa's sin. Beneath the gathering gloom the earth became a black expanse, as though the fire of all other kings' splendour had been quenched. The heavens strewed thick their constellations bright as opening *Tagara*-blossoms, like flowers for the twilight levee of the ruler of the earth. Dust-grey[1] in the sky shone Airāvata's track, as though he had rushed towards the fragrance of the ichor of the scent elephants in the camp. Abandoning Indra's quarter, as if infected by the sniff of the angered tiger-king, the lover of Rohiṇī[2] mounted the firmament. Over the ten quarters the moon's rays sped, thrilling, like rumoured invasion, the hearts of proud ladies. Agitated in the play of their creatures[3], the lords of rivers shook as if sick with terror at the emperor's new march. Leaving all the realms of space, the weft of darkness passed into the cave hollows, like anxiety into the hearts of kings[4]. [246] From the night-lotus beds, as from the eyes of hostile neighbouring chiefs, sleep waned away.

At that hour the sovereign, who was lying beneath an extended awning, dismissed his servants with the words 'Begone now,' and then to Haṃsavega said 'Explain your errand.' With a low bow the other began his narrative:— 'In former times, your majesty, the holy earth, having through union with the Boar become pregnant, gave birth

[1] The dusty colour is taken as due to the dust of Airāvata's speed.

[2] *Rohiṇīramaṇas*, 'the moon,' may also mean 'bull,' which is supposed to be frightened by the tiger's scent. The tiger-king is Harṣa.

[3] Or—otherwise—'the lords of armies in all the functions of their spirits.' The 'lords of rivers' are the oceans.

[4] Or—with the usual pun—'mountains.'

in hell to a son called Naraka. Before this hero's feet, while he was still in his boyhood, the crest-jewels of the lords of nations were apt to bow. Without the command of this stout-armed ruler of the world the sun himself, though scanned with angrily bent side-glances by the female *cakravākas* of the domestic lotus tanks, went not to his setting, and Aruṇa reversed his chariot wheels in fear. It was he who won this umbrella, this external heart of Varuṇa. In the posterity of this hero, when many great Meru-like kings, such as Bhagadatta, Puṣpadatta, and Vajradatta, had passed away, there was born a Mahārājādhirāja named Susṭhiravarman, a splendid hero famous in the world as Mṛigāṅka: great-grandson of Mahārāja Bhūtivarman, grandson of Candramukhavarman, and son of Sthitivarman, who wore the unshaken majesty of Kailāsa. This king was born with a pride which seemed unborn. Even as a boy he dealt out presents to all Brāhmans through affection, and reverses[1] to all enemies through hate. In him was seen at its best the so unattainable sweetness of Glory, that child of the salt ocean. For he took away the conch-shells of the lords of armies[2], not their jewels; grasped the stability of the earth, not its tribute; seized the majesty of monarchs[3], not their hardness. To this auspiciously named king was born by his queen Çyāmādevī a son and heir Bhāskaradyuti, otherwise named Bhāskaravarman, as Bhīṣma was born to Çantanu by Bhāgīrathī. Now from childhood upwards it was this prince's firm resolution never to do homage to any being except the lotus feet of Çiva. Such an ambition, so difficult of attainment in the three worlds, may be reached by one of three means, by a conquest of the whole earth, [247] by death, or by a friend like your majesty, peerless hero of the world, burning the heavens with a blaze of impetuous valour. The friendship of monarchs again commonly has regard to utility.

[1] *Pratigraha* is used in a double sense, (1) = presents given to Brahmans, (2) = the rear of an army.

[2] Or 'lords of rivers,' = oceans. The use of conchs was a sign of independent rule.

[3] Or 'mountains.'

And what possible contribution of utility could incline your majesty to friendship? Wealth is but a remote consideration to your majesty, whose aim is to amass fame. One who relies upon his arm alone has no occasion for desiring the assistance of his other members, much less of a stranger. To one greedy to seize the four combined oceans what gratification is there even in the proffered gift of a part of the earth? Even the alluring present of a beauteous maiden is nothing to one whose eye wantons with the sight of glory's lotus face. Seeing, therefore, that ours is an object attainable only by impossible expedients, let your majesty, graciously regarding a mere petition, hear. The sovereign of Assam desires with your majesty an imperishable alliance, like that of Kuvera with the foe of Kāma[1], that of Daçaratha with Indra, that of Dhanañjaya with Kṛiṣṇa, of Vaikartana[2] with Duryodhana, of the Malaya wind with the month Mādhava. If your majesty's heart too is inclined to friendship and can comprehend that friends enter upon a slavery disguised under a synonym, then enough! Commission me to say that the sovereign of Assam may enjoy your majesty's, as Mandara Viṣṇu's, hearty embrace, so that the crushed bits of bracelet[3] gems may grind as they clash against the jewelled edges of great arm rings. In this moonlike face, pouring forth a ceaseless ambrosial flood of pure beauty and magnificence, let the glory of the sovereign of Assam at length indulge[4] to satiety the longing of her eyes. If your majesty accepts not his love, command me what to report to my master.'

When he ceased speaking, the king, who from previous reports of the prince's great qualities had conceived a very high respect for him and whose affection had been raised to a climax by the affair of the umbrella Ābhoga, replied almost bashfully with profound respect:—'How could the mind of one like me possibly even in a dream show aversion, Haṃsavega, when such a great and noble spirit, such a

[1] I.e. Çiva. Cf. Megha-D. 76, *a*. [2] Karṇa, the son of the sun.

[3] *Kaṭaka* by a pun (='the slope of a hill') applies also to Viṣṇu and the mountain.

[4] Or with the Kashmir reading *kṣālayatu* 'bathe her eyes.'

treasure of virtue and captain of the worthy, bestows his love as an absent friend upon me? Though keen to scorch the whole world, the rays of him of the piercing splendour fall cool upon the lotus bed that gladdens the eyes of the universe. [248] Who are we, bought by the multitude of his virtues, to be called friends? the ten regions are the unhired servants of the sweet qualities of the noble. Who needed to intercede with the moon on behalf of the night lotus, which exhibits its likeness in a nature absolutely bright and open[1]? The prince's design too is excellent. Stout-armed himself, with me, a devotee of the bow, for his friend, to whom save Çiva need he pay homage? This resolve of his increases my affection. The heart respects the lion, though a brute, for his pride: how much more a friend! Therefore use your endeavours that my yearning to see the prince may not torment me long.'

Haṃsavega responded:—'What else remains? Even your majesty's generous words give a pain to my noble master. The good are timid of dependence, and herein especially our haughty Vaiṣṇava line. But not to mention my master's family, let your majesty consider:—When towards servitude inclined by overwhelming calamity, like a wicked mother, old in years; spurred on by greed like an unsatisfied wife; harassed by ill imaginings with their manifold cravings, begotten of youth, like bad children; beholding circumstances over-ripe, like an elderly daughter in his house, and suggesting recourse to another man; urged to exertion by all planets of distress, like poor kinsmen; pursued by foul deeds, like aged servants, of long standing and not to be shaken off: when thus, cherishing in his heart in vain the desire of grasping the whole round of delights, as though the power of all his senses were blighted, a man makes up his mind to enter a palace, as a malefactor[2] a

[1] The argument is that every one, however exalted, is *at once* attracted by that which is perfect in itself,—the sun by the day lotus, the ten regions by the noble, the moon by the night lotus,—and I by your king.

[2] The notion of the malefactor and the causes which lead him to crime runs through the whole of the preceding.

cowdung fire, to the burning torment of all his frame,—first of all, withering like a festoon spray at the very portal, he has the distress of being shut out by lackeys. Entering at the door, he is beaten by others like a deer, dashed away time after time, like the dummy in elephants' practice, by buffets from the hands of a group of lackeys[1], downbent through greed of wealth, like a tree branch over a treasure. No petitioner, he is turned away and shot forth [249] by the mean[2], till he flies into desperation: no thorn, he is plucked away, as he clings to the feet, and hastily hurled aside: no Kāma, he is annihilated by the scorching glance of a master[3] angered by his unseasonable approach. Like an ape, he changes not colour when angrily reprimanded: like a Brāhman-slayer, he performs degrading offices, forbidden to touch, his shaven poll seared by daily obeisances: like Triçaṅku, he stands day and night with downbent head, excluded from both worlds[4]: like a horse, he submits for a mouthful of food to be driven at will[5]: like a fasting monk, he wastes his frame, retaining[6] the desire of life in his heart: like a dog, he turns away from his proper spouse and in bondage to vile habits consumes himself: like a dead man, he receives his ball of meal in gruesome[7] quarters: like a crow, he lives for nought a wastrel[8] life, his manly vigour subservient to a greedy tongue[9]: like a ghoul frequenting graveyard trees, he hovers about royal favourites made rough by their accursed

[1] *Pratihāramaṇḍalakara* may also mean 'trunks surrounded by 'gloves'.'

[2] *Amārgaṇasya* may also mean 'no arrow' and *udvegaṃ vrajatah*, 'speeds on its flight.' 'No arrow, he is drawn far back, turned outwards, and driven swiftly away.'

[3] Sc. Çiva or a king.

[4] Râm. I. lx.

[5] *Sukhavāhya* = (1) 'easily driven,' (2) 'exiled from happiness.'

[6] Or—as applying to the monk—'with death (*jīva-nāça*) determined in his heart.'

[7] *Anucita* may be divided *anu-cita* = 'post-burial,' i.e. 'cemeteries.'

[8] There is a pun in *vihitāyuṣo*, which might be divided *vi-hita-āyuṣo* = 'having a life fit for a bird.'

[9] Or—as applying to the crow—'through greed of tongue devouring human ordure.'

success[1]: like a child, he is innocently duped by the talk of parrot kings, conferring delight by a false tongue and showing affection[2] only on their lips: like a vampire, [250] there is nothing he will not do under his master's spell: like a painted bow, he is for ever bent in the one act of distending a string of imaginary virtues[3], but there is no force in him[4]: like a heap of dust sweepings gathered by a broom, he carries off toilet-leavings[5]: like a phlegmatic patient, he is daily worried by acrid doorkeepers[6]: like a Buddhist, he has attained to life-weariness through learning the vanity of things[7], and longs for the yellow robe: like the meal offered to the Divine Mothers, he is cast out into space even at night: like one under a taint, he aggravates a wretched existence by poor lodging[8]: like a pumping machine, he has left all weight behind him and bends even for water: degraded below the worm, he worships even with his words the feet of those uncontented with his head alone. Abandoned by shame, as if she were alarmed by hard strokes from chamberlains' canes: avoided by self-esteem, as if stifled in a heart contracted by meanness: parted from magnanimity, as if angered by his condescension to low acts; through devotion to riches he heaps up troubles, increasing his contemptibleness under the idea of magnifying his means. Fool! though there exists a wood[9] fragrant with the scent of myriad flowers, he does homage to a mirage: though a noble, he trembles like a malefactor as he draws near: though of good presence, his being is fruitless as a painted flower: though learned, his speech is as blundering as a fool's: though

[1] Or 'made rough by the ashes of the burnt.'

[2] Or 'redness.'

[3] *Alīkaguṇādhyāropaṇa*=(1) 'ascribing unreal virtues,' (2) 'stretching an unreal string.'

[4] Or 'but he has no force of an arrow.'

[5] There is a pun here, as *nirmālya* might mean 'purity.'

[6] *Kaṭuka* may mean either (1) 'doorkeeper' or (2) 'hot flavours.'

[7] The reference is to the nihilist tenets of the Buddhists. 'Through vain petitions' or 'through nihilist doctrines.'

[8] Or 'by lodging on the ground.'

[9] *Vane* may also mean 'water' in reference to the mirage. The literal sense is that the courtier might have recourse to a life in the woods.

capable, he folds his hands helplessly, like a leper. Roasted without fire at the elevation of his equals, dying without expiring [251] at the rise of his inferiors, tossed like a straw by insults, burned without respite by the fire of pain, though partial unportioned, though cold to pride yet scorching his kin, though of humble carriage[1] yet making no way, though his weight is fallen from him yet gravitating downwards, though void of spirit yet a seller of human flesh[2], though free from intoxication yet not master of his actions, though no hermit[3] yet giving up his soul to pensiveness, a burnt-poll[4] bowing as soon as he gets up, a domestic fool for ever dancing to amuse the wise, a household firebrand burning his stock, a human ox bending his neck to get even a wisp of grass, a mass of flesh born only to fill his belly, a sore of his mother's womb, for his sins a servant,—for him what atonement is there? What means of reformation? Whither shall he go to find peace? What is his life like? What manly pride is his? What possible pleasures? What dream of enjoyment? This dreadful name of servant, like a torrent of mud, lays everything low. 'Ah me!' he sighs, 'to hell with such wealth, perdition seize such advancement, hail to such worshipful enjoyments, my service to such grandeur, away with such glory, joy go with such pomp, for the sake of which my head must seek the earth.' An eunuch whose love is but words, a worm of inodorous carrion, a mannikin of no account[5], a walking footstool all grey atop with the dust of feet, [252] in coaxing notes a human cuckoo, in gratifying cries a peacock, in bosom-rubbing a land tortoise, in mean fawnings a dog, in modulated notes a pipe, in strainings of body a harlot's person, in the rice-fields[6] of manliness a straw, in jerkings of head a lizard, in curling himself up[7] a hedgehog,

[1] Or 'though a chariot,' *vimāna*.

[2] I.e. his own. Human flesh is offered to goblins or spirits.

[3] Or 'hapless.'

[4] This was the name of a sect of ascetics.

[5] Or punningly 'a hell of dishonour.'

[6] The word *-çāliṣu* is ambiguous=(1) 'rice field,' (2) 'possessor of.'

[7] Of the servant 'in shrivelling up his soul.'

in rubbing of feet a very footstool[1], in slappings with hands a ball[2], in beatings with sticks a lute board,—if a wretch of a servant belongs to the world of men, then a *rājila* snake is a cobra, and a withered stalk the best of rice. Better for a manly man is a moment of manliness; at the price of bowing the wise deem not even the joy of a world-sovereignty worth a bow. Therefore let your majesty, approving of our love, bethink himself that the king of Assam died only a few days ago.'

So much said, he became silent, and shortly after bowed and took his leave. The king spent that night with a heart held captive by yearning for a sight of the prince: for over the great self-devotion works as a charm that needs no simples. On the morrow he sent Haṃsavega away with a load of answering gifts in charge of eminent envoys. For[3] himself he thenceforth advanced by ceaseless marches against the foe. One day he heard from a letter-carrier that Bhaṇḍi had arrived with the Mālwa king's whole force, conquered by the might of Rājyavardhana's arm, and was encamped quite near. At this news the fire of brotherly grief awoke again; his courage gave way, and he retreated into the darkness as it were of a swoon; laying aside all his occupations, remaining in his own quarters [253] with his attendants noiseless and still through the chamberlains' prohibitions, he waited awhile with his royal retinue for Bhaṇḍi's arrival.

Soon with a single horse and a retinue of a few nobles, he came in sight. His soiled garb, his breast filled with the points of enemies' arrows, like an array of iron pins implanted to restrain his heart from bursting, his beard resting like reverence for his master in his bosom, all betokened his grief. On his arm, flabby from neglected exercise, dangled for an ornament a remnant of his charm bracelet. His parched lip, faint in colour from careless application of betel, protruded under the force of long sighs,

[1] There is some obscure pun in *pratipādaka* (='leg of a couch' text p. 7, l. 2).

[2] Read *kanduka* for *kaṭuka* with the Kāshmir text.

[3] Or 'by himself.'

like a coal from a heart burning with sorrow's flame, and with a stream of tears for a shawl he hid his face, as though abashed by the crime of preserving his life after his master's removal. With limbs enfeebled he appeared to shrink through shame into himself: and his long sighs seemed to vomit forth the now purposeless prowess of his arm. Like a sinner, a criminal, a malignant he seemed, like a man plundered and deluded, a young elephant despondent at the fall of the monarch of the herd, a lotus bed robbed of its loveliness by the sunset, Droṇa's son distracted by Duryodhana's death, the ocean deprived of its jewels.

In this guise he drew near the king's portals, and, dismounting from his horse, entered the residence with downcast looks. While still some distance away, he uttered a cry and fell at the king's feet. But he, on seeing him, rose, and advancing with tottering steps, uplifted him, and clasping his neck in a close embrace, wept long and piteously. The fury of his grief relaxing, he turned back again and sat as before upon his seat: finally, when Bhaṇḍi had wiped his face, he wiped his own. A little time having elapsed, he enquired the facts of his brother's death, and Bhaṇḍi related the whole story in full. Next the king asked what was Rājyaçrī's plight. 'Your majesty,' was the response, 'I learnt from common talk that after his majesty Rājyavardhana was taken to paradise and Kānyakubja was seized by the man named Gupta, queen Rājyaçrī burst from her confinement, and with her train [254] entered the Vindhya forest. But not to this day have the numerous searchers sent after her returned.' 'What care I,' the king answered, 'for other seekers? Where she has gone, I myself, abandoning all other calls, will go. Your honour also must take the army and advance against the Gauḍa.' So saying, he rose and went to the bath chamber; and when Bhaṇḍi had caused his mourning beard to be shaved, had bathed in the chamberlain's apartments, and had received signs of favour in the shape of clothes, flowers, unguents, and ornaments for the body, the king ate and spent the day alone in his company.

On the next day Bhaṇḍi, approaching the king, said:—

'Let your majesty inspect the Mālwa king's army and royal equipage, won by the power of his majesty Rājyavardhana's arm.' The king consenting to this being done, he displayed the booty, such as elephants in thousands, great as moving boulders, with muddy cheeks whose temples were hairy with swarms of bees clamouring about the intoxicating scent of incessantly dripping ichor, elephants booming with deep roars like clouds alighted upon the earth, and, like concentrated autumn days, emitting the fragrance of full-blown *Saptacchada* groves: horses swift as antelopes and gay with lines of gold-bedight chowries: ornaments of divers kinds, raining floods of morning radiance and by their light covering the heavens with many a rainbow: wondrous pearl necklaces that had toyed with the scent of the bosoms of love-intoxicated Mālwa women, like stars and yet flooding the heavens with a torrent of unborrowed light: yak-tail chowries, like Harṣa's own glories, white as a mass of moonlight: a white umbrella with a golden stock, like the lotus dwelling of Çrī: beauteous women, like Apsarases come down out of fondness for valour redolent of many a fight: regal paraphernalia such as lion thrones, couches, and settees: all the Mālwa king's adherents with their feet restrained by iron fetters: the whole of his treasure chests, heavy laden with wreaths of ornaments and provided with written records of their contents.

The inspection over, the king appointed overseers to take charge of the booty according to their several functions. The next day [255] he set out with the horse in search of his sister, and in a comparatively few days' march reached the Vindhya forest referred to. Entering, he saw while still at some distance a forest settlement, distinguished by woodland districts turned grey by the smoke from granaries of wild grain in which heaps of burning *Ṣaṣṭika*[1] chaff sent up a blaze. Wherein were huge banyans, encircled with cowpens formed of a quantity of dry branches; tiger-traps, constructed in fury at the slaughter of young calves[2]; zealous

[1] A kind of rice ripening in sixty days, commonly called *sāṭhī*.

[2] *Vatsarūpaka*: cf. *vatsarūpa* p. 257 l. 3 from end, Bombay ed., and Comm. *svalpā vatsā · vatsarūpāḥ*.

foresters violently seizing the axes of trespassing wood-cutters; and Durgā arbours built of tree clumps in the thickets. The outskirts being for the most part forest, many parcels of rice-land, threshing ground, and tilth were being apportioned by small farmers, and that with no little vigour of language, since it was mainly spade culture and they were anxious for the support of their families. No great amount of coming and going tramped the earth owing to the difficulty of ploughing the sparsely scattered fields covered with Kāça grass[1], with their few clear spaces, their black soil stiff as black iron, the branches bursting from the tree trunks set up here and there, their growths of impenetrable *Çyāmāka*, their wealth of *Alambusa*, and their *Kokilākṣa* bushes not yet cleared away. Near the tillage scaffolds constructed above ground suggested incursions of wild beasts.

In every direction at the entrance to the forests were drinking arbours made of wayside trees, which by their coolness seemed to dispel the summer heat: arbours, where the shade was dappled by fresh shoots made grey by the dust of travellers' stamping feet, where were *Nāgasphuṭa* bushes planted in the vicinity of freshly dug tanks bedecked with bunches of *Sāl* flowers easily obtained from the woods, tiny huts formed of close-woven wattles, heaps of crocks dotted with meal and encircled by twisted braids of flies, stones of rose apples which travelling folk had eaten scattered over the ground about them, masses of *Dhūlī-Kadamba* flowers with the pollen formed, wooden stands surmounted by an array of bristling[2] water jars to steal away thirst, cool porous vessels with dripping bases for allaying weariness, pitchers black with moist aquatic plants for the purpose of keeping the water cold, bits of pink gravel taken from ewers to cool the air, cups having pink flowers tied by straw whisps about their necks, tree trunks bristling with bunches of juicy young mango fruit forbidden to wither by bundles of dew-besprent twigs, and successive troops of resting pilgrims drinking the water.

[1] The Kashmir text and A read *kāçilaiḥ*.

[2] *Kaṇṭakita*='containing grass stalks'? cf. c. v. p. 139.

In other places again [256] blacksmiths were almost intensifying the heat by burning heaps of wood for charcoal. On every side the prospect was filled with the inhabitants of the district, who dwelt in the surrounding country, entering the woods to collect timber and enveloped in the provisions guarded for them by old men stationed in the hamlet houses of the vicinity. Their bodies they had anointed to prepare themselves for their hard sylvan toils. On their shoulders were set strong axes, and about their necks hung their breakfast bundles. They wore ragged clothes for fear of thieves. Their water they bore in jars having mouths covered with corks of leaves and attached to their necks which were encircled by triple collars of black cane. Strong oxen marched before them in couples[1].

Ranging on the outskirts were hunters, who grasped snares with intricate loops formed of animals' sinews[2], and bore coiled traps and netted nooses fastened to a quantity of screens used in shooting wild beasts. Fowlers roamed hither and thither, loaded with cages for falcons, partridges, *kapiñjalas*, and the like, while their boys loitered about with aviaries hanging from their shoulders. Troops of childish trappers wandered in eager pursuit of female sparrows caught with twigs[3] whereon a little castaway pulse broth was smeared. Young hunters, practising bird-catching, coaxed on a tribe of dogs frightened at partridges hidden in clumps of grass.

There were people moving along with bundles of *Çīdhu* bark, hued like an old ruddy-goose's neck, countless sacks of recently uprooted *Dhātakī* flowers of the colour of red ore and of cotton plants, plentiful loads of flax and hemp bundles[4], quantities of honey, peacocks' tail-feathers, wreaths of compressed[5] wax, barkless *Khadira* logs frilled with hanging *Lāmajjaka* grass, large bundles of *Kuṣṭha*, and *Rodhra* yellow as a fullgrown lion's mane. Village wives hastened en route for neighbouring villages, all intent on thoughts of sale and

[1] Or *yuga* may mean 'yoke': for *balad* read *balavad* with the Kashmir text, or with A *puraḥsaradbalīvarda*.

[2] *Mṛigatantu*?

[3] The MS. A reads *lagna* for *vadhū*.

[4] Read, with A, *atasīçaṇapūlakānām*.

[5] Or 'easily obtained'?

bearing on their heads baskets filled with various gathered forest fruits.

Here and there the preparation of unsightly fields of barren soil was being effected by numerous lines of wagons, bearing heaps of manure [257] from old dust heaps and yoked to strong young steers, while to the creaking of their loose and noisy wheels were added the angry cries of the dust-grey ploughboys[1] who sitting on the poles urged them on. The surrounding country was black with numerous sugar cane enclosures, showing wide carefully tended branches, buffalo skeletons fixed on stakes to scare with their sharp points the rabbits which devastated the rising buds, and high bamboo fences which the antelopes lightly leapt when startled by ox-drivers' sticks which the watchers hurled at them.

At very wide intervals were the dwellings of the forest householders, girt with orchards of emerald-bright *Snuhā*, entangled with thickets of bamboo suitable for bows, and difficult of access owing to rows of thorny *Karañja*. They had garden enclosures with clumps of *Garmut*, *Gavedhukā*, *Granthiparṇa*, *Çigru*, *Sūraṇa*, *Surasa*, *Vaṅgaka*, *Vacā*, and the castor plant, and a network of *Kāsthāluka* creepers, reared upon tall painted uprights, provided a shade. Young calves[2] were tied to *Khadira* stakes fixed in the ground in circular jujube arbours, and crowing cocks more or less indicated the positions of the houses. At the foot of *Agasti*[3] trees in the yards tanks and drinking vessels[4] for birds had been constructed, and pink masses of jujube were scattered around. The walls were formed of partitions made of [258] slips of bamboo, leaves, stalks, and reeds, while for ornament *gorocanā* pigment and *Kiṃçuka* flowers were used[5]. There were piles of charcoal tied with *Valvaja* grass, numerous

[1] Reading *sairika* (·*hālikaḥ*) with Comm. and A. The texts have *sairibha*, 'ox.'

[2] *Vatsarupāḥ svalpā vatsāḥ* Comm.: cf. *supra* note.

[3] Read *aṅganāgasti*- with the Comm.

[4] *Kṣiprapūpikā*? The Comm. *pakṣipūpikā* · *pakṣāṇāṃ vetravalāni bhāṇḍabhedāḥ* points to a reading *pakṣipūpikā*. The Kashmir text has *kṣiprapakṣipūpikā*. A has *pakṣiprapikā*.

[5] Read with MS. A *kiṃçukagorocanāviracitamaṇḍaṇair valvaja*—.

heaps of cotton from the *Seemul* tree fruit, stores of *Nala* rice, waterlily roots, candied sugar, white lotus seed, bamboos, and threshed rice ready at hand; also collections of *Tamāla* seeds[1], mats worn from being used to pound ashes and disposed upon heaps of *Kāçmarya*[2], a wealth of withered *Rājādana* and *Madana* fruit, abundance of *Madhūka* fruit decoctions, pots of safflower in excellent cupboards, no lack of *Rājamāṣa*, cucumber, *Karkaṭikā*, and gourd seeds, and collections of living pets, such as wild-cats, *māludhāna* snakes, ichneumons, *çālijātakas*[3], and the like.

[1] MS. A reads *tamālavījaiḥ*.

[2] A (?) B read *bhasmamalinamlānakāçmaryakūṭavyāpṛita-*, 'mats used for heaps of *Kāçmarya* and so worn and dusty'?

[3] MS. A *-çālijātakādibhir*, cf. p. 235, *infr.*

Here ends the seventh chapter--entitled The Gift of the Umbrella—of the Harṣa-Carita composed by Çrī Bāṇa Bhaṭṭa.

CHAPTER VIII.

[259] As it produces at once all the objects which desire could ask,
Even Fate seems to pay beforehand[1] its homage to the fortunate;
By association with learned men, and by the joy of beholding a kinsman who has been loved and lost,
Who would not be made happy in the world[2], and by the attainment of a costly jewel[3]?

Next morning the king rose up and going out of that village went into a forest of the Vindhya; and there he roamed hither and thither for many days. But one day as he was wandering, the son of Çarabhaketu, a tributary chief in the forest, named Vyāghraketu, taking with him a young mountaineer, came up to the king. Now the young mountaineer had his hair tied into a crest above his forehead with a band of the *Çyāmalatā* creeper dark like lampblack, and his dark forehead was like a night that always accompanied him in his wild exploits, with an involuntary frown which branched in three lines; his ear had an ear-ring of glass-like crystal fastened in it, and it assumed a green hue from a parrot's wing which ornamented it, while his somewhat bleared eye, with its scanty lashes, seemed by its native colouring to distil hyena's blood[4] which had been applied as a medicine,—his nose was flat, his lower lip thick, his chin low, his jaws full, his forehead and cheek-bones projecting, his neck a little bent down [260] while one half of his

[1] Cf. Bombay ed. p. 140. 1. [2] *Bhuvane*, MS. A.

[3] Çrī Harṣa will gain all these blessings in the course of the eighth book.

[4] Pliny says that hyena's gall "illitum frontibus lippitudini prodest," XXVIII. 27.

shoulders stood up[1],—he seemed to mock the broad rocks of the Vindhya's side with his brawny chest, which was broadened by exercise and hardened by incessantly bending his bow, while his arms, which were more solid than a boa-constrictor, made light of the tallest *Çāla*-trees of the Himālaya; he wore a tin armlet, decorated with white *godanta* beads[2], which was placed on his fore-arm, the back of which was covered with a bundle of the rootlets of *Nāgadamana*[3] fastened together by the bristles of boars; he had a thin belly but a prominent navel; his huge broad loins were rendered formidable by a sword,—the end of which was anointed with quicksilver and its handle was made of polished horn,—it was wrapped in a short black antelope skin as in a woven covering, and its sheath was adorned[4] with the spotted skin of a *citraka* snake, placed between two strips of the skin of an *ahīraṇī* snake. His brawny thighs were covered with the flesh that had as it were fallen down from his waist which had grown thin and spare in his early youth; his dark body[5] seemed as it were to blossom with a leathern quiver on his back, made of a bear's skin, wrapped round with a spotted leopard's skin, its woolly hair black with the bees that clustered on it, and filled with arrows bearing mostly crescent-shaped heads; he carried a hunter's extemporised box of colours with him in a partridge whose red palate was displayed through its open beak, while its neck was strung on the end of the sharp notched extremity of the bow, and a hare whose soft white hair on its breast was clearly seen by reason of its body being stretched out (as it hung suspended), while its nostrils were stained with a line of blood red like a *Bandhūka* flower and an extempore *svastika* sign was produced by one of its legs which was caught in a hole cut by an arrow in the other

[1] *Skanna* may mean 'fallen, drooping.'

[2] *Godanta* is said to be a white fossil substance, apparently an earthy salt. The Scholiast calls it a snake.

[3] A plant used as an antidote against poison.

[4] MS. A reads *çārīkṛita* for *tārakita*. This passage is obscure.

[5] AB *kārṣṇyam*.

one,—it hung head-downwards on his stout bamboo-like arm which bore a bow resting on his left shoulder and which was adorned with a profuse pigment of peacock's gall, and was full of fierce vigour and with its sinews fashioned of Khadira roots[1], while the top of the arm[2] was gay with a blue jay's tail fastened on the upper part[3]. His right hand seemed busily engaged with a *vikarṇa*[4] arrow, having its point dipped in a potent poison, and looking like a black snake which had been stupefied by certain roots[5]. He was like a moving dark *Tamāla* tree on the side of a mountain or a pillar of solid stone artificially wrought[6], or a moving mass of black collyrium [261] or a melting block of iron from the Vindhya,—a very fever to the elephants, the noose of death to the deer, a comet of ill omen to the lions, the last day of the Durgā-pūjā[7] to the buffaloes, the personified essence of destruction, the embodied fruit of sin, the cause of the Kali age, the lover of doom's-night.

Having made him stand at a distance, the chief addressed the king, "My lord, there is a general of the Çabaras named Bhūkampa, the lord of all this Vindhya-range, the leader of all the village chiefs,—this is his sister's son Nirghāta, who knows every leaf in this Vindhya forest, and still more its localities; let your majesty ask him,—he is able to carry out every command." Nirghāta laid his head on the ground and made his obeisance and offered the partridge and hare as his present. The king respectfully asked him, "Sir, you are acquainted with all this region, you love wandering at this season; has a noble lady come within the general's sight or that of any of his attendants?"

[1] This line is obscure; but the MSS. AB give no help, having the same reading.

[2] Should we read *bāhuçikhara* which means 'shoulder' in Bk. VI. (p. 204, l. 1)?

[3] Or perhaps "three parts standing out."

[4] So Kashm. text.

[5] Or 'held by the tail.'

[6] Or perhaps 'torn up by a lever,' cf. Bombay ed., pp. 104. 9, 123. 8–9, 169, l. 12.

[7] A day especially celebrated by sacrifices of goats, sheep, and buffaloes.

Nirghāta, feeling himself honoured by being thus addressed by the king, bowed and thus respectfully spoke, "Sire, scarcely the deer can wander here unnoticed by the general, much less then women, or such a distinguished lady. Still according to your command every day a search is carried on by diligent messengers. And in a great thicket of trees, reverenced by munis, which grows at the foot of some mountains a league from this place, there dwells near a mountain stream a wandering mendicant who lives on alms, named Divākaramitra, with a train of disciples,—haply he might learn some tidings." The king reflected, "I have heard that a follower of the Maitrāyaṇī çākhā, the boy friend of the deceased Grahavarman of auspicious name, having abandoned the three Vedas, when he was a leading Brāhman teacher, though still young in years, turned his studies to the Buddhist doctrine and assumed the red dress. [262] Now even the sight of a friend generally gives much comfort to one's heart, and the good qualities of every one are worthy of a visit, and who would not shew respect to a *muni*? And, again, religious asceticism, fit mate to virtue, causes honour to be paid even to a fool,—still more to a really wise man who wins the hearts of all men. Since my heart has been continually desirous of seeing him, this is a lucky chance that has come in my way,—we will visit him as we have so earnestly sought for such an interview." Aloud he said, "Shew me, Sir, the place where the mendicant dwells." So saying, he proceeded in the direction indicated.

As he went on, there rose in his view all sorts of trees, some full of fruit, *Karṇikāras* in blossom, *Campakas* in abundance, large *Phalegrahis*, *Namerus* bowed down with fruit, palms and *Naladas* with dark green leaves, *Sarala* pines and the yellow *Nāgakesaras*, lines of *Kuruvakas*, bristling with their opening buds; every direction was painted with the beauty of the shoots of the red *Açoka*, while a beautiful grey hue was thrown over them by the pollen of the blossoming *Kesaras;* the *Tilakas* had their surface covered with their own pollen as with sand, while assafœtida spread everywhere. Betel nuts abounded on all sides, the *Priyaṅgus* were brown with quantities of flowers,—everywhere was heard the pleasant murmur of the bees gathered on the sprays which were red with pollen, [263] while the undisturbed rubbing of the elephants' cheeks was revealed by the tell-tale trunks of the *Mucukunda* trees, which were stained by the dark ichor. The grassy glades were all bright with the young antelopes skipping about without fear, while the *Tamāla* trees darker than midnight obscured the sunshine; the *Deodars* were spangled with their clusters of flowers, while the lines of rose-apples and *Jambhīras* were studded with patches of flickering betel-vines; the air was kissed by clumps of *Dhūlīkadamba*-trees white with the powder of their flowers, while the ground was moist with the dropping honey; the nostrils were refreshed with perfume; the hollow trunks of the *Kuṭujas* were tenanted by the hens with their new broods, while the young sparrows uttered their cries as they were tended by the mother-birds, and the beaks of the *cakora* birds were busy in feeding their mates, and the *bhuruṇḍas* were fearlessly eating the ripe brown-red fruit of the *Pīlu* trees, and the merciless parrots were piercing the never-failing fruit of the *Kaṭphalas*, while they dropped the unripe berries; the young hares basked on the smooth rocks; lizards rolled about securely in the roots of the *Çephālikā* water-plants; the antelopes were free from fear, the ichneumons played in peace, the soft-voiced kokilas devoured the opening buds, the deer lay ruminating in the mango-groves, troops of *nīlāṇḍajas*[1] rested at their ease, and the female gayals as they gave milk to their young were watched by the motionless wolves, [264] the drum-like flapping of the elephants' ears grew languid in the pleasant sleep induced by the lulling sound of the cataracts falling from the mountain slopes near by; the *ruru* deer listened well-pleased[2] to the songs of the neighbouring *kinnarīs*, the hyenas were delighted, the snouts of the young boars were stained with

[1] The Schol. explains this as a sort of deer; the name would seem to denote some kind of bird.

[2] MS. A *ramamāṇa*.

the juice of the *Pītadru* trees which was yellow when freshly pierced, polecats were making a low noise in the *Guñjā* shrubs, and tribes of *çālijātakas*[1] lay asleep in the nutmeg-trees, while the young monkeys, angry at being bitten, tore in pieces the nests of the red worms, and the baboons, eager for the bread fruit, leaped on the *Lavalī* shrubs; the water-basins at the foot of the trees had been made with sand, the mountain-streams were checked in their rush by the zigzag lines of waterpots, while pitchers hung on the thick boughs and branches, and the bowers were full of empty begging-bowls suspended by looped strings; models of caityas stamped on pink clay were set up in the neighbouring hermits' huts; the ground was stained with the water which was coloured by the dye of the brown rags; the peacocks raised their storm of cries as if the thickets were so many clouds; the branches of innumerable trees met in confusion like the *çākhās*[2] of the Veda; the trees assumed dark forms as if made of rubies, they obscured all eyes as if made of darkness, they seemed to lift great dark lakes of verdure into the air like so many Yamunās, they were like pleasure-hills of the spring, dark-hued as with emeralds, or like flowering mountains of collyrium—they seemed children of the Vindhya born in the forest, or masses of hell's darkness which had burst up from the earth or close neighbours of the days of the rainy season or partial avatārs of the nights of the dark fortnight, or palaces of the wood-nymphs constructed of sapphires.

The king reflected, "The venerable mendicant cannot be far off." [265] Having alighted, and washed his mouth in a mountain stream and having made his troop of cavalry halt in that place while the forest glades were deafened by the neighing of the horses as they welcomed the sudden rest, and in his heart having assumed a deportment suitable for a visit to such a holy man, and leaning with his right hand on Mādhavagupta's shoulder, he proceeded on foot attended by a few tributary kings.

Then in the middle of the trees, while he was yet at

[1] MS. A has *jātayaḥ* for *valayaḥ*.

[2] I.e. texts current in different schools.

a distance, the holy man's presence was suddenly announced by the king's seeing various Buddhists from various provinces seated in different situations,—perched on pillars, or seated on the rocks or dwelling in bowers of creepers or lying in thickets or in the shadow of the branches or squatting on the roots of trees,—devotees dead to all passion, Jainas in white robes[1], white mendicants[2], followers of Kriṣṇa[3], religious students, ascetics who pulled out their hair, followers of Kapila, Jainas, Lokāyatikas[4], followers of Kaṇāda, followers of the Upanishads, believers in God as a Creator[5], assayers of metals, students of the legal institutes, students of the Purāṇas, adepts in sacrifices requiring seven ministering priests[6], adepts in grammar, followers of the Pañcarātra and others besides, all diligently following their own tenets, pondering, urging objections, raising doubts, resolving them, giving etymologies, disputing, studying, and explaining, and all gathered here as his disciples. Even some monkeys who had fled to the 'three Refuges[7]' were gravely busy performing the ritual of the caitya, while some devout parrots, skilled in the Çākya çāstras, were explaining the Koça[8], [266] and some mainas, who had obtained calm by expositions of the duties of the monastery life[9], were giving lectures on the law, and some owls, who had gained insight[10] by listening to the ceaseless round of instruction, were muttering the various births of the Bodhisattva, and even some tigers waited in attendance who had given up eating flesh under the calming influence of Buddhist teaching, while the fact that some young lions sat undisturbed near his seat shewed at once what a great sage he was, as he thus sat as it were

1 The Jaina Çvetāmbaras.

2 Hindu ascetics in white robes, who had abandoned Buddhism.

3 *Bhāgavatāḥ*.

4 An atheistical school.

5 Followers of the Nyāya.

6 Or containing seven leading types, see Sāyaṇa, R.V. x. 124. 1.

7 I.e. Buddha, the Law, and the Assembly.

8 The Buddhist dictionary by Vasubandhu, see Burnouf's *Introd.*, p. 563.

9 The ten *çikshāpadas* are precepts regulating the monastery life.

10 The Kashmir text reads *gṛihītālokaiḥ* for *gṛihītālīkaiḥ*. This is opposed to their usual blindness by day.

on a natural lion-throne. His feet were licked by some deer who seemed to drink in ascetic calmness; he propitiated universal charity by means of a young dove which sat on his left hand like a lotus dropped from his ear and ate wild rice, while he dazzled the spectators by the rays which streamed from the nails of his other hand, as he poured water on a peacock, which stood near with its neck uplifted, like an emerald water-jar, or strewed grains of panic and rice for the ants. He was clad in a very soft red cloth, as if he were the Eastern quarter of the sky, bathed in the morning sunshine, teaching the other quarters to assume the red Buddhist attire, while they were flushed with the pure red glow of his body like a ruby freshly cut; with his gently bright eye bent down in humility, before which the lotuses in the lake closed their buds, he seemed to rain ambrosia to revive the little insects which the crowd had unwillingly crushed,—he was the Supreme Buddhist[1] Avalokiteçvara, compacted of all the letter-atoms of all the çāstras,—absorbed without faultering in penances,—revealing the real nature of all things to the student, like the light,—one whom Buddha himself might well approach with reverence, Duty herself might worship, Favour itself shew favour to, Honour itself honour, Reverence itself revere,—the very source of muttered prayer[2], the circumference of the wheel of religious observance, the essence of asceticism, the body of purity, [267] the treasury of virtue, the home of trust, the standard of good conduct, the entire capital of omniscience, the acme of kindness, the extreme limit of compassion, the very finality of happiness,—Divākaramitra, who was still in the prime of life. His reverence was excited by his calm and reverent appearance, and he devoutly (sādaram) saluted him while still at a distance, with head, mind, and voice.

Divākaramitra, being by nature full of kindness, was charmed with his visitor's dignified bearing, which, being

[1] For *paramasaugata* cf. Fleet's *Gupta Inscriptions*, p. 232. There may also be a pun, "a supreme Buddhist and yet recognising an Īçvara."

[2] The Kashmir text and A have *japasya*, which is also required by the alliteration.

such as he had never seen before, surpassed all men and seemed worthy of a supernatural world and shone forth in the fulness of his magnanimity, and also with his courtesy which at once revealed noble birth; and without hesitation he welcomed him with his eye and his heart. Heroic in mind though he was, he sprang up hurriedly from his seat and gathered together his robe which was somewhat disordered by his sudden movement as it hung from his left shoulder, and, being skilled in courteous compliments, he raised his right hand which was graced with all the lines and signs of a great man, and greeted the king in a gentle voice and with hearty welcome and every good wish; and, shewing all honour to him as to a guru, he invited him to share his own seat.

Then he said to a disciple by his side, "Bring water for his feet in an ewer." But the king reflected, "The kindness of the noble is a fast bond, though it is not made of iron; with good reason my old friend Grahavarman, devoted to all merit, often described his virtues to me." He then said aloud, "This favour which you shew me seems superfluous after the blessing which the very sight of you confers; after you have proved your kindness by welcoming me as your own with your testing eye, the labour of offering me a seat seems only to make me a stranger. The very ground[1] in your presence is too high a station; and when my *whole* body has been sprinkled with ambrosia by the gracious address of a saint like yourself, [268] water for the *feet,* which deals only with a part[2], is needless,—let your highness sit down,—I am seated well enough," so saying he sat down on the ground.

The seer said to himself "The courtesy of the great is the true adornment,—gems and the like are mere stones,"—so, when the king, however much pressed, would not consent, he resumed his old seat. Having paused awhile with his heart bound fast in the fetters of his eyes, which were fixed on the monarch's lotus-face, he thus addressed him, seeming to wash away the sin of the Kali age by the bright gleams of his

1 Read with the Kashmir text *atibhūmir bhūmir eva.*

2 Read with the Kashmir text *pradeçavṛitti.*

teeth, and exhaling as it were, when he opened his lips, a bower of spicy plants, bright with a mass of blossoming flowers, which had sprung from his life-long vegetable diet,—"From to-day this world of ours, displaying its essential goodness, is not merely not to be blamed, it is positively to be praised. What marvel is not seen by mankind, when this form of thine appears unexpectedly to our view? Such heart-delights help us to infer what our good deeds in former lives must have been. Our penances have given us their fruit even in this life, when they let us look on a favourite of the gods whose sight is so hard to be attained. Our eyes are satiated with ambrosia,—our minds desire not even the happiness of nirvāṇa; it can only have been by great previous merit that our eyes can rest on such a paragon. Happy was the day of thy birth! Fortunate was thy mother who bore thee who givest life to all living creatures. Blessed indeed are those merits, of which thou art the fulfilment. Preeminently meritorious are those atoms which make up the total of thy limbs. Fortunate is that good fortune which has visited thee,—blessed is the human nature which is thine. For verily, though I have been longing for liberation, the sight of thee has made me once more believe in human birth,—without my own will I have seen Kāma himself. The eyes of the wood-nymphs have to-day won their desire; these forest-trees have attained the end of their being, since thou hast come within their range. Thou art all ambrosia—thy words must be only sweet. [269] But ponder as I may, I cannot imagine what earthly being could have instructed thee in courtesy, when thou art still such a boy. The range of virtues was void till thou wast born. Happy is the king in whose family thou hast arisen like a precious pearl. My mind is bewildered when I think how we can gratify such a worthy visitor come so unexpectedly. What are we indeed, who share a diet of roots and fruits and a drink of the mountain-stream with every forester? But this wretched body of ours is only for another's service,—all we have is left for the welcome of our friends. Our few drops of learning are at our own disposal, but our friendship cannot hesitate how to make use of them. If it does not hinder some moment of action[1], and if the secret can be openly uttered, be pleased to make it known; my heart is all eager to hear. Under what burden of anxiety have you come into this inhospitable place, and how long will you go on wearying yourself with wandering about this empty wood? why is your body thus worn, unfit to bear such hardships?"

The king respectfully replied, "Reverend Sir, you have performed everything by your zealous words which ceaselessly rain forth ambrosia-like honey to gladden my heart,—I am indeed fortunate that a venerable saint should thus consider an insignificant person like me worthy of respect. Be pleased to learn what is the cause of my being fatigued with wandering in the forest. For I have only one young sister left, who is the sole link that keeps up my life, now that I have lost all my loved kindred. Now she, while wandering fearful of outrage from her enemies in consequence of the loss of her husband, entered the thickets of this Vindhya forest, swarming with hordes of vile foresters and unnumbered troops of elephants, and terrible beyond measure with its lions and çarabhas, [270] and having its paths infested by huge buffaloes, and impassable with sharp spear-grass, and full of pits everywhere. Night after night we have been ceaselessly exploring the wood in search of her, but we have not found her. Be pleased to tell me if any tidings of her have reached your ears from some forester."

The holy man made answer with some agitation, "No tidings of this nature have come to me; we are not worthy to bring to your highness such welcome narrations." But while he was thus speaking, a mendicant of tranquil age suddenly came up in bewilderment, and folding his hands before the ascetic spoke in a compassionate tone with his eyes full of tears, "O my lord, it is indeed a sad occurrence. A young woman overpowered by heavy misfortune, though apparently highly prosperous in former days, in helpless despair is even now mounting the funeral pile. Consider that she is not yet

[1] Read with the Kashmir and Calcutta texts *kañcit*.

dead,—come to her aid with suitable topics of consolation; even a poor worm in pain which found no rest has often ere now experienced the sage's compassion."

Fearful for his sister, melting within with grief from his fraternal affection, and having his heart greatly agitated, speaking with difficulty in broken accents, with his voice choked and his eyes full of tears, the king made inquiry, "O Mendicant, how far off is the woman whom you describe and can she be still alive? If you asked who she was or to whom she belonged or from whence she came or why she entered this wood or why she mounted into the fire,—I want to know in full what she answered to each question, and how she came into your sight and what manner of person she was."

The Mendicant replied, "Listen, noble Sir. I had offered my worship in the early morning to the sun and I was wandering on and on by the soft sand of this river-bank. [271] In a bower of creepers near the mountain-stream I heard a monotonous mournful bewildering sound of women's weeping like the murmur of lute-strings[1] in a very loud note, or the hum of bees distressed at a sudden frost cutting their lotus-beds. With a sudden feeling of pity I turned to the spot; and there I saw a woman surrounded by a troop of other women, whose eyes were closed with the sharp pain of the spear-points of the *Çara*-grass which had pierced their heels, and whose feet were swollen beyond the power of moving by the fatigue of a long journey, while their toes were bleeding with the wounds from the jagged stones; who had birch-bark tied on their ankles which were aching with the wounds from stakes, while their legs were fevered and lame with blisters, and their calves were white with dust, and their knees were torn by the matted fibres of the date-palms, and their thighs were wounded by the *Çatāvarī* shrubs; their silk skirts were torn by the *Vidārī*-plants, their jackets rent by the sharp ends of the bambu branches; their soft hands were pierced by the thorny *Badarī*-creepers as they pulled them down in their wish to gather the fruit, their arms were wearied by the quantities of bulbs, roots and fruits which they had

[1] The Kashmir text and the Comm. read *varṇatantrīṇām.*

dug up with the horns of the deer; they chewed the soft myrobalans to relieve the dryness of their mouths without their favourite betel, while they used red arsenic as an ointment for their eyes which were swollen and bleeding with the blows of the flowers of the *Kuça* grass, and their curls were torn by the thorny creepers; some used boughs as umbrellas against the sun, others held plaintain-leaves as fans, others carried water in the hollow of a lotus-leaf, others took the fibrous lotus-roots as their provisions, others carried pine oil[1] in cocoa-nuts balanced on loops made of strips of China silk hanging from a yoke; while the rest of the crowd were bewildered eunuchs[2], humpbacks, dwarfs, deaf, barbarians, (and all the other mis-shapen guards of the gynæceum). [272] The centre figure which lay prostrate in the wood, though in deep misery, was still clothed in the grace and dignity of high birth,—her body dyed[3] by the reflected boughs of the creepers near by, as if it were covered with the freshly bleeding wounds of her desperate grief,—her feet red, as with the customary lac, through the blood pouring from the wounds made by the hard spikes of *Darbha* grass, her face pale though shaded by a lotus-leaf which one of the women held up by its stalk,—seeming to be more empty than the desolate ether,—made as of earth in her insensibleness, made as of air in her incessant sighing, made as of fire in her constant fever, made as of water in her streaming outflow of tears,—like the sky in her want of all support, like the lightning in her tremulousness, like sound in her ceaseless wailing, like the kalpa tree of paradise[4], dropping off her silken garments, jewels, flowers, gold, and painted decorations. She lay on the ground like Ganges after her descent, while her limbs still shewed their insolent power ready to humble imperial heads (as Ganges trampled on Çiva's head when she fell upon it); her feet[5] were grey with the pollen of the wood-

[1] *Saralatailena* Kashm. and MS. A.

[2] Read *-çokavikalakalamūka-*.

[3] Read *-pāṭalīkriyamāṇa-* (A *-pāṭalīkṛita-*).

[4] The Kalpa tree *dropped* everything which its votary desired. Cf. p. 73, l. 9. Note puns in Comm. in *mukta* and *vana*.

[5] With a pun in *pāda* which also means 'rays.'

flowers, and she herself longing for another world like the paling moon of early morning,—her long bright eyes dimmed with the outflow of tears, and she herself fading like a lotus-bed of the Mandākinī,—passing a weary time like a bed of night water-lilies withering beneath the fierce rays of the sun; pale and thin like the flame of a lamp at morning, deceived by its exhausted wick[1]; like a female elephant plunged in a lake and only rescued by the care of her companions,—lost in the forest and in thought, [273] bent upon death and the root of a tree, fallen into calamity and on her nurse's bosom, parted from her husband and happiness, exhausted by wandering and emptied of her youth, bewildered in her dishevelled locks and in pondering how to end her life, pale with the dust of the road and the pains of her limbs, burned with the fierce sunshine and the woes of widowhood, her mouth closed with silence as well as by her hand, and held fast by her companions as well as by grief. I saw her with her kindred and her graces all gone, her ears and her soul left bare, her ornaments and her aims abandoned, her bracelets and her hopes broken, her companions and the needle-like grass-spears clinging round her feet, her eye and her beloved fixed within her bosom, her sighs and her hair long, her limbs and her merits exhausted, her aged attendants and her streaming tears falling down at her feet, her band of followers and her life reduced to a scanty remnant,—languid in opening her eyes, ready only to shed tears, continuous in anxieties, broken short in hopes, wasted in her body, thick in her sighs, filled with misery, emptied of courage, dominated by fatigue, deserted by her heart, immovable in her purpose but shaken from her self-command,—herself the home of calamities, the receptacle of cares, the abode of ever varying conditions, the fixed site of want of fixity, the seat of fainting fits, the centre of calamities, the goal of misfortunes, the very dismay of dismays, the special object of pity, the ne plus ultra of helplessness. As I saw her, I reflected, 'Strange! do calamities assail even such a form as this?' But even in that destitute condition she bowed her head respectfully as I came up. I

[1] *Daçā* also means 'state.'

thought to myself, as, in my great compassion I wished to speak to her, 'How shall I venture to address such a noble lady? If I call her 'my child' it will be too affectionate, 'mother' will be too flattering, 'sister' will be giving myself too much honour, 'your majesty' would be the address of her attendant, [274] 'princess' will be too general, 'lay sister' will be only my hope, 'mistress' will be to accept the position of her slave, 'lady' would be suitable for other women, 'long-lived one' would be cruelty in the circumstances, 'fortunate one' would be mockery in her present plight, 'moonfaced' would be an improper idea for a muni, 'girl' would be disrespectful, 'venerable' would too much imply old age, 'holy' would not be borne out by the fortune which has befallen her[1], 'madam' would be too applicable to everybody. Moreover, 'who art thou?' would be rude, 'why dost thou weep?' would remind her of the cause of her grief, 'weep not' is not to be said unless one can remove the cause of her tears, 'be consoled' has no foundation to rest on, 'welcome' is flat and stale; 'are you well?' is false.

"While I was thus reflecting, a woman of venerable aspect but overwhelmed with sorrow, came out from that crowd of women, and laying her partially grey head on the ground, scalded my feet with her tears which expressed the vehement emotion of her bosom, and my heart with her mournful words. 'Holy father, the nature of a religious mendicant is always compassionate for all beings; and the Buddhists are skilled in the self-devotion of relieving every sorrow, and the doctrine of Çākyamunī is the family-home of pity, and the Jaina saintship is ever ready to help everybody, and the religion of the Munis is a means to attain the next world, and no higher kind of merit is known in this world than saving life. Young women are naturally the objects of compassion,—still more so when they are overwhelmed in misfortune; and the good are the 'happy land' of the mourners. This our mistress, being helpless through the death of her father, the loss of her husband, the absence of her brother, and the disappearance of all her other relatives, in her excessive tenderness of heart

[1] Cf. Acts xxviii. 4.

and childless desolation, naturally wise but overwhelmed by the cruel insults of her base foes—her delicate nature tortured by her weary wandering in the forest and her heart bewildered by these continually fresh calamities inflicted by accursed fortune, [275]—unable to bear her dreadful misery any longer,—rejecting her older friends as they tried to hinder her, whom she had never gone contrary to before even in her dreams,—and despising the friends of her youth who tried to reason with her and whose love had never known a break even in play,—and spurning away her attendants who, helplessly weeping, tried to dissuade her and whose words she had never before scorned even in thought,—she is now entering into the fire. O save her! Even a saint like thyself may employ in her case those words of thine skilled in such counsels as can remove even unendurable sorrow.' As she spoke these mournful utterances, I raised her up and still more distressed myself gently addressed her, 'Madam, it is as you say. This noble lady's grief is however beyond the reach of my words; but your request will not be in vain, if we can save her but for a moment. My own teacher is near at hand, who is like another holy Buddha. When I tell him this occurrence, he will certainly come, boundlessly compassionate as he is. He will guide our pious sister into the path of wisdom by the good words of Sugata which pierce the mists of sorrow, and by his own wise counsels, illustrated with apt examples and weighty with various sacred texts.' When she heard this, she fell again at my feet, urging me to make haste. So I have come in haste, announcing to my teacher this startling and mournful occurrence, which threatens death to so many helpless young women."

The king at once understood the mendicant's agitated words, which were interrupted by his tears, even though his sister's name had not been mentioned; and with his mind oppressed by grief, and with all uncertainty dissipated by the reflection that her condition so exactly agreed with every circumstance told about her, and with his ears burning at the tidings, said to the chief mendicant, "Holy Sir, this is indeed my poor sister,—base, hard-hearted, cruel and unfortunate as I am, I have left her to fall into this condition through pitiless undeserved misfortunes,—my torn heart only too surely tells me so." [276] Then he turned to the inferior mendicant and said, "Rise up, holy sir, shew me where she is; make haste[1], we will go at once to win the merit of saving these many lives, if by any means we can imagine her to be still alive," and as he uttered the words he himself sprang up.

Followed by the holy man who was attended by all his disciples, and followed by all his tributary kings who had alighted from their horses, which they led after them, the king made the Buddhist disciple go in front to shew the road, and went on foot after him, seeming to devour the way with his rapid strides. As he drew near, he heard from between the trees various utterances such as suited the emergency from that crowd of women all anxious to die, "O holy Yama, come quickly,—where art thou, O goddess of our family,—O divine Earth, dost thou not support[2] thy wretched daughter? —whither is Lakṣmī gone, the matron of [3]Puṣpabhūti's house? O lord of the Mukhara family[4], why dost thou not restore to consciousness this thy widowed wife, distracted with her various griefs? O holy Sugata, thou art asleep to thy distracted worshippers. O Royal Duty, ever fostering the house of Puṣpabhūti, why art thou become so indifferent? I raise my hands in fruitless supplication to thee also, O Vindhya, thou friend in calamity! O Mother forest, dost thou not hear the cries of this distressed daughter? O Sun, save this devoted wife, helpless in her misery. O thou, saved with difficulty, ungrateful Honour, thou utter barbarian in conduct, dost thou not save the princess? what have her royal marks secured for her? O queen Yaçovatī, devoted to thy daughter, thou hast been carried off by the robber fate! O king Pratāpaçīla, dost thou not fly to rescue thy daughter from the flames? thy paternal love is indeed weak. O king Rājyavardhana, dost thou not hasten? thy love for thy sister

[1] The Kashmir text and A read *yatasva*. [2] *Dhārayasi* A.

[3] An ancestor of Çrī Harṣa, see ch. iii.

[4] Rājaçrī's slain husband was Grahavarman of the Mukhara family.

is indeed cold, the world of the dead is indeed deaf to pity! Away O fire, art thou cruel enough to kill a woman? art thou not ashamed of thy blaze? O brother wind, I am thy suppliant,—hasten to tell the king Harṣa that the princess is burning, he is the consoler of all who are in trouble. O pitiless barbarian, Sorrow, thou hast thy desire! [277] O demon Separation, thou mayest well be content! In this lonely wood, whom shall I call? to whom shall I speak? to whom fly for refuge? to which direction shall I turn? what shall I do in my forlornness? O Gāndhārī[1], this bundle of creepers is mine. O savage Mocanikā, cease that quarrelling over the gathering of boughs. O Kalahaṃsī, why do you still smite your head? O Maṅgalikā, why do you still weep so passionately? O Sundarī, your companions are all far away. O Çabarikā, how will you stay in this horrible camp of corpses? O Sutanū, will you too go into the fire? O Mālāvatī tender as a lotus-fibre, you are fainting. O mother, Mātaṅgikā, have you too accepted death! O dear Vatsikā, how will you dwell in the hated city of the dead? O Nāgarikā, you have gained glory by this loyalty to your mistress! O Virājikā, you are made famous by your resolution to die in your mistress' calamity! O pitcher-bearer, you are happy in knowing how to face the fall from a precipice! O Ketakī, how will you ever find again such a mistress even in dream? O Menakā, may the God Fire, when he burns your body, give you a service under the princess in every successive birth! O Vijayā, fan the fire! O Sānumatī[2], Indīvarikā bows her farewell, longing to go to heaven! O Kāmadāsī, give me room to circumambulate the pile! O Vicarikā, make the fire! O Kirātikā, strew a heap of flowers! O Kurarikā, cover the pile with *Kuruvaka* buds! O chourie-bearer, clasp my neck for the last time[3]! O Narmadā, you must forgive my excessive bursts of laughter provoked by our jests! O Subhadrā, may your journey to another world be fortunate! O

[1] These are the names of various attendants who are preparing to enter the funeral pile with their mistress.

[2] Or 'on the mountain.'

[3] The MSS. read *caramam* for *cāmaram*.

Grāmeyikā, who lovest the virtues of the noble, may you rise to a happy birth! O Vasantikā, make room! O queen, thy umbrella-bearer bids thee farewell,—give me a last look! Your beloved Vijayasenā abandons life! Muktikā, the manager of your dramas, wails aloud near you! Patralatā, your loved betel-bearer, O princess, falls at your feet! O Kaliṅgasenā, [278] this is our last embrace, press me tightly to your bosom! O Vasantasenā, my life is departing! O Mañjulikā, how often do you wipe these eyes dimmed with a thousand tears of intolerable sorrow, and how long do you weep while you embrace me? Created existence is always like this, O Yaçodhanā! O Mādhavikā, why do you still hold me fast? Is this a situation for consolations? The time is past, O Kālindī, for reverential salutations to your companions! O distracted Mattapālikā, it is a useless waste of time to fall humbly at the feet of your beloved ones! O Cakoravatī, loosen thy hold of my feet, passionate one! O Kamalinī, why these repeated reproaches against fate? The happiness of union with our friends is over only too soon! Farewell, O revered chamberlain Taraṅgasenā! O dear Saudāminī, I have at least seen you! O Kumudikā, bring the flowers with which to worship the fire! O Rohiṇī, give me your hand to support me as I climb the pyre! O mother nurse, be firm; verily such is the retribution of those who have sinned! I give my last salutation to your honoured feet! O mother, this is my last bow of farewell as I depart to the next world!—O Lavalikā[1], at the time of death why is there this joyful shouting in my heart! with what foreboding do my limbs bristle and thrill with delight? O Vāmanikā, my left eye throbs! In vain, O friendly crow, do you keep alighting on a milky tree[2] in front of me born to ill-fortune! O Hariṇī, I hear to the north the neighing of horses! O Prabhāvatī, whose is this lofty umbrella which I see between the trees? O Kuraṅgikā, who is it that has

[1] This sudden change from sorrow to joy implies Çrī Harṣa's approach.

[2] This seems to be a good omen—a crow seen on one's right hand is a good omen in the Bengālī poem 'Caṇḍī.'

uttered my lord's auspicious name? O queen, thou art indeed happy in the joy of the coming of King Harṣa!"

As he heard these various voices, the king hurried up and saw Rājyaçrī fainting as she prepared to enter the funeral pile, and full of agitation, he pressed her forehead with his hand as she lay with her eyes closed in her swoon. [279] At that reviving touch of her dear brother's hand which seemed to diffuse a life-restoring power as if healing plants were fastened to his arm, and to drop a mysterious influence as of amulets in his bracelets, and to rain ambrosia from the moonbeams of his nails, and to bind on her forehead a moon-gem crest which dropped a cool dew like that which falls when the moon rises, and to calm her fevered heart with his fingers cold like lotus-fibres and to bring back her wandering life, Rājyaçrī instantly opened her eyes. Clasping the neck of her brother thus unexpectedly restored to her as if seen in a dream, and pouring forth a flood of tears from her eyes which were like the channels of two rivers, with the stored reservoir of grief overpowering all her soul and bursting out violently at his sudden appearance,—she cried out, "O father, O mother, O friends." Meanwhile her brother, as he tried to comfort her, covered her mouth with his hands, and kept calling out in a loud voice through the agitation caused by his fraternal affection, "O my child, be firm,"—and the holy teacher exhorted her to obey the words of her elder brother, and the courtiers implored her, "Dost thou not see, O queen, the condition of the king? cease now to weep!" Her attendants said to her, "O Mistress, have pity on thy brother," and her aged relations restrained her, "O daughter, cease for the present and weep again at some future time," and her young friends counselled her, "Dear friend, how long will you weep? be silent, you greatly pain the king." Though surrounded by all these various comforters, the princess wept violently for a long time with a loud outburst of grief, her throat choked by the tears which broke forth to shew the pressure of the griefs which she had so long pondered over, and her soul filled with the weight of her distress; but when the first vehemence of her emotion was spent she allowed her brother to lead her away from the fire and sat down at the foot of a tree near by. [280.]

The holy teacher, having slowly recognised that it was Harṣa himself, felt a still deeper feeling of reverence, and, after a short pause, made a secret sign to his disciple, and, the latter having brought some water, he himself presented it to the king in some lotus leaves that he might wash his face. The king also, having respectfully accepted it, first washed his sister's eyes which were flushed from her continued weeping and seemed like a red lotus sprung[1] from her long flow of tears, and then washed his own. When the king had washed his face all the spectators stood silent as if painted, and then he turned and spoke gently to his sister, "My child, salute this holy man. He was your husband's second heart and is our guru." At his words the princess made her obeisance, while tears again filled her eyes at the sudden shock of the news that he had known her husband; and the holy man, who felt that his stoical calmness was threatened by the tears which gathered in his own eyes and could only be kept back by an effort, turned away his eyes for a while and heaved a long sigh. After standing still for a time, he tenderly spoke in a gentle voice, "O virtuous monarch, you have wept long enough, and your royal attendants have not even yet ceased their weeping,—let the due rites of ablution be performed,—when all have bathed, it will be well for us to return home."

Then the king, in compliance with right custom and the teacher's words, rose and bathed in the mountain stream, and proceeded to that place with his sister. There he devotedly waited upon her in her sorrow and made her and her attendants partake of the food prepared for the funeral offerings in honour of her husband; and then afterwards ate of them himself. Then he heard from the attendants the full story of his sister's misfortunes from her imprisonment onward,—how she was sent away from Kānyakubja, from her confinement there during the Gauḍa trouble[2], through the

[1] The MSS. read *jātam* for *jālam*.

[2] A. reads *Gauḍasambhramaguptito*, B. *-sambhrame-*.

action of a noble named Gupta[1],—how she heard the news of Rājyavardhana's death, and refused to take food, and then how, faint for want of food, she wandered miserably in the Vindhya forests and at last in her despair resolved to mount the funeral pile. [281] Then the teacher came to the king, as he was sitting quietly at the foot of a tree with his sister in a lonely place away from all their attendants,—at first he sat down and waited; and then little by little he thus addressed him, "My lord, listen,—I have something to say to you. Yonder ear-ring of night, the inconstant Moon, in his pride of youth despised all his many wives, however radiant in their youthful bloom, and carried off Tārā the wife of Bṛihaspati the priest of Indra, wishing to make her his own wife, and fled from heaven, and wandered about in many pleasant places with her whose eyes were as beautiful as those of the timid partridge and who was lovely in every limb, and responded to his love[2]. But at last through respect for the words of all the gods he restored her to her husband, the lord of speech,—still in his heart he was continually burned, though without fuel, by the fire of absence from her.

"One day, as he was rising from the Eastern mountain, he beheld his own reflection in the pure water of the ocean, and as he gazed he fondly remembered Tārā's smiling face, and, stirred with passion, even though in heaven, he dropped big tears from his eyes, which were as bright as if they had drunk up the radiance of all the lotuses. The pearl-oysters swallowed all these tears as they fell into the sea. When they had become pearls in the bellies of the oysters, the King of the snakes, Vāsuki, dwelling in hell, somehow became possessed of them; and he made of them a single wreath which shone even in hell like a cluster of stars; and he called it Mandākinī. By the power of the holy Soma[3], the lord of all plants, it became an antidote against all poisons, and in consequence of its having been produced from the moon which is the ever-cool fountain of ambrosia, its touch relieves the pain of all creatures. Vāsuki therefore

[1] See *supr.* pp. 178, 224.

[2] *Abhikāmayā*, A.

[3] The Moon.

always carried it about with him to soothe the burning heat of poison [282].

"As time passed on, one day a mendicant named Nāgārjuna was brought to hell by the nāgas; he begged it from the snake-king as a gift and received it. When he went out of hell, he gave it to a king, his friend, Sātavāhana, the lord of the three oceans[1]; and in course of time it came into our hands by the regular succession of pupil-hood. Although to offer a present to one so exalted as yourself is almost an insult, still I pray you to deign to accept it in consideration of its potency against poison, since you know the virtues of medicines, and, as you are ever engaged in helping all living beings, your life well deserves to be guarded." So saying he uncovered the pearl-wreath Mandākinī, which was wrapped up in the skirt of the mendicant who was standing near by.

When the pure bright mass of rays suddenly gleamed forth as the jewel was unveiled, illumining the different quarters of space, it was as if the trees burst out from their very roots as longing for their twining creepers to bud[2],—as if troops of wild geese in the lakes hurried as it were eager for new lotus roots, making the sky white with their flapping wings,—as if orchards of Ketakī-trees blossomed, white with the pollen as the clusters burst open through their weight, and bright with the needle-like anthers[3] made visible by the opening of the calyx,—the lotuses seemed to awake, rough with their unfolding leaves,—the lions moved about, seeming as if they filled the horizon with their tossing light-coloured manes—the wood-nymphs smiled, as though besprinkling the forest-glades with the flashing of their teeth,—thickets of Kāça grass blossomed, as though laughing openly with their filaments bursting out of their buds,—herds of yaks roamed about, looking white as they waved their bushy tails,—the mountain streams seemed to dash along, rolling their waves which swelled and foamed and danced—

[1] He therefore ruled Jambudvīpa, Plakṣadvīpa and Çālmalidvīpa.

[2] Lit. 'budding creeper-brides'.

[3] Or is it 'the sharp long leaves'?

the full moon seemed to rise as though rejoicing in gaining a new set of stars, as its circle of spreading rays filled the different quarters of the sky,—the day seemed to be made clean though its horizon had been grey with the ashes of the forest-fires, and the faces of the women soiled with tears were as it were washed once more [255].

The king, after repeatedly opening and closing his eyes which were dazzled by the mass of rays in front of him, at last with a great effort beheld the wreath filling all the quarters of the heavens as if it were the collected spouting of all the elephants of the sky, or the cloudless[1] autumn moonlight drawn in lines there, or the path of the new moon's motion with its steps clearly traced, or the wreath of the seven ṛishis dropped motionless from their hands[2], or a digit of the moon in the North-east quarter, eclipsing the splendour of all the ornaments in the world[3], or beauty embodied with its quality of whiteness in perfection, risen from the milky ocean, or Ganges, which takes away all misery, come down to the successive mountains of our earth, or a banner of silk ceaselessly fluttering which announces the coming of embodied Imperial power, or the teeth of Çiva seen directly in front, white like camphor, or Lakṣmī's garland which she gave at her svayaṃvara, fulfilling her bridegroom's desires, or the joyous smile of the goddess of Earth[4] hardly visible beneath her concealing hand, or the rosary of personified Royal Duty, intent on its three great objects, counsel, treasure and an army, or the tablet inscribed with the catalogue of Kuvera's treasures, ornamented with his own seal[5]. As he gazed, he was filled for a long time with astonishment.

Then the teacher, taking it up, bound it on the king's noble shoulder, and the king, shewing his pleasure, thus

[1] Or—punningly—'having great pearls'.

[2] Or—punningly—'without the constellation *hasta*'.

[3] Or—punningly—'eclipsing the ashes worn by Çiva the ornament of the whole world'.

[4] The Kashmir text and MS. A have *sudhāyāḥ* for *vasudhāyāḥ*.

[5] *Samudra* may punningly refer to the sea.

addressed him, "Reverend Sir, men are unworthy of such gifts. This is all the result of your ascetic observances or the special favour of the gods. [284] Who are we even to have control over our own selves,—still less to presume to accept or reject your gifts? Ever since I beheld you I have been devoted to you, with my heart captivated by your preeminent virtues. This body of mine is placed unreservedly at your disposal till death. You are now absolutely free to do with it what you please."

After a while, when the courtiers had discussed the beauty of the wreath, Rājyaçrī, having gained courage, called her betel-bearer Patralatā and whispered something in her ear; and the latter turned respectfully to the King and said, "Sire, the queen bids me say that she never remembers to have uttered before a loud remark in your highness' presence, far less a command; but this outrageous tyranny of sorrows makes her speak, and this sad plight brought about by evil fate makes her forget her due respect[1]. A husband or a son is a woman's true support; but to those who are deprived of both, it is immodesty even to continue to live, as mere fuel for the fire of misery. Your highness' coming stopped my resolution to die, even on the point of accomplishment; let me therefore in my misfortunes be allowed to assume the red robe." The king heard her and remained silent for a time.

Then the teacher spoke gravely, "O lady, verily sorrow is a synonym for 'demon,' another form of epilepsy, the heyday of darkness, a peculiar kind of poison, an undying[2] King of the city of the dead; it is a flame which has no *nirvāṇa*, a consumption which never ends; a Janārdana[3] where no Lakṣmī dwells, a mendicant[4] who has nothing to do with holiness, a destroyer of sleep, yet without wisdom[5], [285] a

[1] MSS. A and B read *iyaṃ hi çucām asahyatā vyāhārayati hata-daivadattā ca daçā çithilayati vinayam*, which we adopt. But we might read *-ādeçān* in the Bombay text as governed by *vyāpārayantī*.

[2] Or "other than Yama."

[3] A name of Kriṣṇa as 'agitating mankind.' Every epithet in this speech is susceptible of two or more meanings.

[4] Or "a destroyer."

[5] Or "a kind of sleep with no waking."

very crisis of fever like fire[1], a Vināyaka[2] who is no attendant of Çiva, a host of evil planets with no Mercury in their rear, a flame with nothing auspicious in it[3], an outburst of madness from love, a fire rising out of the mind[4], a fury of passion out of a tender heart[5], parching out of softness, utter gloom out of affection[6]. This wound of the heart ever running with tears[7], this thief of life, stealing in under the long dark night[8], this cause of chaos, overpowering all beings[9], this lord of misrule skilled in destroying all bodies, this lingering sickness ruthless with wasting, sighing, and delirium, this evil constellation, foreboding destruction to all the world, this thunderbolt not produced from the clouds, life-destroying and with a long-lasting flash[10],—even all the hearts of the wise cannot stand against it, though illumined by all the lightning-flashes of perfect knowledge and profound in grasping all the secret meanings hidden in deep books, [286] ripe with the lore of many poems, laden with the weight of many çāstras,—far less the hearts of women tender like the flowers of the new jasmine, and weak like the fibres of the juicy lotus stalk.

"Say therefore, O faithful to thy vow, what is it that thou art doing, who is reproached, to whom art thou wailing thus loudly, and telling thy heart-consuming sorrow? We mortals must bear everything, closing our eyes, without bewilderment. O holy lady, these ancient ordinances,—who can alter them? The long ropes of the water-wheel,—birth, old age, and death, —go round and round, night and day, to the five races of men; the hard all-sweeping ordinances of Yama are cunning to trace out the ways of all the minds which preside over the five different families of the five kinds of great beings[11]. In

[1] Or "ever active." [2] Gaṇeça and also "an obstacle."
[3] Or "a light without *yoga*." [4] Or the Mānasa lake.
[5] Or "dust out of moisture." [6] Or "colour (*rāga*)."
[7] Read with Kashmir text *ajasrāsra-*.
[8] Or 'under the bewilderment of many faults.'
[9] Or "all the elements.' [10] The lightning is *Kṣaṇaprabhā*.
[11] This is obscure. Perhaps it means the five races of embodied beings,—Gods, men, the Manes, cattle and birds. Or perhaps *pañca-kula* means 'the assembly (the *pançāyit*) of the elements.'

every home the hours of time, never waiting even[1] for a moment, flow on and on, cunning to reckon the years[2] of life. The stern command of Yama goes forth at once through the world, offering the sacrifice of the lives of all beings. The drums of the Lord of the dead keep incessantly clanging, skilled in announcing the departure of all living beings. The messengers of fate roam in companies in every quarter and in every city, with eyes red like hot iron, and bodies black like the Kālakūṭa poison and carrying black nooses in their hands. The proclamations of the dreadful onset for the destruction of all living beings pass from house to house, striking terror through the din of the bells of Yama, as they are shaken in the hands of the awful messengers. In every direction run the broad highways of the travellers to the other world, with the young jackals which haunt the cemeteries howling for joy, [287]—highways crowded with the biers of the dead, discoloured with the hair scattered by the widows, and echoing with their wailings of grief,—while the eyes of the vultures eagerly watch the banners of the King of the dead, as they flutter grey with the smoke of the funeral piles. The tongue of the goddess of Doom's-night, black like the charcoal of the funeral piles and covered with blood, licks up the lives of living beings, like a cow that licks her calf's shoulder,—eager to swallow all creation as a mouthful. The hunger of the god of death, as he devours all beings, never learns satiety. The stream of the transitory rushes on ever speeding. The meetings of the company of the five elements last only for a moment. The sticks that compose the body's machine[3], which encages the soul, are apt to fly asunder in the night. The atoms which build up this corporeal frame, are ready to crumble, helpless against the onsets of good or evil fortune. The threads of the cords that bind the living principle break at a touch. Nothing is self-depending,—all is ending.

"Considering all this, O wise woman, thou surely wilt

[1] The MS. A reads *Kṣaṇam apy akṣamamāṇāḥ.*

[2] The Kashmir edition and A read *āyuḥ-kalā.*

[3] The Kashmir edition and A read *gātrayantra.*

not allow darkness utterly to overwhelm thy tender mind. A single moment of reflection steadies the soul. And though sorrow has made a wide inroad, is not thy elder brother to be regarded by thee, who is as a guru and as a father? Were it not for him, who would not honour thy noble resolve to assume the red dress? A holy mendicant life is the surest consolation for every sorrow; this is the best home for the wise. But he now stops thy desire, for thou must only do what he commands. Whether thou regardest him as a brother, as an elder, as one beloved, or as a virtuous man, or as a King,—thou must in any case obey his decree."

When he ceased, the King replied, "Who could speak thus except your reverence? You and your fellows are the pillars, created by destiny, of its own will and unasked, to support the world under its grievous calamities. [288] You are the lamps of religion, softly bright with kindness and powerful to dispel the darkness of delusion. But excessive affection like mine, when emboldened by kindness thus lavishly shewn to it, learns to covet what is properly beyond its reach; and to receive great favours, emboldens even a cautious man to venture, urged on by his levity of heart, and self-love teaches even a retiring man to thrust himself forward, forgetful of all considerations of what is proper or improper. But the noble will always on their part recognise the constraining influence of a request, as the ocean-tide recognises its shore; and your highness made over to me this your body, unsolicited[1],—primarily to shew me hospitality. Therefore I would prefer a petition to my honoured lord[2]. My sister, so young and so tried by adversity, must be cherished by me for a while, even if it involves the neglect of all my royal duties; but I also made a vow in the presence of all the world, when I bound myself to obey my right arm which was uplifted to destroy the insolent enemies who had slain my brother; and unable to endure the insult offered, I surrendered my whole soul to

[1] Scil. when he accompanied Harṣa; the Kashmir edition (but not A.) reads *abhyarthitena*.

[2] He here uses the Buddhist term '*bhadanta*.'

righteous vengeance. Will your highness therefore deign to employ himself for a while in this business of mine? Grant this body of yours to me your guest[1]. From this day forth, while I discharge my vow, and console my subjects in their sorrow for my father's death, I desire that she should remain at my side and be comforted with your righteous discourses, and your passionless instruction which produces salutary knowledge, and your advice which calms the disposition, and your Buddhist doctrines which drive away worldly passions. At the end, when I have accomplished my design, she and I will assume the red[2] garments together.—What will not the magnanimous grant to a suppliant? Dadhīca, that ocean of constancy, made the lord of heaven win success by the gift of his bones[3]. How often did not Buddha, the chief of Sages, when his compassion was appealed to, disregard his own life, and offer himself as a victim to carnivorous animals? You well know other instances besides these." [289] Having uttered these words, the King was silent.

The Buddhist sage replied, "The fortunate do not need to utter their wishes twice; at once by means of the thought alone you make your virtues receive the homage of the offering of your servants' bodies[4]. The service of one so incapable of true service is tied to your command whether in a great or a small matter." Pleased at the way in which the other so warmly accepted his friendship, the King, after staying there that night, the next morning dismissed Nirghāta, well satisfied with gifts of garments and ornaments, took his sister with the holy man and went back, in a few marches, to his camp stationed along the bank of the Ganges.

As he was relating there to his friends the story of the recovery of Rājyaçrī, the sun completed his journey through the heavens; and the day, dear to the *cakravāka* pairs, folded

[1] I.e. become in turn my guest.

[2] *Kāṣāyāṇi.*

[3] The myth of Dadhyac (later Dadhīca) occurs in the Rig-veda; the bones were used as thunderbolts against Vṛitra.

[4] The MSS. A and B read *guṇās tāvakāḥ.* Put a stop after *janena.*

up its light like a lotus-bed tawny-coloured with thick honey. The Sun absorbed again in his body the web of his sanctifying[1] rays, which had been spread far and wide to the ends of the world, red like freshly spilt blood, just as the preceptor Çākalya swallowed back the Yajur-veda[2] vomited by his disobedient disciple Yājñavalkya. Then in gradual succession, the Sun, bright with its gathering mass of deepening colours, seemed to be like the congenital crest-jewel[3] which Bhīma carried off from Açvatthāman's turban, horribly red with the fresh blood;—or like the begging vessel consisting of Brahmā's[4] skull, filled with the blood from the veins of the bald heads, which Çiva flung down in his furious eagerness to present a Rudra-alms,—or like the far-stretching lake of blood[5], made by Rāma (Jāmadagnya) when incensed at his father's murder, [290] and filled through a thousand channels from the throats of the vile Kṣatriyas, which were cut by the axe which cleft the bull-like shoulder of the monstrous Kārtavīrya,—or like the tortoise Vibhāvasu[6] as it rolled in the sky, bereft of life and with head, paws and feet contracted through fear in its round shell and covered with blood from the attacks of Garuḍa's cage-like claws,—or like the egg which contained Aruṇa's half-formed embryo body when its mother Vinatā broke it[7];—or like a cliff of Meru, rich in metallic ore, tossed up by the goddess Kālī, vexed at the long delay of the world's destruction beyond its appointed time,—or like the awful cauldron of Bṛihaspati[8], bearing signs of the cooking of an oblation in some magic rite for the destruction of the demons, and having its inside red with the

1 *Pāpamuṃṣi.*

2 One or two words have been supplied here from the Commentary. For the legend see Viṣṇu Pur. iii. 5.

3 Mahābh. x. ch. 14, 15.

4 This seems to allude to the legend of Brahmā's fifth head having been cut off by Çiva.

5 This alludes to Paraçurāma's slaughter of the Kṣatriyas, when he cleared them from the earth seven times and filled five lakes with their blood.

6 Mahābh. i. 29.

7 Mahābh. i. 16.

8 The priest of the gods.

bloody stew,—or like the yawning gulf of Mahābhairava's[1] mouth, fearful with the smeared blood of the demon Gaja, as his body was rapidly swallowed.

Then the evening appeared, leaning on the clouds which shone with the sun's many forms as reflected in the ocean,—like a goblin who has just seized his fill of raw flesh,—while the ocean had its waves dyed in the evening glow as if it were once more crimson with the blood of the demons Madhu and Kaiṭabha, when crushed by the brawny thighs of Viṣṇu. At the close of the evening-tide, the moon was brought to the King as a respectful offering by the Night, as if it were the impersonated Glory of his Race bringing him a cup from the pearl Mountain, to slake his boundless thirst for fame,—or the impersonated glory of the Kingdom bringing him the stamp of the primeval King[2] on the silver patent of his sovereignty, to encourage him in his resolve to bring back the golden Kṛita age,—or the Goddess of the Future[3] conducting a messenger from the White Dvīpa to animate him to the conquest of all the seven Dvīpas[4].

Here ends the eighth chapter in the great poem, the Harṣa-Carita, composed by Çrī Bāṇa Bhaṭṭa, the son of Citrabhānu, and crest-jewel of the company of great poets.

[1] A name of Çiva. [2] Manu or Pṛithu Vainya.

[3] Or perhaps 'Majesty' (*āyati*).

[4] This concluding description, like all such in the book, is at least semi-symbolical ('the pathetic fallacy'). The sunset is described in terms suggesting bloody wars and the fall of Harṣa's enemy, followed by the rising of the moon of Harṣa's glory.—Bāṇa's narrative abruptly ends here which was begun in p. 79.

APPENDIX A.

I.

The following is the description of Mālatī omitted p. 25.

[35] 'Under the semblance of her form's radiant halo she seemed to be bringing with her all the pure water of the river. Like Gaurī on her tiger, she was mounted upon a great maned steed, in colour resembling a bunch of opened *Atimuktaka* blossoms. Sportively inserted in the girth of her horse, which turned prick-eared to listen to the clear tinkle of the anklets, her feet, glowing with clotted lac and stained with saffron on the upper surface, poured out on either side bright red streams of light, as if she were trailing forests of sprouting red *Açokas*, attracted by morbid cravings for her kicks[1]. [36] About her loins a girdle rang like a proclamation devoting to murder and rapine the hearts of all the animate world. Hanging down to her toes, a gown of white bleached silk, lighter than a snake's slough, concealed her creeper-like form. Visible through the robe's thin fabric, her limbs, white with viscous sandal, suggested a lake with lotus fibre-stalks discernible 'mid the translucent water. Underneath gleamed a petticoat of safflower tint and variegated with spots of different colours, as if she were a crystal ground enclosing a treasure of jewels. Dotted as with clusters of large bright planets by a collar of pearls round as *Āmalakī* fruit, she recalled the autumn

[1] A reference to the superstition that the *Açoka* cannot blossom until kicked by a woman, cf. p. 149 *supra*.

sky, overcast with a mass of thin white cloud. Above bosoms like full cups she wore a necklace with jewelled pendants, spraying forth red and green rays, like a festoon of wild flowers signalizing the entrance of some happy man into her heart. Set upon her forearms, each golden bracelet, having an emerald crocodile-shaped signet, made green the ends of heaven with a texture of light like land lotus-beds accompanying her under the idea that she was Lakṣmī. Her joined lips, darkened by a deep black stain of betel, seemed to pour forth, mingled with the afterglow, a dusk swallowed up by her moonlike face. A thick swarm of bees, settling eagerly upon the blooming blue lotuses of her eyes, covered half her face like a veil of dark blue silk. Attached to her left ear, a peacock-blue earring, of a tint borrowed from indigo, resembled a patch of dark cloud amid her lightning radiance. [37] From a pair of pendant ear-ornaments, formed of three pearls comparable to *Vakula* fruit, she poured a rain of light, as if besprinkling her soft creeper-like arms. Her right ear being provided with a pendant in the shape of a string of leaves containing *Ketakī* flowers[1], it seemed as if the moon's tongue were through greed for her beauty licking her cheek. Her face, Love's sum of riches, bore, as it were, for a seal, a round sectarial mark, black as *Tamāla*-bark and dispensing a fragrance of civet. Dancing upon her forehead and kissing her hair-parting was a frontal jewel, whose upward-streaming flickering radiance formed, as it were, a shawl of red muslin about her head. With tresses hanging loose from careless fastening and swaying at her back, as if wearing a streamer of dark chowries, she resembled the pennon of Kāma with her crest-jewel for its crocodile[2]. She might be described as the moon's family goddess, the simple which could restore to life the God of the flowery bow, the shore of love's ocean, the effulgence of youth's moonrise, the great river of passion's

[1] The *Ketakī* flower is white, and therefore compared to the moonlight.

[2] The MS. reads *-āvacūlinī* and *-patākeva*; we have read *iva* in both places.

ambrosia, the efflorescence of dalliance's tree, the primer of archness, the moonlight of beauty, the strength of steadfastness, the sanctum of reverence, the nursery garden of bienséance, the conference of excellencies, the wisdom of magnanimity, the satiety of youthfulness.

[38] Behind her, mounted on a tall mule, came the bearer of her betel casket, a girl composed, as it were, of flowers, her eyes being long like a string of blue lotus petals, her lips rosy, her teeth gleaming like jasmine blossoms, her arms soft as *Çirīṣa* chaplets, her hands delicate as red lotuses, her breath fragrant as *Vakula* buds, and her aspect bright as the *Campaka*.'

II.

The following is the description of Bhairavācārya omitted p. 87.

[113] 'Soon amid a great throng of recluses he beheld Bhairavācārya, who thus early had bathed, presented the eightfold offering of flowers, and attended to the sacrificial fire. Seated on a tiger-skin, which was stretched on ground smeared with green cow-dung, and whose outline was marked by a boundary ridge of ashes, he was wrapt in a black woollen cloak, as though, apprehending an entrance into an Asura cavern, he were rehearsing a dwelling in the darkness of hell. Like realgar paste purchased by the sale of human flesh[1], his flashing splendour, lurid as lightning, cast a glow upon his disciples. With his hair, knotted at the top and showing the round shells of his rosary hanging from one braided part, he seemed to be imprisoning the saints, who, presuming upon a smattering of knowledge, roamed overhead. [114] His time of life, marked by a few white hairs, had just passed five-and-fifty years. The hair-line on his skull was giving way to baldness, the orifices of his ears were covered

[1] The *manaḥçilā* or realgar stone is very precious.

with hair, and his forehead broad; while a slanting forehead-mark, made with ashes, produced the effect of a white line of skull bone burst by the heat of burnt gum repeatedly held over half his head[1]. A natural frown, contracting the interval between his brows, seemed by the meeting of these to give him one long unbroken line of brow tawny in colour. His very long eyes, somewhat yellow as with *gutta serena* in the pupils, sparkling bright in the centre, and from their red corners sending out a film of rays, appeared to trace round him a many-coloured circle like a rainbow, and to shower about the parts of space an oblation to Çiva variegated with rows of white, yellow, and red symbolical marks[2]. The tip of his nose was curved like the end of Garuḍa's beak, his cheeks narrowed by the wide gash of his mouth, and the outgoing light of his teeth, somewhat indented, whitened the stretch of heaven as with the light of the moon, the crest of that Çiva who was ever treasured in his heart. As if overweighted by the whole Çaivite canon resting on the tip of his tongue, his lip hung a little downwards. A pair of crystal earrings, dangling from his pendulous ears, suggested that Venus and Jupiter were pursuing him in the confidence of acquiring a knowledge surpassing gods and Asuras. Upon one forearm, having an iron bracelet and bound with the line of a charm-thread of various herbs, he wore a bit of shell like one of Pūṣan's teeth broken by the holy Çiva and out of devotion converted into an ornament. His right hand shook a rosary, like a Persian wheel containing the buckets for raising water from the well of all delightful emotions. His beard, dangling upon his breast and somewhat tawny at the end, was like a broom sweeping away all the dust of passions therein contained. Covered with a circle of very thick black hair, his bosom seemed scorched by the illumination won through meditation. The ring of a rather loose-hanging wrinkle ran round his middle: [115] the flesh upon his buttocks swelled out in bulk: his girdling loin-cloth was of pure white linen: while

[1] For this custom cf. p. 135 *supra*.

[2] R. R. Kale explains this of a rice oblation smeared with yellow turmeric and reddish saffron.

circling round him in a tight *paryaṅka* band was an ascetic's wrap in hue white as ambrosia foam, as if Vāsuki, manifested by the power of many unfailing charms, were performing the circuit of honour about him. His feet, whose soles were tender like red lotuses, appeared by the clear woven rays which fell from their nails to be crushing hell to pieces in the delight of carrying away its great treasures. They were constantly attended by a pair of pure white water-washed slippers, like a pair of *haṃsas* become intimate with him during his pilgrimage to the holy fords of the Ganges. Constant at his side was a bamboo staff with a barb of iron inserted in the end, which might be compared to a goad for driving away the god whose function it was to remove obstacles to the full attainment of knowledge[1]. Rarely speaking, slowly smiling; every man's benefactor, and chaste as a boy; supreme in austerities, surpassing in wisdom; restrained in anger, unrestrained in kindness; graced, like a great city, with unfailing native nobility[2]; delicately tinted[3], like Meru, as with the sprays of the Tree of Paradise; like Kailāsa, having his head purified by the dust of Paçupati's feet; like Çiva's heaven, the resort of Māheçvara throngs; like the ocean, cleansed by many a male and female stream; like the Ganges flood, made pure by visiting many a sacred bathing-place: dwelling of dharma, *tīrtha* of truth, storehouse of sincerity, burgh of purity, hall of high character, domain of patience, rice-plot of unassumingness, pedestal of constancy, support of steadfastness, mine of mercy, home of happiness, pleasance of pleasure, palace of propitiousness, [116] mansion of venerableness, congress of refinement, genesis of good feeling, end of evil: such was the holy Bhairavācārya, a very Çiva incarnate.'

[1] *Scil.* Gaṇeça was himself only an obstacle. But MS. A reads *anapanayana* 'the not driving away.'

[2] R. R. Kale shews that these words contain a pun when applied to 'a great city,' since by Pāṇ. 6. 2. 89 the word *nagara* does not lose its accent when compounded (*adīnaprakṛiti*).

[3] *Chāyā* contains a pun. Bhairavācārya is *tinted like*, Meru *shaded with* the sprays.

APPENDIX B.

ADDITIONAL NOTES AND CORRECTIONS.

(*The black figure refers to the page, the plain figure to the line.*)

6 8–10 For *pattrabhaṅgamakarikā* cf. *Kād.* p. 115, l. 15, and for *makarikā Kād.* p. 211, l. 14 (*sīmantamakarikā*) and below, text, p. 37, ll. 8–9 (*cūḍāmaṇimakarikā*) [Peterson's 2nd ed.]. The word *makarikā* appears to denote a *makara*-shaped forehead ornament, perhaps with an erotic signification, the *makara* being Kāma's token. *Pattrabhaṅga* appears to be regularly used of personal ornamentation, probably in the shape of leaves (*vide* text, p. 146, l. 3 with the pun on *pattra* and cf. B. and R.): *apāçrayapattrabhaṅgaputrikā* (text, p. 140, l. 2, cf. also p. 153, l. 18) is in this last respect exceptional.

The reference to the chess-board in this passage is perhaps due to the fact that one of the Indian chess-men was a *makara* in the sense of being an elephant. *Kāla* punningly refers, no doubt, to the *black* army on the chess-board. Thus *kṛitakālasannidhānām* has three senses, (1) 'with the *black* at hand' of the chess-board, (2) 'with Yama at hand' of the wives of Yama, (3) 'with blackness at hand' of the ascetic's forehead.

13 20–3 The verse contains puns in *akaluṣamānasa* ('pure of mind'= Brahmā) and *paṅkajālaya* (=abode of Brahmā, cf. B. and R.).

17 1 Or we might read 'drinking in,' as a flower drinks in the sunshine.

17 9 For 'heavens' read 'world.'

17 14 For 'coral trees' read '*Pārijāta* scent,' the reference to the Tree of Paradise being merely a pun.

17 28 sqq. Read 'for the two ruddy-geese of a loved one's breasts.' For the comparison cf. *Kād.* p. 83, ll. 14–15. The 'sand-bank' is that surrounding the ocean, cf. p. 160, ll. 1–2 *infra*.

18 19–20. Read 'in the air and falling with the force of their curvetting to tear up the earth,' *valitavikaṭam* going with *patadbhir*.

19 1 *Siddhyayoga*='one who possesses an infallible charm': in this youth happiness possesses just such a charm.

19 7 Read 'on a horse with no person in attendance.'

19 18 'Took it all in': we have translated *pratītya*, but the reading of MS. A (*pratinivṛitya* 'having returned') is better.

20 2–4 Read *ārohati* (for *āropayati*) with MS. A. *Atinamre* might mean 'towards the very courteous.'

20 9–10 It will be better to take these words as referring to *Vikukṣi* 'that appears in a favourite of heaven like yourself.' *Devānāmpriya* is similarly employed below, text, p. 268, l. 14.

22 12 Insert 'with a lip' before 'wearing etc.'

24 6–8 Read '...my misdemeanour, as if committed in a previous birth, has wrought its fruit.'

25 9–10 Or more correctly '...high birth is not devoid of true nobility,' or 'through your lord's nobleness high birth acquires a meaning.'

26 27–30 Read 'Who am I to grant attention as a favour, or to command body or life? Even without asking the charming and lovely are masters of our all (or 'of everyone').'

27 6–12 Some of the puns in this passage are omitted.

27 13–14 For 'your heart will tell you that' read 'that is honouring oneself,' and cf. *Kād.* p. 199, ll. 17–18.

27 17 'That implies experience' is probably wrong for *nipuṇopakṣepaḥ*, but the correct rendering is not clear. Comparing *Kād.* p. 180, l. 10, we may suggest that it means 'a polite insinuation' or 'threat'; for the use of *nipuṇa* cf. also *Kād.* p. 220, l. 8.

29 11–12 'Spent that fair night': literally 'wooed that lovely woman.'

29 28 *Bhrātṛi* is probably a proper name, as Dadhīca has no brother, and it would be unnecessary to describe his brother or cousin as a Brāhman. It might mean 'foster-brother.'

30 8–9 and n. 1 As *-kūṭa* was a common termination in place names, it will be better to keep the Sanskrit name *Prītikūṭa*. That this was the name of Bāṇa's home appears below, p. 45.

30 19 For the reference to herons and cats cf. Manu IV. ç l. 30. The 'Cock' rules required the eating of food of only the size of an egg.

30 n. 2 We may here note some of the puns in this passage: *pravardhamāna* = (1) as in text, (2) 'giving forth a roar as it rises from the footprint of the patriarch Viṣṇu'; *sakalakalāgama* = (1) as in text, (2) 'deep and singing as it goes'; *mahāmuni* = (1) 'great saints,' (2) 'Jahnu'; *vipakṣakṣobhakṣama* = (1) as in text, (2) 'potent to shake the hills'; *kṣititalalabdhāyati* = (1) 'renowned over all the earth,' (2) as in text; *çrauta* = (1) as in text, (2) 'cant'; *janapaktayaḥ* = (1) as in text, (2) 'the cooking of the people'; *agṛihītagahvarāḥ* = (1) as in text, (2) 'not retreating to holes' like snakes. The punning expression *bhāgīrathīpravāha iva vipakṣakṣobhakṣamah* recurs on the inscription *Ind. Ant.* XIII. p. 78, l. 15.

31 22 For 'a mountain' read 'the weight of the earth.' *Caturudadhigambhīra* = 'deep with four oceans.'

33 6 A verse in the Comm. defines *hairika* as 'a goldsmith's supervisor.'

33 n. 3 On *asuravivara* v. n. p. 193, n. 3 and also *Kād.* p. 227, l. 2. In the note, p. 193, *vātika* is probably interpreted wrongly, as the sense 'madmen' ('inspired') will suffice. The word occurs *Kād.* p. 287, ll. 11–12 *bhujaṅgavṛittayo mahāvātikāḥ* and below, p. 152, l. 7.

37 8–9 'Moonlight': *soḍupāḥ* punningly means also 'possessing rafts.'

37 21 Read 'the ripe (red) clusters of the grislea tomentosa.'

38 2–3 Read 'as the summer grew more mature.'

39 16–18 Read 'Insects baked..., which were studded with etc.'

39 26 'Wearing matted locks': or punningly 'resting on rootlets': the pun in *jaṭā* occurs above, text, p. 14, l. 5 and *passim*.

40 31 For 'brother' read 'cousin' or 'half-brother.'

45 n. 2 On *pañcāṅgula* cf. Fleet, *C. I. I.* III. p. 146. It recurs *Kād.* p. 41, l. 13.

46 1 It is not clear who this brother was: perhaps *bhrātari* here means 'cousin' or 'fosterbrother'; cf. note on p. 29, l. 28 *supra*.

48 29 Cf. Colebrooke's *Essays*, I. 190.

49 8 Read *Parāçara*.

50 5–6 Read 'with the huge pearls which studded it.'

50 10 Or 'let your worship treat him etc.' *Kalyāṇābhiniveçin* is used, *Kād.* p. 104, l. 7, p. 136, l. 6, as a synonym for *kalyāṇin*, which itself occurs, text, p. 117, l. 11 below, and *Kād.* p. 102, l. 1.

50 32–3 Or read 'grow longer owing to one hoof being extended behind by means of a footrope': for this method of hobbling, the object of which was to give the horse a certain carriage of body, cf. J. L. Kipling, *Beast and Man in India*, p. 170.

53 30–2 Read 'his head, which was constantly cooled..., he carried high etc.'

54 24–5 *Dalantam*, the Kashmir reading (which is supported by the alliteration) would require the rendering 'he seemed to burst with pride.'

57 9 sqq. In this sentence we have probably a reference to the facts underlying Hiuen Tsang's story (Beal, *Si-Yu-Ki*, I. p. 213) that Harṣa at the advice of a Bodhisattva refrained from mounting the *siṃhāsana* or 'lion-throne.' For the *lakṣaṇāni* clasping his members cf. *Kād.* p. 186, ll. 17–18.

58 2–5 Or perhaps 'he gave away to the Kings from the coruscations of his ornaments thousands of rainbows, which had been sent to him by Indra as presents; in his conversations he rained wine (sc. sweetness) which he himself had abandoned' (cf. note 2).

59 26–7 For *makaramukha-* the Kashmir text has *mukha-*, which gives a better sense.

61 30 Omit 'self.'

62 27–8 For this conceit cf. *Kād.* p. 192, ll. 5–6. We read *-darçanusukharasarasarāçimantharitapakṣmaṇā*: cf. the Kashmir text.

64 10–11 Read 'to the creators the day of their final bath etc.'

65 12 Omit 'royal.'

65 26 Read *aparavaktrā*.

66 9–11 Read 'the other by his silence seemed not to comprehend the speech—Bāṇa having paused a moment in silence etc.'

67 1 MS. A has *atyanuvṛitti*, which is doubtless right.

67 5 Or 'that they unfailingly grasp people's characters.'

67 35 to end of the paragraph A great portion of this passage recurs nearly verbatim in the *Vāsavadattā* (Hall), p. 168, l. 6–p. 171, l. 3.

72 1–6 It would be perhaps better to take *sukhitayā* with *kiyanmātraṃ naḥ kṛityam* 'We have but little concern with happiness so long as etc.'

73 19–74 2 The epithets have different senses according as they apply to the lives and to the studies of Bāṇa's cousins. In their *lives* they are 'men of mild (or 'pure') ways, believed when they speak, holders of the status of preceptors (or 'a high status'), conscientious in speech, weighty owing to their application to virtue, and renowned for goodness.' In their studies they are 'expounders of texts, devoted to exegesis, engaged upon difficult words, logicians, deep in the study of able works, and averse to all infelicitous language.' For similar passages cf. *C. I. I.* III. p. 175, *J. R. A. S.* (Bomb.), x. p. 78, ll. 32–3, *Epigr. Ind.* I. p. 87, ll. 22 sqq.

74 12 For 'respectfully' read 'affectionately.'

74 14–75 15 Most of this passage recurs verbatim *Vāsavadattā* (Hall), p. 273, l. 1–p. 276, l. 4.

74 20 The punning sense of *mārgaṇavyasana* is 'addiction to pillaging expeditions.'

75 1–10 In a few cases we have in this paragraph placed the wrong alternative in the text; the whole should run:—In Nṛiga's becoming a chameleon a confusion of colours was seen. By Sandāsa, the murderer, the earth was confounded. Nala, inadequately skilled in dicing, was overcome by Kali.... Kārtavīrya was slain for persecuting a Brāhman by reason of his cows. Marutta...was not highly honoured by the Brāhman of the gods.' The alternatives should go in the notes.

75 12 *Vane* punningly means 'in the water' and *madanarasāviṣṭo* 'drunk with *Madana* juice.'

76 8–10 This passage refers, as Bühler has shown (*Ind. Ant.* XIX. p. 40), to Harṣa's conquest of Nepal.

78 10 Read 'being fed with oblations.'

78 15–16 MS. A has *sandhyām avadhīrayati* 'dishonouring the twilight.'

80 10 For *prasphoṭita* 'bursting out' (*nīrājanīkṛita*) v. note on p. 226, l. 20 *infra*.

80 17 For 'tinged by' read 'indistinguishable from.'

80 34 The reeds were used for the sacrificial fire, cf. Kātyāyana Çr.-S. 22. 10. 25: or should we read *varṇair*?

81 4 We may take *mahattara* in the sense of a 'village head,' cf. *C. I. I.* III. p. 169, n. 7. It is 'a title' *Epigr. Ind.* I. p. 275.

81 10 According to the Comm. *mathitapayaḥ* may punningly mean 'buttermilk and milk.'

81 12 *Kudṛiṣṭayaḥ* punningly = 'weak eyes.'

81 n. 1 Read *gunin* (sic).

82 11–12 Read 'might of king's raids,' the reference to Çiva's arrow being merely a pun.

82 16 For 'lover's retreat' read 'home of Kāma.'

82 24 On *asuravivaravysanin* and *vātika* v. note on p. 33 bove.

82 n. 2 If *vikṣepa* (which appears in MS. A) is to be kept it doubtless means 'camp,' regarding which sense v. *Ind. Ant.* VII. pp. 62 and 252, XI. p. 161 n. etc.

82 n. 6 Read 'Or—punningly—"Gaurīs yet not attached to Çiva".'

83 15 Read 'their hair-nets but the fashion of young ladies.'

83 last line Bühler suggests (*Epigr. Ind.* I. p. 70) that the name should be read as *Puṣyabhūti*, as many proper names in *-bhūti* have the name of a constellation for their first member.

84 9–10 Read 'a Budha in the assembly.' It is to be noted that these proper names are significant, *Pṛithu* meaning 'broad,' etc.

86 19 Or 'bamboo sieve for straining earth.'

88 15 Or *pratipattayaḥ* may mean 'manner of address.'

88 29–30 and n. 4 But MS. A has *anukteṣu*, which requires the rendering 'friends are masters of our bodies even if unmentioned.'

89 1 Or 'on the following day.'

89 24 Or 'a hilt of ivory.'

90 9–10 Or 'which is but little skilled in the contempt gained by accepting the property of others.'

90 26–7 *Mahākālahṛidaya*='having Mahākāla (sc. Çiva) for its centre,' cf. p. 104, n. 3.

91 7 Or 'at such and such an hour.'

91 35–7 The murmur of the bees corresponds to the muttering of the charms; their clusters to braids of hair.

92 1 Read 'mystic hand-clasps.'

92 21–2 Or 'and the incense and smoke of resin, transfused (literally 'broken up') with the light of magic lamps, filled the heavens etc.'

93 29–31 With reference to the temple the long compound means 'having its top adorned with thick crisp curls of sleek, dark cloud.'

93 35 Read 'globes.'

94 10–11 For 'raised...leg' read 'raised the right leg crosswise in a bent shape,' cf. below, p. 174, l. 23.

94 22–3 Read 'who is made an instrument by such Çaiva outcasts as you.' For the use of *upakaraṇīkar* cf. text, p. 35, l. 9.

95 30 For 'coral beds' read 'coral-tree sprays.'

95 35 Or 'from the prison of a close encampment.'

96 last line An instance of such 'victory columns' (*jayastambhāḥ*) is the Mandasor stone pillar with Yaçodharman's inscription, *C. I. I.* III. pp. 142 sqq.

97 33 Read 'having been enslaved by your virtues and having attained my true self.'

98 14 We read with Kashmir edition *naḥ*. MS. A here reads *tvadvirahakāraṇaṃ karaṇīyaṃ na siddhir.*

101 2 sqq. The Kashmir text reads *-pravarāt* and MS. A *-prasarāt* for *-prabhavāt*. We may here note the puns in this paragraph which we have left unmentioned: *Kṛitamukhāt* = (1) 'beginning of golden age,' (2) 'clever'; *tejonidheḥ* = (1) 'source of light,' sc. the sun, (2) 'treasure of splendour or valour'; *vigraha* = (1) 'forms' (of the hills), (2) 'armies'; *brahmakarāt* = (1) 'Brahmā's hand,' (2) 'prayer-maker'; *ghanāgamāt* = (1) 'approach of clouds,' (2) 'possessed of profound learning'; *nandanāt* = (1) 'heavenly garden,' (2) 'giver of delight'; *çrīdharāt* = (1) 'Viṣṇu,' (2) 'sovereign.'

102 last line Lakṣmī clasps Viṣṇu's breast (*parahṛidaya* 'the supreme (spirit's) breast' or 'the greatest (king's) heart').

102 n. 6 MS. A, eight of the best other MSS., and the Madhuban Inscr. have Yaçomati, cf. Bühler, *Epigr. Ind.* I. p. 70.

103 22 Better '*loveliness*' boon-winning.'

103 last line–**104** 1 Read 'the centre of the king's existence, love etc.'

104 12 The *Ādityahṛidaya* is still a common *stotra*, cf. Bühler, *Epigr. Ind.* I. p. 70.

105 30–1 The Comm. here suggests a rendering 'red as a firefly' for *indragopakarucā*.

109 10 Read *dhavalantyo* with MS. A and the Kashmir text.

109 n. 2 In the first quotation read *sauhārdād*, and in the second *alaṅkārāṃçukādikam* and *pūrṇakam*.

110 25 and n. 7 Read 'leaving her husband, the disc-wielder.'

111 8 Or 'old ladies of the family could be seen.'

111 14 Or 'the Mothers incarnate.'

112 27 The echoes *repeat* the festival.

112 n. 1 MS. A has *vikaṭavīkāṃçca*: cf. *tāmbūlavīṭikā Kād.* p. 183, l. 11, p. 191, l. 23 etc.

112 n. 2 MS. A has *caraṇavikuṭṭana*, doubtless the right reading, confirming our conjecture: cf. *Kād.* p. 73, l. 19

113 18 Or perhaps 'the soft ring of the brazen gong was clearly heard.'

114 15 We read *utsavayantyo* with MS. A.

117 12 *Dakṣiṇa* 'courtly' also means by a pun 'southern.'

117 18 For 'gateway' read 'structure.'

117 25 The word *kṛitayugayogyau* has two senses, (1) 'fit for the *Kṛita* age,' (2) 'taking exercise together.'

119 14 'Unwatched': or 'considerately treated.'

119 23 Or 'Mālwa nobles,' but cf. p. 66, l. 7.

119 n. 1 *Kṣudrāḥ* also has two senses, (1) 'mean persons,' (2) 'small.'

120 28 The red *Āmlātaka* flower is punningly compared to loyalty; *anurāga* = (1) 'redness,' (2) 'loyalty.'

121 5 and n. 1 For 'dignity' read 'fairness.'

121 6–8 This noble's glory is 'going forth' in the sense of 'spreading abroad,' cf. p. 90, ll. 4–5 *supra*.

122 13 *Guṇavattā* might be translated 'the possession of attributes': the Kashmir text has an easier reading *guṇavṛittā* 'as if become an attribute,' with doubtless puns in *guṇa* and *vṛitta*. *Cintā* would be better rendered by 'anxiety.'

122 33 *Dharaṇīdharāṇām* = (1) 'royal houses,' (2) (with reference to Çiva's footprint) 'hills.' The word *māheçvara* doubtless implies that the Mukharas were, like Harṣa himself, Çivaites.

123 10–11 The reading of MS. A (*yathā neyam*) gives better sense 'that all our lives she may incur no trouble, 'tis for my lord to provide.' A. reads *ācitāṃ* (?), the Calc. ed. *nādhitāṃ*, and, in a note, *ārttitāṃ*.

124 21 *Sarasātarpaṇahasta* means '*hand-marks* of liquid pigment,' if the Comm. rightly explains *ātarpaṇa* as *piṣṭapañcāṅgula*, for which cf. p. 123 n., and compare *nihitaraktacandanahasta* *Kād.* p. 224, ll. 16–17, and *ātarpaṇapañcāṅgulayaḥ*, *Vāsavadattā* p. 183, l. 3.

124 35 The reference is to the *viçeṣaka* or 'beauty-spot.'

125 6 *Bhakti* we have translated 'cutting' in accordance with the Comm., who explains it by *vicchitti*: we might translate 'adorning,' a sense which both *bhakti* and *vicchitti* will bear.

125 15 The sense is not quite clear; with our transl. cf. *Ind. Ant.* XIII. p. 77, l. 7 of inscr.; we might compare *Raghu V.* XVII. 25 *haṃsacihnadukūlavān* with S. P. Pandit's note: MS. A has *-haṃsatūlaiçca* (?=' beds of goose down').

126 5 *Yauvarājye* exactly = an installation of the heir to the throne, a time of great jubilation.

126 29 Sc. *red* lotuses.

128 2 For *mukhena patati* in this sense cf. *Kād.* p. 35, l. 6 (with Peterson's note) and p. 38, l. 2.

128 24 *Laṅghayan* means—punningly—'leaping over' (of the lotus beds).

129 11 Read Rati (sic).

129 20–21 The reading of MS. A *adhomukhīm* gives better sense 'while with downcast face she seemed to chide her friends and heart etc.'; cf. p. 120, ll. 25–6.

129 30 sqq. We have puns in *sudhā* = (1) 'plaster,' (2) 'ambrosia,' and *bhūbhṛid* = (1) 'mountain,' (2) 'king.'

130 1–4 and n. 1 Read 'enemies' faces' (sic). We should perhaps translate 'enemies' faces with coloured masks.' Also *sekasukumāra* may mean 'oil-besprent,' and the words 'which had' ought perhaps to be omitted. We have taken the instrumentals as connected with *añjalikārikābhiḥ*.

131 4 The 'night bowl' *nidrākalaça* is no doubt employed as a charm at the bed's head; cf. *Kād.* p. 68, l. 7, p. 178, l. 14.

133 13 The red eyes of the *cakora* are referred to below, p. 170, n. 2 and also *Kād.* p. 140, l. 6, *Raghu-V.* VII. 22.

134 21 Read 'to have his horse (or 'the horses') saddled.'

135 30 Or 'young devotees' or 'squires,' 'apprentices': the word *navasevaka* appears to have a semi-technical sense, cf. p. 200, l. 22 and *Kād.* 76, l. 20, p. 207, l. 6, p. 331, l. 16.

138 30–33 It would be *possible* here to read '*their* dry mouths' and '*their* cravings.'

139 3–4 *Çalākā* is explained by Kailās c. as 'collyrium stick': the Comm. says *pāṣāṇakaṇikāḥ* 'bits of stone.'

139 11 Read 'porous jar.'

142 18–21 The Sanskrit sentences may here be differently divided:— 'I know, my boy, your filial affection. At times like this an over tender heart distracts even a sober man's mind. Hard to resist is family affection, all-confounding.'

143 2 For 'fathers' read 'parents.'

149 6 For 'pallid' read 'parched.'

151 n. 2 MS. A has *kulaputraiḥ çvasitaiçca.*

154 21 Read 'glory, of' (sic).

154 n. 1 Query *vanaṃ vāpi?*

155 n. 1 Read *uparirudhyamāna* (sic).

158 19–21 Place comma after *manorathānām* and read 'the paths of men's desires are sundered, their Eldorados are laid desolate etc.' Cf. *Kād.* p. 312, l. 23 *bhagnā panthāno guṇānām*, and the whole passage.

159 30 For 'humps' read 'frontal globes.'

159 n. 5 MS. A has *prabhātasamaye* and *samuccīyamānāsu.* Read *samuccīyamānāsu* (sic) in note.

160 14 'With eyes aflame'; sc. the prince could not bear to look upon the objects which met his view.

160 n. 1 *Çāva*=(1) grey, (2) belonging to a corpse.

161 27–8 Or better 'made bright the afterglow of their love.'

161 n. 1 MS. A has *babhañjuḥ.*

163 12 Read 'love.'

164 6–9 Rather 'As the twang of the broken sapling, by robbing the lion of his sleep, redounds to the elephant's own destruction, So, by awaking a hero's wrath, to the villain's own ruin turns the foul blow dealt upon the confiding.'

167 7 and n. 2 *Kālakramopacayānām* is probably right after all, cf. *Kād.* 176, l. 20; the impossibility of gradual increase implies the sudden intensity of the sorrow.

167 31 sqq. The Sanskrit has here a complicated simile; the prince's washed face and throbbing lip are compared to the autumn sky at the close of the rains, when the lightning has almost ceased, his white eye to the opening lotuses. MS. A has *jijayiṣateva.*

168 26 Çrī, the goddess of sovereignty, is roaming, sc. not yet settled with a new king. The paragraph contains several significant allusions ('the pathetic fallacy'). The red sunset is a sign of bloody wars; the separation of the ruddy-geese of the separation of the brothers; the buzzing bees of arrows; the rise of the blotted moon of the rising power of the Gauḍa king. The last is important as the word used for the moon (*Çaçāṅka*) confirms the Comm.'s statement in p. 195 (text) that this was the Gauḍa king's name (Hiuen Thsang's Che-chang-kia). One MS. of the Harṣa-Carita names him Narendra-Gupta, v. Bühler *Epigr. Ind.* I. p. 70.

169 7–8 'Softened etc.'; this however may go with 'you,' after 'tractable.'

170 15–18 MS. A reads corruptly *-kṛitapaṭāvaguṇṭhanījanadrumāṅganām iva*, and *nirākartum* for *tyaktum*. The reading *janaṅgamāṅganām* is probably the right one, as the conception of Çrī as a Caṇḍāla woman runs through this speech and its reply.

170 n. 5 *Guror* contains a second sense 'an *elder's* will.'

171 14–15 Read 'freed from fear by my sire's death.' Sc. Puṣpabhūti had held it in check.

172 n. 3 The meaning might be 'Why not take the sovereignty—worn out as it is—with you?' But Rājyavardhana had himself compared Çrī to old age.

173 30 The Mālwa king is identified by Bühler with the Devagupta of the Madhuban Inscr. (*Epigr. Ind.* I. p. 72), and Kānyakubja he regards as Grahavarman's capital. Mālwa may, he says, be the Mālwa in the Punjab near Thānesar.

174 12 Or perhaps the river writhes *with* Kāliya's brood.

174 16–20 The hand is here compared to a spray (*pallava*) used for sprinkling water. The 'sweat' in the next sentence is a common Hindu erotic idea.

176 1 For 'you desire' read 'it desires.'

177 n. 2 MS. A here agrees with the Kashmir rendering, which should be adopted 'which, breached within and timid through brotherly affection, seemed as it were in flight.' The reading is confirmed by *antarbhinnahṛidayatvāt*, *Kād.* p. 273, l. 18.

180 24 The *senāpati* had really risen from a bed of *reeds* (*çara*). Cf. *Vāsavadattā*, p. 297, l. 9.

183 2 For 'his' read 'this.'

183 7 Rather 'dream of aught dishonourable.'

183 19 The serpent Çeṣa supports merely the earth (not the oceans) and does not enjoy the earth (v. next sentence).

185 8 *Cakṣūrāga* appears to be a technical word with an amatory sense, as it occurs in similar passages below, p. 283, l. 11 (text) and *Kād.* p. 41, l. 1.

186 22–25 and n. 2 The notion in this sentence is that Bhīma is pleased with the taste of carnage, since it is sweetened by the kisses of his demon wife.

187 24 The title *sandhivigrahādhikṛita* besides *vyāpṛitasandhivigraha* and *sāndhivigrahika* is found also on inscriptions, e.g. *C. I. I.* III. pp. 10, 35, 104, 108, 128, 167; *Ind. Ant.* XIII. pp. 84, 118; *J. R. A. S.* (Bomb.) x. p. 27; *Epigr. Ind.* I. p. 88, l. 50.

188 7 The Kashmir text inserts *iti* after *parāgato'ham*, perhaps to mark the end of the quotation. We ought apparently to translate *parāgato'ham* by 'I am arrived,' cf. *Kād.* p. 262, l. 13, p. 264, l. 11, and our text, p. 243, l. 3.

189 12–14 We may better take *suciram* with *ruditam* 'I have not abandoned myself for long even to tears.'

189 25 Skandagupta is probably the same person whom Harṣa names on the Madhuban Inscr., *Epigr. Ind.* I. p. 73.

190 3 Take 'uplifted' with 'thickets.' With reference to the Vindhya this compound means 'with bamboos, creepers, woods, and thickets adorned with peacocks' tails.'

190 n. 2 Omit the note.

192 28–9 It would be possible with Dr Bhau Dhāji to render *çailūṣamadhyam adhyāsya* by 'having joined a company of actors.'

192 n. 1 Read *ābhijātyasya*.

193 5–7 We have here omitted *Caṇḍīpatiḥ* (which might mean 'lord of Caṇḍī,' so Hall) with the Kashmir text and read *Çaiçunāgiḥ* with MS. A. *Kaṇṭhaçca* is read by MS. A and the Kashmir text. MS. A reads akārya*kutūhalī* 'curious where he should not be.'

193 13 MSS. AB have 'Mount *Govardhana*.'

193 15 Mekala is part of the Vindhya Mountains.

193 16 Read 'the Pauṇaki prince' (MS. A has *Pauṇika*).

193 26 The Kashmir text and the Comm. read Dadhna.

193 n. 3 Concerning *asuravivara* and *vātika* cf. note on p. 33 *supra*.

194 3 We might translate 'ensconced in a reed grove with an uplifted thicket of reeds in their hands.'

194 12 For 'sweet-toothed' read 'drunken.' Dr Bhau Dhāji's MS. apparently read *madhumoditamadhuraka-* in one word. For *madhuraka* MS. A has *madhurasa*.

194 14 Probably MS. A is here right in reading *Jārūthyām* 'in *Jārūthī*.'

194 n. 6 Read *-kūladūtadṛiṣṭayaḥ*.

198 7–10 We have here read *saṃvibhajya kliṣṭakārpaṭikakulaputralokam* ucitaiḥ *prasādadānair, vimucya bandhanāni.*

198 24 The word *ākṣapaṭalika* 'one in charge of *akṣapaṭala* i.e. documents' occurs frequently on inscriptions, cf. *C. I. I.* III. p. 180, l. 76 and p. 190, n. 2. We have a 'notary-in-chief' (*mahākṣapaṭalika*) id. p. 177, l. 46, and a 'village notary' (*grāmākṣapaṭalādhikṛita*) id. p. 257, l. 15. *Mahākṣapaṭalādhikaraṇādhikṛita* occurs on Harṣa's Inscr., *Epigr. Ind.* I. p. 73.

199 17 For *balādhikṛita* cf. *C. I. I.* III. pp. 109 n., 210 n.; *Kād.* p. 331, l. 14.

199 22 Read *kaṭukakaṭuka-*. For *kaṭuka* = 'officer' cf. text, p. 250, l. 4.

200 22 On *navasevaka* v. note on p. 135, l. 30 *supra.*

200 27–8 The apes are carried for superstitious reasons (*rakṣārtham*), Comm.

200 n. 3 The sense of *jāghanika* is uncertain: possibly it means 'debauchee,' cf. *jaghanya.* We translate *jāghanīkara.*

200 n. 4 The translation suggested in the notes is supported by *Kād.* p. 88, ll. 4–5, p. 97, l. 21, p. 191, ll. 2–3, p. 212, l. 17 etc., and *supra* p. 106, l. 6.

200 n. 5 *Nāsīra* means 'vanguard,' *Kād.* p. 331, l. 14, which confirms the meaning 'vanguard' here.

201 28 MS. A reads *trastavesara-* '*frightened* mules.'

202 5 *Antarāsana* 'the inner seat' occurs in a similar passage, *Kād.* p. 112, l. 5. Perhaps the sense is 'a near seat.'

202 n. 1 MS. A has *tilaka.*

203 21 Read 'inlaid ruby' for 'ruby inlaid at its top,' as *upari* goes with *dhriyamāṇena.*

204 n. 2 We have followed MS. A: otherwise it would have been necessary to read *draṣṭrīn* for *draṣṭrīṇām.*

205 5 Read 'palace peacocks,' and for the idea cf. *Kād.* p. 183, ll. 6–7.

205 16 'Spread': for *tastāra* intransitive cf. *Kād.* p. 76, l. 21, p. 368, l. 11. MS. A has *tatāra.*

206 4–6 We have read *haritakṛitāḥ* for *haritīkṛitāḥ*: MS. A has *harīṇāṃ kṛitāḥ.*

207 2 For 'old fellow' read 'standstill.'

208 16 'The whole body of nobles': or *asaṃvibhakta* might mean 'the *not specially provided* nobles.'

208 19 'Fools of grant-holders': *āgrahārika* occurs on inscriptions in the sense of 'an officer in special charge of an *agrahāra*,' *C. I. I.* III. p. 52, n. 2, p. 257, l. 12.

208 27 *Āyuktaka* is a regular word for 'official' on inscriptions, e.g. *C. I. I.* III. p. 166, l. 20: we have *āyuktapuruṣa*, id. p. 8. *Cāṭa* 'knaves' is the word which Fleet renders (*C. I. I.* III. p. 98 n.) by 'irregular soldiers.' MS. A has *ceṭa*.

208 n. 4 Here (Bombay ed. p. 238, 1) the texts read *uddhūyamānadhūlipaṭalam kvacid ekāntapravṛittāçvavāracakracarvyamāṇāgāmigauḍa vimṛigyamāṇasasyasaṃrakṣaṇam*, which as far as *gauḍa* recurs below, continuing with *-vigraham*. It is clear that in the first passage only *mṛigyamāṇasasyasaṃrakṣaṇam* is needed. The repetition must be due to some homoeoteleuton (perhaps *abhidadhānair* and *dhāvamānair*). The MS. A is here right and reads *-carcyamānā-*.

209 1 'Ripe': we read *niṣpanna* with Comm. and the Kashmir text.

209 27 'Collisions': or *saṃghaṭṭa* may mean 'races,' as *supra* text, p. 65, l. 3.

211 23–4 For this custom of touching on the back cf. *Kād.* p. 230, l. 19, p. 335, ll. 9–10 and Hiuen Thsang, *Si-Yu-Ki* (Beal), I. p. 85; (Julien) I. 86.

213 13 There is doubtless a pun in *danta*, implying that the umbrella has circles of *ivory*. For *maṇḍalaka* MS. A has *maṇḍaladyuti*.

214 14–15 'And of the hue etc.': the Sanskrit adjective may here go with the next clause. The Kashmir text in this line reads the adjective *āgurava-*.

216 15 'Rushed towards': or perhaps 'fled from,' as the *gandhadvipa* is a terror to all other elephants. The Moon in l. 18 refers to Çaçāṅka, the Gauḍa king (cf. *sup.* note on p. 168).

216 20 The 'ladies' are the wives of Harṣa's enemies, whose lands are soon to be seized.

216 22–3 *Vimuktasarvāçā* may punningly mean 'abandoning all hope.'

217 25 Hiuen Thsang visits Bhāskaravarman, king of Kāmarūpa.

218 n. 4 MS. A also has *kṣālayatu*, which is to be preferred.

219 17–18 Or perhaps 'What any more can torment my noble master, thus addressed by your majesty?'

219 26 After 'daughter' insert a comma.

221 16–17 We might here translate 'he worships men's feet even with his words, uncontented with his head alone.'

222 last line 'A hedgehog': or 'polecat.'

222 n. 5 Or 'an uncounted hell.'

223 9 We have translated *parāgataḥ* by 'died' (cf. *pareta*) because the ambassador comes from the *Kumāra*. But v. note on p. 188, l. 7 *supra*. We might translate 'the king of Assam will arrive in a few days' or 'has come home only a few days' or 'for a few days.'

223 32–3 Read 'dangled as his sole remaining ornament his charm bracelet,' comparing S. P. Pandit's note to *Vikramorvaçī*, p. 84.

223 n. 3 For the instrumental *ātmanā*='on his own part' cf. *Kād.* p. 25, l. 16, p. 163, l. 15, p. 340, l. 2 etc.

225 last line 'Zealous' is our translation of *yantrita*; but the Kashmir text has *ayantrita*, which probably means 'furious,' literally 'unrestrained'; cf. B. and R. MS. A reads *āviṣṭagopālakalpita*.

226 20 'Dust of travellers' stamping feet': for this use of *prasphoṭita* (the dust *flying out*) in almost the same word cf. *Kād.* p. 223, l. 15 *kārpaṭikaprasphoṭitacaranadhūlidhūsarakisalayalāñchitopakaṇṭhaiḥ*.

228 11 Or '*white* skeletons.'

229 10 We have accidentally omitted the concluding sentence 'There the king stayed,' or with MS. A 'There the king passed the day.'

233 13 According to Dr Bhau Dhāji (*J. R. A. S.* Bomb. x. p. 40) the Maitrāyaṇīya Brāhmans are still found at Bhaḍgaon and in neighbouring villages near the Saṭpuda Mts.

233 29–**235** 5 Part of this passage recurs nearly verbatim, *Vāsavadattā* (Hall), p. 263, l. 4–p. 266, l. 3.

236 8 The *keçaluñcana* ascetics appear to be mentioned *Si-Yu-Ki* (Beal) I. p. 76; (Julien) I. 69.

250 31 The Kashmir text has *patitapiṇḍa*, and MS. A *pratipiṇḍa*, which would support the rendering 'taking food with an effort shown at every mouthful.'

255 n. 11 Cf. *pañcamaṇḍalī* *C. I. I.* III. p. 31, l. 6. *Pañcakula* is the title of an office, *Epigr. Ind.* I. pp. 160, 170; cf. *Ind. Ant.* XI. p. 221, l. 21, p. 242, l. 9.

256 30 'In the night': but MS. A has a better reading *gātriṣu* 'in those who have bodies,' to be taken with *mahābhūtagrāmagoṣṭhyaḥ*.

INDEX OF PROPER NAMES, ETC.

I.

II.